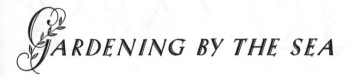

GARDENING BY THE SEA

Other Gardening Books by the Author

GROUND COVERS FOR EASIER GARDENING
GARDEN FLOWERS IN COLOR
VEGETABLE GARDENING IN COLOR
ANNUALS FOR YOUR GARDEN
GARDEN BULBS IN COLOR

GARDENING

By DANIEL J. FOLEY

BY THE SEA

From Coast to Coast

PARNASSUS IMPRINTS
BOX 335, ORLEANS, MASS. 02653

To

GEORGE TALOUMIS

Acknowledgments

To Mr. Duane Doolittle, I am deeply indebted. Also to Mr. Paul A. Darling, Mr. Kenneth Drayer, Mrs. W. W. K. Freeman, Mr. Paul E. Genereux, Mr. J. P. Roche, and Mr. George Taloumis for the use of photographs.

To Lorraine Crabtree, Elizabeth Hunt, Marcy Merrick, Susan N. Papin and Elsie Wright for assistance in typing the manuscript are due a large measure of thanks.

To Mr. James Atwell, Miss Eunice Brown, Mr. and Mrs. John A. Burnham, Mr. Andrew Bye, Miss Marjorie Cawthorne, Mr. Warren Hassmer, Mrs. Arthur S. Heitz, Mrs. Robert H. Larkin, Dr. G. L. Laverty, Mrs. Philip H. Lord, Mrs. Alvah Roberts, Mr. William Theriault, Mr. Robert Thomson, Mrs. Frances Williams, and countless other friends who helped me to locate plants and gardens and other details relating to the preparation of this book, I am most grateful.

To Mrs. Oliver Ames	Mr. and Mrs. Lewis Garland
Mrs. Joseph Batchelder	Mrs. W. Griffin Gribbel
Mr. Cary Bok	Mr. Samuel W. Haddock
Mr. and Mrs. Roland Booma	Mr. and Mrs. T. C. Haffenreffer, Jr.
Mr. and Mrs. William Breed	Mr. Carl Hoblitzelle
Mr. Steven Calef	Mrs. Calvin Hosmer, Jr.
Mr. and Mrs. Theodore Carangelo	Mrs. Edward P. Jastram
Cider Hill Greenhouse	Mr. and Mrs. Nils R. Johaneson
Mrs. T. Jefferson Coolidge	Miss Viola B. Kneeland
Mr. and Mrs. Marcus E. Cox	Dr. G. L. Laverty
Corliss Brothers, Inc.	H. V. Lawrence, Inc.
Miss Marion Crowell	Mr. and Mrs. Philip H. Lord
Mr. Henry Dolan, Jr.	Mr. and Mrs. Hollis Lovell
Mr. Rick Eaton	Miss C. Sally Low

Massachusetts Horticultural Society   Mr. and Mrs. Raymond Shea
Mr. and Mrs. George Moore   Mr. and Mrs. C. Fred Smith, Jr.
Mr. and Mrs. Harold Morse   Mrs. Lois Spanel
Mr. Brian O'Neill   Thomson Nursery
Mr. Leonard J. Raymond   Mr. and Mrs. Maurice Weiner
Mr. and Mrs. Gordon Roaf   Mrs. Foster Whitney
Salem Public Library   Mrs. Helen Snow Wilson

who have contributed in various ways by sharing their gardens for photographing, or by allowing me to test my pet theories in their gardens or by contributing their professional skill.

To my family, to my associates, to Mr. William Lickfield, my heartfelt gratitude for their patience and forbearance.

DANIEL J. FOLEY

Salem, Massachusetts

Contents

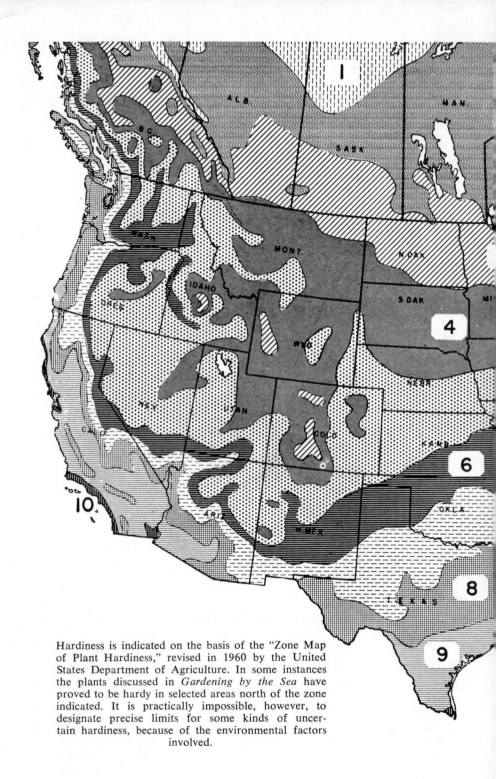

Hardiness is indicated on the basis of the "Zone Map of Plant Hardiness," revised in 1960 by the United States Department of Agriculture. In some instances the plants discussed in *Gardening by the Sea* have proved to be hardy in selected areas north of the zone indicated. It is practically impossible, however, to designate precise limits for some kinds of uncertain hardiness, because of the environmental factors involved.

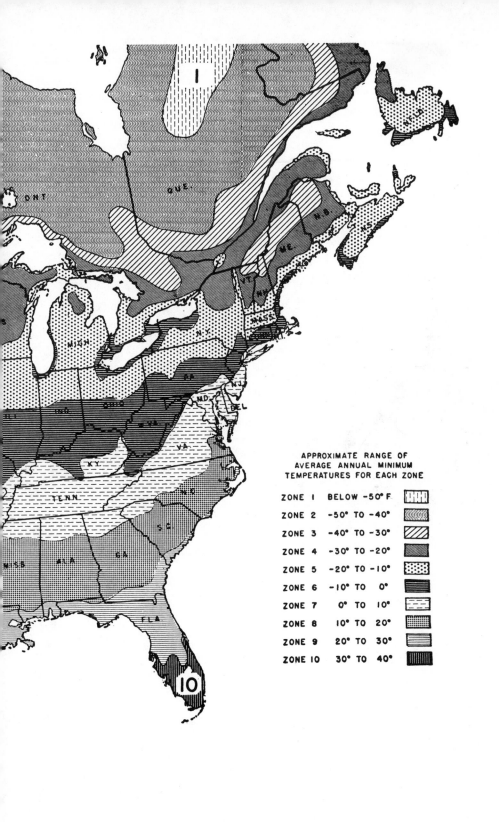

APPROXIMATE RANGE OF
AVERAGE ANNUAL MINIMUM
TEMPERATURES FOR EACH ZONE

ZONE 1   BELOW -50° F.

ZONE 2   -50° TO -40°

ZONE 3   -40° TO -30°

ZONE 4   -30° TO -20°

ZONE 5   -20° TO -10°

ZONE 6   -10° TO   0°

ZONE 7   0° TO 10°

ZONE 8   10° TO 20°

ZONE 9   20° TO 30°

ZONE 10 30° TO 40°

GARDENING BY THE SEA

CHAPTER ONE

The Lure of Seaside Gardens

F I HAD MY CHOICE, it would be a garden by the sea! A place where untempered winds and ocean spray often challenge the most competent of gardeners. A place where sunlit dew makes even the tiniest plants appear like jewels in the early morning sun. A place where the mingled fragrances of flowers, mixed with the salt of sea breezes, give the air a bracing freshness.

Within reach of the sea, plants frequently assume curious and picturesque forms, contorted by the prevailing winds. Nature with all the force of her power holds dominant sway, often using wind pruning and salt spray to sculpt trees and shrubs in the most elemental of art forms, stripping ruthlessly leaf and flower, twig and branch.

Ernest H. Wilson, the most extraordinary plant hunter of the twentieth century, has described the great struggle of the forces of nature vividly in *Aristocrats of the Trees*. In a chapter entitled "Trees and the Heart of Man" he wrote: "The Monterey Cypress and other coastwise trees may be dubbed Coastguards, defenders of their rockbound homes. Wind is their great enemy and the feud between them is eternal. From youth to old age the struggle persists and marvelous is the fight the trees of the shore put up against their unrelenting, death-dealing enemy, wind. The struggle may go on through centuries yet sooner or later victory is with the wind, but nothing in the tree world commands admiration more than the magnificent fight an old Pine or Cypress puts up. . . . One can imagine the jaws firmly set, every fiber of the tree's existence stressed to hold its own and proudly floating from the treetop its flag inscribed *nil desperandum*. There is something sublime in the masterful struggle between the organic and inorganic forces and methinks old Mother Nature stands as umpire witnessing the noble game."

The colors of blossoms and foliage appear to glow brighter, the tints and shades are more distinct. The blues are bluer and the pinks are pinker

1

Annuals and perennials make a setting for an unusual garden ornament.

and dew-drenched flowers in the morning light have a freshness that is not found in gardens inland. The subtle softness of silvery dusty miller, blue-green sea hollies, and gray lavender is all the more apparent in ocean-side plantings. Henry Beston, who spent a year living on the great beach of Cape Cod, recorded his experiences in an enchanting book entitled *The Outermost House*. He wrote vividly of many things and not the least of them was the dusty miller. One of the loveliest of all, a gray-leaved perennial native to the shoreline of the northeastern United States, it is often grown in seaside gardens. Of it he noted: "It jumps from the dune rim to the naked slopes, it even tries to find a permanent station on the beach. Silver gray-green all summer long, in autumn it puts on gold and russet— golden colorings of a singular delicacy and beauty."

What is it that gives coastal gardens their rare enchantment? Is it the sun on overcast days filtering through the recurring mist and fog, or is it the vast backdrop of sea and sky that encompasses them? Or could it be a combination of both? Or, in a different mood, is it the gleaming brilliance of that same sun on cloudless days that lights and warms the world so comfortably, all the while enhancing the landscape with a strange kind of glow that relaxes the spirit and makes everything about us pleasant and vibrant? For those who have lived near the ocean, on the East coast or the West, the lure of the sea is an unforgettable experience, and all the more so when your house is in or near a garden.

There is more to gardening by the sea than the sheer enjoyment of color. It is not just one delightful day after another spent weeding and cultivating, tying up plants and removing dead flowers. There are times when storms come suddenly, full of wind and rain, taking their toll of beds and borders. Seaside gardening has its hazards; the relentless wind often leaves its imprint in various ways. Yet there are always plants that survive the roughest of weather, and gardeners too begin each spring with new courage and enthusiasm.

Many of the earliest dooryard gardens planted along the Atlantic seaboard faced on the ocean or on some inlet from the sea. Enclosed by fences of wattle, rough pickets, or simple rail construction, these little plots were filled with herbs, culinary and medicinal, and favorite flowers of the Old World. In many ways they provided a nostalgic link with gardens left behind across the sea. In describing this deeply rooted tradition, Nathaniel Hawthorne once wrote: "There is not a softer trait to be found in the character of those stern men than that they should have been sensible of those flower-roots clinging among the fibres of their rugged hearts, and felt the necessity of bringing them over sea, and making them hereditary in the new land."

John Josselyn, writing in the mid-seventeenth century, reminds us that not all the roots and seeds brought to the New World flourished. For some, the ground in winter was too damp, for others the severe cold was more than they could stand, but this did not deter the sturdy Englishwomen who tended them. They soon found ways to combat the weather, even winter gales and heavy snow. Their love of gardens was inborn.

The surrounding landscape that formed the background and setting for the simple houses and tiny gardens of the Pilgrims and the Puritans was a far cry from what they had known at home. Yet many of the plants that grew naturally in this untamed wilderness reminded them of the land

3

In the herb gardens at Plimoth Plantation, thyme, sage, yarrow, and other fragrant plants flourish in the sun by the sea.

they had left. Not the least of these were the holly and the wild roses they found in great abundance growing near the shore. To be sure, our American holly does not have the glossy leaves so typical of English holly but the bright red berries and the general aspect of both English and American holly are similar. The wild roses sprawling over great boulders and ledges along the coast or growing in grassy meadows and upland pastures had all the sweetness, the color, and the texture of the eglantine and the rose wildings so typical of the English countryside. Thus Nature, the Art of God, as Sir Thomas Browne expressed it, sustained their courage in the New World.

Then, too, there were the stately red cedars, singly and in groups, standing like sentinels along the windswept coast, and beneath them in shallow pockets among the rocks, sprawling junipers formed an evergreen carpet. Bayberries, blueberries, elderberries and strawberries among the grasses, "the sweetest we ever eat," together with innumerable native bushes and trees of all sizes dotted the landscape. Lilies blossomed in many places

4

Old time herbs were essential for culinary, medicinal and general household use.

and countless strange and curious wild flowers made this wild country a broad flowery meadow.

The brilliant attire in which the maples, oaks, and sassafras decked themselves in autumn was an experience new to the pioneers. They had not known such spectacular pageants of fall color at home. True, some trees and shrubs of the English countryside change color as summer wanes, but generally the effects are much more subdued than what they witnessed in the new land. The golden days of October and early November were indeed an inspiration for these homesick settlers, ill-equipped to face the rigors of the wilderness, but determined to establish themselves and their way of life. Somehow, they survived and flourished and those "flower-roots clinging among the fibres of their rugged hearts" actually took root in the virgin soil of Colonial America. From this dedicated beginning, the inherent love of gardens transported as one of their most treasured possessions became a part of our American heritage.

5

Thus it remains today. The engaging hobby of gardening has become an endless adventure for countless thousands of gardeners. Experience has taught them that the greater the challenge, the richer the rewards to be enjoyed. As a result, some of the most beautiful and fascinating gardens in America are those which flourish by the sea. Despite the vagaries of wind and weather and the ever-changing reflections of sky and water, it is that rare translucent quality of light near the sea which gives flowers and foliage their true color value—making contrasts in form and texture all the more subtle and memorable.

Gardening near the edge of the sea often leads to the discovery of life on the dunes and the salt marshes where curious forms of plant and animal life exist. There, the engaging study of birdlife takes on new dimensions. The simplest forms of plant life that float in the shimmering water and are often tossed up on the beach after a high tide or a storm, make one realize that here, too, are marvels of plant life with an enchanting appeal of their own. "A day spent in the dunes

> *On the firm packed sand, Free*
> *By a world of marsh that borders a world of sea;*

with the roar of the waves and the cries of the gulls in one's ears, the breath of the marsh and of the ocean in one's nostrils, the wild beauty and loneliness of the scene in one's eyes, is indeed an inspiration, a memory worth treasuring."

Dr. Charles Wendell Townsend made these observations more than half a century ago in *Sand Dunes and Salt Marshes*. The ageless attraction of this wild beauty has not diminished, nor is it likely to. And it is perhaps best enjoyed and interpreted by those who have a zest for gardening in some form within sound of the sea, for

> *There is rapture on the lonely shore,*
> *There is society where none intrudes,*
> *By the deep sea, and music in its roar.*

CHAPTER TWO

Making the Most of Your Site

*T*HE possibilities, limitations, and success of any seaside garden are to a large extent determined by wind, sand, salt spray, and tide. When the garden site is perched high above the shoreline, tides have little or no immediate effect, but all the other compelling forms of nature that an ocean exposure conjures up are present in one form or another. For centuries, despite hurricanes and tornadoes, vegetation of a special kind, both woody and herbaceous, has endured the buffeting of wind and salt spray. Not even the shifting dunes of Cape Cod or those of the Jersey shore, or the seemingly endless stretches of Florida's coastline and the constant pounding of the surf on the Pacific shores, have eliminated the beach grass, the bayberry, the beach plum, the dusty miller, the beach pea, the seaside aster, and other denizens of these ever-changing strands that line our coastline east and west.

As we study the attempts that have been made to stabilize the shoreline in various parts of the country and to make gardens, we find that our forebears have not always used native materials exclusively to solve their problems. From the Orient they introduced the Japanese black pine and the rugosa rose. The sea buckthorn and the Russian olive are native to the coastal regions of Europe, and both the Scots and Austrian pines came to us from the Old World. So too did the heath, the heather, the sea lavender, and others. Along the South Florida coast we find the Australian pine (*Casuarina equisetifolia*) which rates high for endurance under salt spray and thrives in sand. Pittosporums for hedges and windbreaks were brought from Australia, New Zealand, and the Orient, and lilyturf came from Japan.

From Oregon to California other exotics equally adaptable have found the coastline to their liking. The sea is a great leveler even in the plant realm. Indeed, both Australia and New Zealand have contributed notably to the coastal gardens of the United States (tropical and subtropical). Amer-

7

icans visiting the South of France are surprised to find California wildings flourishing on the Riviera. Man's search for plants well suited to difficult sites as well as the perpetual lure of the exotic have taught us that there is a continuing and stimulating challenge for those who garden—particularly by the sea. It is essentially a kind of battle against nature, while using nature's far-flung materials to win the fight.

On the other hand, there are many native trees, shrubs, ground covers, and perennials that are by nature adapted to seaside conditions. A considerable number of them have more than average eye appeal and distinct landscape value, but they are seldom utilized unless they are found growing on the property. Even then, they are likely to be ignored or removed in favor of exotics. Weedy kinds like sumac, black cherry, scrub oak, pitch pine, and others may have to be thinned to make room for more desirable natives. However, where any kind of shelter-belt planting exists in the way of trees or shrubs or a combination of both, regardless of how weedy, tangled, and unkempt it may be, it should be analyzed carefully before pruning or uprooting. Often by cutting back and clearing undesirable growth, useful plant material can be fed heavily to encourage new fresh growth. This can be interplanted with desirable shrubs and trees.

Another reason why nature's seaside bounty has not been as widely utilized as it should be is that many native plants are not easily obtainable. Comparatively few nurseries list wild blueberries, bayberry, beach plum inkberry, shadbush, bearberry, and others. One has to shop and select from catalogs, checking with specialists, or arrange to order these items through garden centers and nurseries. This takes time. In the spring, when garden fever is at a high pitch, operators of nurseries and garden centers are far too busy to handle requests for these plants in small quantities. Therefore, considerable advance planning is essential during the winter months. It is a mistake to select too many exotic plants when there are desirable natives better suited to coastal sites.

Maintenance is a continuing challenge to any gardener, and thought must be given to the over-all design so that constant care is kept to a minimum. Even the smallest garden may require more attention than is at first realized. In this respect, mulching is of prime value. See Chapter 18.

The soil in which plants grow to a large extent determines the quality of growth, its vigor and general health. With few exceptions soils in most seaside gardens need improvement. An understanding of soils is basic to good gardening and fulfilling the requirements of plants with special needs is half the fun of this engaging hobby. See Chapter 15 for pointers on soil improvement.

Collecting native plants from the wild and moving them to desired locations is not always as easy or practical as may appear. If the plant is well established in sand, the chances are that its roots are deep and widely spread, and unless it can be moved with a ball of earth, it should not be

Thyme, Baron Solemacher strawberries, nasturtiums, boxwood, firethorn, and other plants make a pleasing setting for a sundial in this small garden.

disturbed. Plants growing in stony ground and in pockets of ledges present similar problems. Small plants and suckers from large specimens are usually safer to handle. Even then they must be watered and shaded until well established. Often time, energy, and money are saved by obtaining well-grown nursery stock, bare root, balled and burlapped or container-grown.

Where outcroppings of rock or great ledges exist, suitable plantings can be introduced to enhance and soften them. Where the soil depth is shallow, earth can be brought in or moved from another location on the property. If the gradient has been altered to any considerable extent, various types of ground cover can be used to prevent washing away of the soil. This method of handling large rocks and ledges is often preferable to making extensive changes in gradient by hauling in loam to level the area. Such procedures are usually costly and often little is gained. It is

9

This ledge planting will be greatly enhanced as the sedums, bearberry, houseleeks, junipers, and various rock plants become established, softening the outline and the surface of this great outcropping of rock.

better to study the existing terrain and its natural features; then thoughtfully exploit them, rather than conceal them.

Whether starting with bare ground or an already developed property, some sort of plan is needed for the over-all harmonization of the place. Assuming that there is a house on the property and that it fits the site, the challenge is to develop the planting so that it enhances both house and site, emphasizing the best features of both. Long-range plans must include the development and improvement of vistas. Every effort made to create pleasing views to and from the house places the emphasis for creating a seaside garden precisely where it belongs. A garden by the sea needs to be so designed that one is ever conscious of the site.

In the fall of 1938 a hurricane destroyed many notable gardens along the New England coast. Among them was the garden of Mrs. Arthur Havemeyer in Martha's Vineyard. Yet the following summer she was impelled to write: "How does nature treat her own gardens by the sea? With a certain austerity. There are great rocks carved into shapes fitted to hold back the oncoming swells—economy of line, beauty of contour. There are dunes which the wind has swept into curves and dips that follow inevitable laws. The rare gay little flowers are all the more telling for this restraint. Seaside plants have no lushness. One has an impression of grays and gray-greens, of rose and purplish reds—beautiful with blue and green water.

"The Japanese say: 'Do not overcrowd the seaside garden with trees and rocks and stone lanterns, for the sea is the principal part of the design.' We, too, should look at the sea undisturbed by petty foreground pictures. Let the flower garden be in the lee of the house or toward its side—a walled garden, a sunken garden, or, as our New England ancestors arranged it, a garden with a picket fence where herbs and flower treasures are protected. A garden by the sea should give relief from the boisterous breezes and the glare. It should be a peaceful retreat with shady places in which to sit and rest the eyes."

CHAPTER THREE

Hedges, Screens, and Windbreaks

INDBREAKS of various kinds are the first line of defense against the elements in most seaside gardens. Protection from the prevailing winds is as essential as that from seasonal storms. The belief that a high fence or wall solves the problem is not always sound. To begin with, the cost and maintenance of such windguards is often out of proportion to the results achieved. Wind often whips in behind solid barriers, causing more damage than when a looser screen is provided. Taking a lesson from nature, we learn that a barrier of shrubs, trees, and ground covers, planted thickly, provides obstacles to break the force of the wind and the salt spray. Then too the roots of these sturdy plants hold the sand.

Writing about wind is like writing about air. Yet too much cannot be said about its damaging effects on growth, nor can these conditions be fully realized until they are experienced. Distortion of form of individual plants is of minor consequence and can often add greatly to the appearance of an entire seaside planting. In fact, nowhere inland can one enjoy the supreme artistry of wind pruning which is far more skillful, adept, and daring than man's work with the shears. But broken branches and twisted stems, battered foliage and flowers, and that brown, burned look are also products of the wind. Thus, while soil and plant food are vital to continuity of growth, windbreaks also are essential before planting can be undertaken in a seaside garden.

Protective planting also limits and disperses to some degree the amount of salt spray likely to be deposited on plants during storms and periods of heavy wind. Salt, carried by the wind and deposited usually as spray, forming crystals as it dries, is neither beneficial nor desirable for most plants, though certain kinds obviously tolerate it and a few apparently thrive on it. As one botanist has observed, the growth of turnips, beets, celery, sea kale, and asparagus is improved when small amounts of salt are added to the soil in which these vegetables are grown. All have an ancestry linked

12

Darling

The effects of wind, salt spray, old age, and hurricanes.

with the seacoast. Salt accumulates in the sap of the plant cells and causes these vegetables to absorb considerable amounts of water, a high ratio in relation to the dry tissue. It would seem that the presence of salt builds up a thirst in plants as it does in humans, causing them to root deeply in search of water and to store it as protection against drought.

However, with many plants that have developed tolerance, the effects of salt in the soil and salt-laden air are sometimes indicated by thinner than normal growth and dwarfing the typical habit of development. Leaves are usually smaller, stems shorter, and the general aspect appears to be reflected in compactness of form. To be sure, wind is also a factor in this development.

Why certain plants are able to endure these conditions is a question frequently asked. Endurance may be attributed to several factors linked with the ecology of seaside plants. Ecology is the science of the home environment of plants. Over the centuries, certain plants in all parts of the world have become adapted to arid soil, long periods of drought, and constant exposure to wind. As a result they have developed defenses for survival including deep roots, special facilities for storing moisture, and protective leaf surfaces to reduce the loss of moisture.

One has only to attempt to dig up a clump of beach pea, dusty miller, bayberry, yucca, or beach plum, growing in sand, to learn how deeply rooted these plants are. These marvelous mechanisms travel far and wide

13

seeking moisture, and this is why established plants are practically impossible to move.

Many seaside plants have long, narrow leaves that stand the wind well. The willows, the sea buckthorn, the tamarisk, and others are typical examples. Acacias have flattened stems instead of leaves and the foliage of the Australian pine is composed of flexible branchlets with leaves and flowers of insignificant size. As a result of this marvel of adaptation, not even the worst hurricane with its constant drenching of salt spray kills these plants. The leaf area is small and rain washes off the salt.

The yucca or Spanish bayonet, the sea grape, the sea holly, yew, the pines, the various hollies, and many other plants bear leaves with glossy or smooth surfaces which serve as protection. A close look at heather, tamarix, the junipers, and many subtropical and tropical plants reveals scalelike foliage which has great wind- and salt-resistance.

Gray or silvery foliaged plants have protective mechanisms in the form of tiny hairs, densely arranged on the leaf surfaces on one or both sides. These catch the salt crystals and protect the leaf itself. They also reduce the amount of moisture given off by the leaves. The waxy surface of the gray fruits of the bayberry and the glaucous character of the foliage of certain plants are other protective measures.

Wind and windblown sand are also damaging to plants. The ways in which nature has modified leaves, buds, stems, and seedpods in size and form and provided them with hard, shiny surfaces and protective hairs, are evidence of adaptability to abnormal conditions for survival.

What to plant, how best to establish these materials, procedures for maintenance, and the ability to replace damaged growth following heavy storms, are the steps involved in building a natural windbreak. The problem is similar to that of mending a dike. It is not always possible to determine the weak spots in advance, nor to anticipate how the storm will affect a particular area. Hurricanes, tornadoes, and northeast storms often behave strangely.

The newcomer to the seaside must observe carefully his own site and those of his neighbors before making elaborate plans. He must learn all he can about the exposure of his property, how the storms affect it, and what plants in adjoining areas have shown the greatest endurance. Growing conditions as they relate to exposure can vary greatly within a distance of 50 to 100 feet of the waterfront. Even within lesser distances, air currents show their influence.

In planting a screen or shelter belt, it is sound practice to use several kinds of woody plants rather than confine selection to a single kind. Under certain conditions big-scale shrubs may assume the aspect of small trees, while trees may become dwarfed by wind pruning to resemble shrubs in appearance. Variety in texture lends interest to any planting, and even when contemplating a windbreak this factor should not be overlooked.

14

See Appendix for lists of plants suited to varying degrees of exposure. Classification is as follows:

Belt I

The first line of defense includes plants that can tolerate full exposure to wind, salt spray, and windblown sand as well as salt in the soil. The plants listed cannot be considered entirely foolproof since they may survive and flourish under one set of conditions while factors such as deficiencies in plant food, inadequate root systems, improper planting, and others not readily apparent, may have an adverse effect.

Belt II

This is the zone where partial protection exists, provided by growth in Belt I.

Belt III—The Protected Area

Material for planting in Belt III should be carefully selected. Plants with well-developed root systems, balled and burlapped or container-grown, are best. If such material is moved from lath shelters (used by many nurserymen) for immediate planting, without hardening for several days, consider-

Japanese black pines take on picturesque growth in windswept places.

Taloumis

able wilt or sunburn may occur when the foliage is exposed to strong winds. The term "hardening," as used here, refers to the placing of nursery stock in full exposure to sun and wind for several days without allowing it to dry out. Container-grown stock kept in the open for a period of time has an opportunity to harden adequately.

Soil preparation as discussed in Chapters 3 and 15 is essential.

Watering must be thorough and frequent until plants are established.

Feeding is best done early in the season so that new growth will have adequate time to harden before winter sets in. See Chapter 17, Winter Protection.

Mulching is sound practice and vital to the conservation of moisture. See Chapter 18 on Mulches and Chapter 17, Winter Protection.

Temporary Protection. Shading tender young growth is not practical except in the small garden and in cases involving special groups of plants. Temporary fencing as discussed in this chapter pays dividends.

Fencing. When and where fencing of any type is used, it should be of sturdy construction and firmly anchored in the ground with posts set even deeper in concrete than might normally be required. Posts are best set closer than would be the case with fences inland. Learning from the experience of others is sound practice especially for the novice or the newcomer to beach property. Pet theories are often shattered after a thorough investigation of local conditions made during all seasons of the year. The weight of the fence, its height, and the type of construction are of prime importance.

Establishing Coastal Sand Dunes. Nature's way is slow but can be hastened in several ways. Federal, state, and local agencies, particularly the National Park Service and the Soil Conservation Service of the United States Department of Agriculture, concerned with conservation and the protection of shorelines, are available sources of information regarding various techniques for different sites.

When properly maintained, coastal sand dunes are the most effective natural defense against damage caused by storm tides, waves, and wind. However, unless the dunes are covered with vegetation to resist erosion from both wind and waves, they do not provide the maximum protection desired. Native beach grass serves the purpose admirably since it traps the wind-moved sand, stabilizing "live" dunes, as they are called, and enabling them to increase in height as the sand accumulates.

During storms of unusual severity, beach grass is sometimes uprooted and washed away. When this occurs, immediate steps should be taken to repair the damage. Otherwise the erosion caused by normal tides and wind may require the use of heavy equipment to reestablish the desired protection, since new dunes must be formed. Where damage is repairable without heavy equipment, barrier dunes can be rebuilt by using sand fences. This

16

Russian olive makes a most effective silvery screen when allowed to grow naturally. A single purpled-leaved plum stands out in contrast.

method traps and holds wind-borne sand as it moves naturally with the wind, providing a new dune on which beach grass can be planted.

Building Dunes. Simple picket fencing, the type used to check drifting snow, is ideal for this purpose. Snow fence is comparatively inexpensive, light in weight, easy to handle, and readily obtainable. When homemade fencing is used, the spacing between pickets should equal that of the width of the pickets. All fencing should be firmly anchored in the sand. Coarse brush and used Christmas trees are also useful and practical for establishing dunes. These materials are best handled by placing them upright so that the branches touch and the stems are buried at least two feet deep. Fence framing (posts and stringers) is sometimes used for anchoring brush.

Sand fences need to be set above or behind the high-water line in two parallel lines 30 to 40 feet apart. Experience has proved that the fenc-

17

Inkberry is the hardiest of all the hollies.

ing needs to be parallel to the water line and as nearly as possible at a right angle to the prevailing winds. Where this arrangement is neither practical nor possible, set a single line of fence, parallel with the sea, and space spur fencing in 30-foot lengths perpendicular to the single line. Spurs spaced 40 feet apart on the seaward side will prevent lateral drift. As the sand fills in around the fencing, additional sets can be placed on the forming dune until the barrier has reached the desired protective height. Then beach grass may be planted to check erosion.

Mulching Dunes. Temporary protection in the form of mulch is possible by spreading salt hay, coarse wood chips, or other coarse materials over the surface and partially covering it with sand. Brush, firmly imbedded in the sand, is useful to prevent scouring. Heavy jute netting, pinned down with wooden or wire stakes, is sometimes used instead of mulch or brush. The Soil Conservation Service has found that these temporary protection measures last about two years and then must be replaced, and their use does not result in any appreciable amount of sand accumulation.

18

American Beach Grass. Despite the use of temporary mulching, newly built barrier dunes need to be planted as soon as possible. American beach grass (*Ammophila breviligulata*), native to the Mid-Atlantic coast, is considered the best species for stabilizing the sand dunes along the East Coast. Once established, it spreads rapidly by underground stems to form a durable erosion-resistant cover. The tough arching foliage with its sharp edges decreases the wind velocity near the surface of the dune, and sand is deposited between the blades. As the sand piles up, the rugged grass grows up through it, establishing a green protective network as the stolons or underground stems develop. Henry David Thoreau, writing of beach grass more than a century ago, stated: "Cape Cod is anchored to the heavens, as it were, by a myriad little cables of beachgrass, and, if they should fail, would become a total wreck, and erelong go to the bottom."

Planting Techniques. Since immediate results are usually essential, planting root divisions of beach grass is preferable to seeding which requires mulching. Even with this precaution, germination is apt to be irregular or uncertain in the shifting sand. Planting stock is most easily and quickly obtained by collecting the grass from established colonies. After digging, shake the clumps free of sand and divide them. Each clump is composed of numerous stems or culms. Separate these, allowing two or three or more culms to each division, using only vigorous young growth. Cut back top growth to a foot in length, removing all dead material to obtain tidy divisions that are easy to handle. Protect divisions by watering them thoroughly and wrapping in wet burlap to keep them moist until they are set out.

Since planting stock of beach grass is available from comparatively few commercial growers, collecting stock as needed is usually the most practical way to secure it.

The period from October 1 to April 30 is the most suitable time for planting. Satisfactory survival of plantings made during this period is generally assured if the sand is not frozen. Usually, summer planting is not recommended, since considerable watering is required for success.

Use a staggered arrangement, spacing plants 18 inches apart each way. One large division or two small ones are needed for each hole. Since erosion-control plantings of this type cover sizable areas, the number of plants required should be determined in advance. In areas where wind erosion is particularly severe, approximately 20,000 large divisions are needed for one acre. If spaced one foot apart each way, 43,560 divisions will be required.

Beach grass needs to be planted at least 8 inches deep to obtain good results as well as to prevent plants from being blown away by the wind. A tiling or ditching spade with a long narrow blade is an excellent tool for making holes. For greatest efficiency, use a two-man crew to plant. The spadesman opens a hole 12 to 14 inches deep and holds the sand from

Pussy willows against the sky.

running back into the hole. His partner inserts the plant to an 8- to 10-inch depth and holds it steady. The spadesman presses his foot next to the plant to firm the sand and eliminate air space in the root zone. As soon as new growth starts, the plants spread by underground stems, filling the bare areas with new shoots. Once established, American beach grass self-sows.

Other Types of Grasses. In the Pacific Northwest, European beach grass (*A. arenaria*) is used, but under severe conditions it has proved to be less hardy than American beach grass. Along the Carolina coast and south as well as along the Gulf Coast a number of coarse grasses have been used successfully. These include:

> Broom sedge (*Andropogon virginicus*)
> Seacoast bluestem (*Andropogon littoralis*)
> Sea oats (*Uniola paniculata*)
> Sea panic grass (*panicum amarum*)
> Veld grass (*Ehrlarta calycina*)
> Volga wild rye (*Elymus giganteus*)
> Weeping lovegrass (*Eragrostis curvula*)

Seed is sown on mulched dunes so that it is enabled to germinate with a protective cover that also shelters it from the wind in the seedling stage. The grasses create striking effects during various stages of growth and have special eye appeal when the seed pods have formed. These are used frequently for dried arrangements.

Importance of Feeding. Heavy feeding is of vital importance in establishing healthy stands of beach grass. Growth and underground spread will occur much faster and earlier protection is possible when the planted areas are fertilized. Apply a complete fertilizer such as 10-10-10 at the rate of 400 pounds per acre in April or May, and make a similar application in July. Fed annually, a heavy growth of beach grass can be expected and the cost is small compared to the expense of restoring an area that has been neglected for several years.

Temporary fencing made with sections of snow fence are practical and easy to handle for a variety of uses. Because of their flexible construction, they make admirable shelter for groups of plants newly set in dunes and along the edge of the shore. In any case, they need to be firmly anchored with wire or wooden stakes driven firmly into the ground.

Problem Sites. In locations where sites present problems of special control of shorelines to meet individual needs, the services of a professional landscape architect should be sought. Often the establishing of dunes requires trespass rights and the cooperation of committees and private landowners. Considerable labor, heavy equipment, and expense may be involved. In the same way, the task of stabilizing bluffs with a bulkhead and suitable plantings is a major operation. Conditions peculiar to a local area involving boundary rights, cooperation with neighbors, heavy construction, the use of creosoted wooden piles, the building of ditches, and the like cannot be detailed or analyzed in this book on seaside gardening. They involve primarily landscape engineering and require the services of professional talent.

CHAPTER FOUR

Adaptable Trees and Their Uses

HE trees discussed in this chapter have been selected on the basis of their adaptability to wind and salt spray. Techniques for planting and the care required until they are established are the same as for flowering shrubs and evergreens discussed in the opening paragraphs of Chapter 5. The list at the end of this chapter includes other worthwhile trees suited to seaside situations in various sections of the country.

AUSTRALIAN LAUREL   6–30′   Zone 8   *Pittosporum* genus

This group of highly ornamental broad-leaved evergreens, mostly from Australia, is the envy of northern gardeners. They flourish only in Florida, the Gulf states, and California, and are completely at home by the sea. Tobira (*P. tobira*) or Japanese pittosporum makes a handsome hedge or specimen plant ranging in height from 6 to 15 feet according to the care given it in pruning. The leathery dark green leaves, 3 to 4 inches long, make a rich background for the creamy white fragrant flowers. The variegated form is particularly striking since the dark foliage is outlined in white. Karo (*P. crassifolium*) is a gray-leaved kind with orange flowers borne on a big-scale shrub or small tree growing to about 25 feet and spreading half as wide if allowed. Victorian box (*P. undulatum*) is a roundheaded tree or large shrub growing to 30 feet or more unless pruned, spreading more than half as wide. Leaves are 5 to 6 inches long, dark and glossy, and the fragrant flowers are white followed by orange fruits.

AUSTRALIAN PINE   30–50′   Zone 10   *Casuarina* genus

Beefwood and she-oak are other common names for the curious Australian pines, so called because the leaves or branchlets resemble the needles of the pines. Because of their curious formation, they are well adapted to wind, drought, and salt spray, so typical of their native habitat in Australia. For these reasons they have been commonly used as hedges and

Taloumis

Native birch adds to the beauty of this protected harbor.

windbreaks in southern Florida where they are widely naturalized and they are also used to some extent in California. The horsetail beefwood (*C. equisetifolia*) of pendulous branching habit and the coast beefwood (*C. stricta*) are much smaller in size and are noted for their rapid growth.

These plants thrive in sandy soil, even brackish conditions, and require no special care.

BEECH   60–90′   Zones 3–4   *Fagus* genus

Few trees can rival the beeches for beauty of form and year-round eye appeal, but they are suitable only for large properties and require several decades to reach any appreciable size. In addition to specimen use, they are most adaptable for hedges. The American beech (*F. grandiflora*) is not as widely planted as its European relative (*F. sylvatica*), which is highly valued for its distinctive varieties. These include the copper, the purple, the fernleaf, the cutleaf, and the weeping beech. While all are tolerant of salt spray, they are not well suited to an exposed shoreline.

For a good start, beeches need well-prepared soil, with plenty of organic matter. They are heavy feeders and respond to annual applications of fertilizer. Hard pruning induces dense, well-shaped growth.

BLACK LOCUST   50–75′   Zone 3   *Robinia pseudoacacia*

Tough, hardy, and fast growing, the black locust is often found in coastal areas. It is a long-lived tree bearing showy clusters of fragrant white pealike flowers. A pink-flowered variety is popular in city gardens and it is sometimes grown as a street tree, as well as in several other selected forms. Its resistance to salt spray and its far-reaching root system for binding soil are reasons for planting it along the shoreline. It is a brittle tree with twigs and branches that fall frequently, and it is also greedy in its heavy root formation. Yet for screen planting and as a windbreak it has considerable merit. See also Honey Locust.

A shrubby locust of treelike aspect that suckers heavily is the rose acacia (*R. hispida*). This woody plant grows to 5 feet or more in height, bearing clusters of showy rose-colored flowers in late spring. Highly ornamental in foliage and general appearance, it is an excellent soil binder and extremely hardy.

Of easy culture, requiring no special soil, the black locust is a weed tree in some areas. The stem borer and the leaf miner are serious pests that sometimes infest this tree.

CAJEPUT TREE   40′   Zone 10   *Melaleuca leucadendron*

Its creamy white flowers resemble those of the bottlebrush (*Callistemon*) and the evergreen foliage is pale in tone. The thick gray bark of this Australian native peels in thin strips. Tough and fast-growing, it is not harmed by salt spray or other adverse conditions.

CALIFORNIA LAUREL   25–50'   Zone 7   *Umbellularia californica*

Also known as California bay and Oregon myrtle, this broad-leaved evergreen can be grown as a big-scale shrub along the entire West Coast where it is native. Glossy aromatic foliage, 3 to 5 inches in length, clusters of small yellowish flowers, and green to purple fruits are among its assets for landscape use.

CALIFORNIA PEPPER TREE   25–40'   Zone 9   *Schinus molle*

A rapid grower, often spreading nearly as wide as it is high, the California pepper tree is of notable ornamental value. The pendulous branches covered with finely cut foliage and the racemes of rose-colored berries that ripen in fall and last through winter are most attractive. Some trees may produce a preponderance of male flowers which results in no fruit yield. This tree is shallow rooted and needs a protected site, as does the Brazilian pepper (*S. terebinthianum*), which bears showy red fruit. Also, this plant is more irregular in habit, with coarser foliage, and is somewhat less graceful in aspect than the more familiar California species.

CRAB APPLE   6–30'   Zones 2–4   *Malus* genus

For their heavy and colorful flowering habit, their showy fruit, clean foliage, variety of form, and ironclad hardiness, crab apples rate high

Crabapples vary in height and form and are well suited to seaside plantings. They are valued for their showy flowers in spring and colorful fruits in autumn.

Genereux

among small flowering trees. Many of the tall-growing species and varieties can be pruned high and thinned for use as substitutes for the fruiting apples formerly grown in gardens as much as for their decorative effect as for fruit yield. Heights vary from 6 to 30 feet according to kind, and they may be roundheaded, pyramidal, broadly columnar, broad-spreading, low and shrublike, or pendulous. Where space permits, they can be used to soften corners of a house, as lawn specimens, in mixed plantings, or in broad masses.

Flowers may be single or double, ranging in color from white to dark red and fruits are either red or yellow, according to kind. Large nurseries offer an extensive list so that selection of favorites is easy. Young nursery-grown specimens are easy to transplant and should be thoughtfully placed since older plants are not easily moved because of their widespreading root systems.

Give crab apples a well-drained location, preferably in full sun. They are reliably hardy, relatively pest free, drought resistant, and require no special care. Many growers offer them container-grown, which makes transplanting easy. It often takes crab apples several years to become established with heavy flowering and fruiting. With all varieties, occasional pruning to improve form is important. In exposed sites, wind pruning will change their naturally symmetrical habit, adding greatly to their appearance.

EUCALYPTUS   30–100'   Zone 9   *Eucalyptus* genus

Gum tree and stringybark are common names for this remarkable genus, mostly native to Australia. West Coast gardeners have a wide selection of species from which to choose as they select for windbreaks, hedges, or specimens. Resistance to disease, aromatic, evergreen foliage of pleasing texture, and moderate-to-rapid growth are attributes of many of the eucalyptuses. More than 500 species are known and a sizable number are available in the California nursery trade.

Drought-resistant kinds and those that tolerate coastal conditions include the sugar gum (*E. cladocalyx*), the yate tree (*E. cornuta*), the dwarf blue gum (*E. globulus compacta*), and others.

Eucalyptus is not particular as to soil and many species grow under adverse conditions. Container-grown plants are easy to handle. They are more easily grown from seed than from cuttings or by other methods.

FALSE CYPRESS   20–80'   Zones 3–5   *Chamaecyparis* genus

The various kinds of false cypress have many points in their favor. Some are forest trees, others are big-scale shrubs, and there are the dwarf Japanese types. Casual pruning keeps them attractive in appearance. In mixed plantings with other evergreens and flowering shrubs, they lend considerable interest because of their threadlike, golden or silvery mosslike foliage, according to the variety grown. For the most part, they are not at

26

their best when constantly exposed to wind. In protected parts of the grounds, the dwarf Hinoki types are desirable for their trim, symmetrical habit of growth, rich green foliage, and slow growth.

Full sun is essential and average garden soil suits them. An annual feeding with evergreen fertilizer keeps false cypress thrifty; otherwise, plants become ragged looking, especially on poor soil. The inner branches need to be washed off annually to remove the dead needles.

HOLLY   2–40′   Zones 3–7   *Ilex* genus

No other plant native to the Eastern seaboard has more nostalgic links with the British Isles than American holly. The shapely trees with spiny leaves and bright red berries that the early settlers at Jamestown, Virginia, Plymouth and Salem, Massachusetts, found flourishing in the new land made them heartsick for the holly hedges and comfortable homes they had left behind. But in later years these sturdy folk and their descendants cherished the holly of the New World, similar in many ways to the English species, and used it as a symbol for recalling the age-old joy of Christmas. In the years following the Civil War, when Christmas became a recognized holiday, American holly was plentiful in the wild, but careless cutting and lack of conservation have caused it to practically disappear. Today natural stands in New England are rare, but farther south, from Virginia to Florida, this handsome evergreen is a familiar plant in the wild.

American holly is a tree of open woods and fields, often found in sandy, stony soil. Holly devotees have spared no effort to study the needs of this plant and have selected a number of varieties, outstanding for the quality and quantity of their fruits, and these have been named. Plants are slow-growing and require considerable care until they reach 4 to 5 feet in height, but once established they eventually develop into trim pyramidal specimens. American holly, like other members of the genus, has hard surface foliage and endures considerable exposure to wind and salt spray, but is more safely planted where it is somewhat protected by a windbreak of trees and shrubs.

In addition to *I. opaca,* Southern gardeners have another native evergreen form with showy red berries (*I. vomitoria*) known as yaupon, hardy from Zone 7 South. It may develop into a small tree 15 to 20 feet or more in height or, in exposed locations near the coast, become shrublike in habit.

Winterberry (*I. verticillata*), also known as black alder, is one of the few deciduous kinds found in moist ground along the Eastern seaboard and inland. When the leaves fall in late autumn, the showy red fruit is particularly striking and lasts well when cut. This shrub grows well in ordinary soil and, if cut back hard every few years, makes a widespreading ornamental shrub 6 to 8 feet high.

English holly (*I. aquifolium*) has proved hardy as far north as Cape Cod and flourishes near the sea as it does in the British Isles. In the North-

American holly, ink berry, yew and other needle-type and broadleaf evergreens give this planting year 'round eye appeal.

west and in California many outstanding varieties are grown in gardens and on holly farms for use as specimens and hedges, as well as for the Christmas trade. Its glossy foliage gives this tree great distinction at all seasons of the year. It is hardy from Zone 6 South.

There are many noteworthy species and selected forms of holly that deserve a place in coastal gardens where they are hardy. In addition, there are evergreen kinds with smaller foliage and black fruit. See Japanese holly and inkberry, Chapter 5.

Although American holly is sometimes found in sandy and gravelly soil, it is best planted in well-prepared holes where the best of drainage is assured, using ample amounts of humus. All hollies need acid soil. Evergreen fertilizer and cottonseed meal applied in early spring are useful for feeding all types of holly. With most kinds, plants of both sexes are needed to produce fruits. Mulching of hollies in seaside gardens is advisable.

Honey Locust   60–100'   Zone 3   *Gleditsia triacanthos*

The common honey locust is a sturdy native tree, completely hardy at the shore. Its chief drawbacks are the heavy spines on trunks and branches and the long brown seedpods which make considerable litter. However, the new thornless varieties, the Moraine, the Shademaster, and other recently named kinds are ideally suited to seaside plantings. All are

28

Newly planted specimens of Moraine locust are likely to be awkward in appearance, but they develop sturdy trunks and pleasing form within a few years after planting. Constant pruning helps to improve their appearance.

29

clean and rapid in growth, graceful in habit, and provide lacy shade. Few shade trees are more adaptable to home grounds or for street use, and they offer less competition to grass growing beneath them. Adapted to hot, dry situations or part shade, they flourish in various types of soil and their sturdy branches are seldom damaged by wind.

The Moraine locust with its round head and somewhat irregular curving trunk and branches, matures as a vase-shaped tree. Rubylace has dark red leaves. The growth of Shademaster is more upright than that of the Moraine locust with a pronounced straight trunk. Sunburst thornless locust is especially conspicuous when the new foliage is unfolding because of its golden yellow coloring, but this novelty needs to be planted with discretion. Skyline is distinctly pyramidal in form, with dark green foliage. The Idaho flowering locust is noted for its pendulous clusters of rose pink flowers in late spring and the Flowering Globe variety has large lavender-purple blooms.

Average soil suits all these varieties and they are reliably hardy, but young trees are shallow-rooted and need to be carefully guyed or supported with iron pipes until well established. Easy to transplant and fast growers, especially in fertile soil, all need to be cut back hard for several years after planting to develop strong trunks. In recent years, the Moraine and the Shademaster locust have been widely planted to replace the American elm.

JAPANESE TREE LILAC   15–20′   Zone 4   *Syringa amurensis japonica*

Not widely planted, but a highly desirable small tree of roundheaded habit, the Japanese tree lilac is distinctive and graceful, with ascending branches. Large creamy white trusses of fragrant bloom appear 2 to 3 weeks later than those of the common lilac, measuring 10 to 12 inches or more in length. Foliage is large with leaves to 6 inches in length, and the yellow-green seedpods are highly ornamental, persisting until dry in the fall. Then they may be cut for dried bouquets.

Of easy culture, well suited to hot, dry situations, it needs only thorough soil preparation when planted and sufficient water until well established. Otherwise, it endures considerable dryness and requires no special care.

LITTLELEAF LINDEN   30–50′   Zone 3   *Tilia cordata*

A dense-headed shade tree of rounded, pyramidal form that shows its mature habit even as a young tree, the littleleaf linden is ideal for lawn use or screen planting. The sweet fragrance of the small, creamy flowers that appear in early summer is another feature. Slow-growing and notably hardy, it is easily obtainable. Other species include: the Crimean linden (*T. euchlora*) valued for its glossy, bright green leaves; the European linden (*T. europaea*) which suckers along the trunk; and the silver linden (*T. tomentosa*) valued for the silvery white undersurfaces of its foliage.

30

The sturdy silver poplar shows the whitish undersurfaces of its leaves with every breeze and endures salt spray with ease.

Lindens thrive in a variety of soils as witness the fact that they endure city conditions when used as shade trees. In exposed situations, where wind, salt spray, and dry soil are prevalent, these sturdy trees have proved themselves. On the whole, they are more satisfactory in the Northeast than on the West Coast.

MAPLE 50′ Zone 2   *Acer* genus

Two of our common maples are frequently seen holding their heads high against the stiff winds from the sea. These are the Norway (*A. platanoides*) and the sycamore maple (*A. pseudoplatanus*). The latter is an excellent tree for windbreaks since it endures salt spray successfully. The foliage is large and rather coarse, but the silvery undersurfaces show to good

31

advantage with every breeze, giving the tree a pleasing appearance. Showy seedpods in sizable clusters appear in summer. The red maple (*A. rubrum*) is found along the coast, often dwarfed and twisted by the wind, but holding its own bravely and conspicuous in autumn when the leaves turn. It is sometimes planted in West Coast seaside gardens.

Maples grow best in full sun, but will tolerate a fair amount of shade and are not particular as to soil. Stake carefully after planting and prune the top for shape. Feed plants in exposed areas to encourage sturdy, compact growth.

MAYTEN TREE   30–40′   Zone 9   *Maytenus boaria*

Rapid in growth until it reaches 15 to 20 feet in height, the mayten tree actually is twice as tall when fully developed, but slows down as it matures. This evergreen with its pendulous branchlets hanging from upright branches suggests a weeping willow in many ways. The narrow leaves are leathery in texture and the flowers are of little significance. Grown by the sea in Florida and California, it rates high as a small tree.

MONTEREY CYPRESS   40′   Zone 7   *Cupressus macrocarpa*

The Monterey pine and this cypress are among the most widely photographed trees in America. They stand against the sea along the Monterey Peninsula, enduring both the constant blasts of the trade winds and the salt-laden spray. Nearly every seaside gardener who has seen them has silently wished it were possible to transplant one of these great patriarchs to his own garden. As a young tree, the Monterey cypress is pyramidal in form but assumes its roundheaded appearance with age. Wind pruning adds the finishing touches to make it highly decorative. The foliage resembles that of juniper and it is sometimes used for hedges.

A rapid grower, requiring only average care, this picturesque tree is not as widely planted as it once was because of its susceptibility to the harmful coryneum canker, which is usually fatal.

MOUNTAIN ASH   30′   Zone 2   *Sorbus aucuparia*

One of the showiest of ornamental trees both in flower and fruit, it has long been a favorite. Large flat clusters of white flowers appear in spring, followed by conspicuous clusters of red fruit in early fall. With the passing of summer, the compound foliage assumes reddish tones. Upright in habit, this tree makes a striking effect in any landscape planting.

Full sun or light shade suits it and the soil requirements of mountain ash are easily met. Be on the lookout for borers near the base, since, if not controlled, their damage can be serious.

NORFOLK ISLAND PINE   90′   Zones 7–10   *Araucaria excelsa*

The Norfolk Island pine, a favorite pot plant in greenhouses because of its symmetrical pyramidal form, is cultivated in the open only in tropical climates. On the other hand, the bizarre monkey puzzle tree (*A. araucana*) native to Chile is hardy from Zone 7 South. The branches are twisted and contorted naturally so that exposure to wind only makes them more so. The needles, which are prickly, persist for many years and showy cones are another feature of this strange tree. The Australian hoop pine (*A. cunninghamii*) produces tufted growth at the ends of its branches and grows to considerable height. All are tolerant of salt spray and belong only in settings where there is ample space for development.

OAK   30–100′   Zones 4–7   *Quercus* genus

A number of oaks are among the limited group of trees suitable for shoreline planting. For cold climates the white oak (*Q. alba*), the black oak (*Q. velutina*), the blackjack oak (*Q. marilandica*), and occasionally the English oak are the kinds best suited to the rigors of the coast. For the southern coastline, the native live oak (*Q. virginiana*), and the holly or holm oak (*Q. ilex*), both with evergreen foliage, are commonly planted. On the West Coast, the California live oak (*Q. agrifolia*) with its evergreen, hollylike foliage has a place in seaside plantings.

Oaks are not as easy to transplant as most kinds of trees. Young nursery-grown specimens balled and burlapped or container-grown are best suited to planting near the sea. Stake carefully after planting. It is a mistake to move specimens of any size unless more than average care can be given.

OLIVE   30′   Zone 9   *Olea europaea*

This familiar Old World tree, brought to America by Spanish missionaries, has many of the required characteristics for a coastal tree. It is adaptable to a variety of soils and resistant to heat, drought, and wind. Willowlike evergreen leaves with silvery undersurfaces and the distinctive twisted character of both branches and trunk give it an unusually picturesque appearance. In California growth is slow; height varies from 15 to 30 feet. The olive has great landscape possibilities when well placed and thoughtfully pruned.

PEA TREE   20′   Zone 2   *Caragana arborescens*

This member of the pea tree family bears showy yellow flowers in clusters in May and is valued for its pleasing habit and clean, lacy foliage. It can be used as a windbreak or screen, for a hedge or as a specimen. Both deep-rooted and long-lived, it has special value in seaside gardens, since it is not particular as to soil. However, it is little known and seldom grown.

PINE   45–100′   Zones 2–9   *Pinus* genus

A dozen or more kinds of pine native to the coastal areas of the United States and several introduced species endure the buffeting of wind and salt spray amazingly well. Many of these species are quite different in aspect when grown inland or even when sheltered from the severity of

33

Pines are usually sturdy, but hurricanes sometimes take them down.

the prevailing winds. Certain types of pine survive extreme exposure, all the while developing twisted, windblown, contorted forms, and this gives them distinct landscape value. This point should be borne in mind when nursery-grown stock is set out; usually it is trim and symmetrical, having been pruned hard. Seedling pines 3 to 4 years old are often planted in quantity to stabilize dunes and sandbanks. Usually they are a bit ragged in appearance until well established, but planting them while small is sound practice. Pines make ideal hedges, screens, and windbreaks and no gardener needs to be told of their appeal as specimen plants or in groups. When planted close to the shore, pines seldom attain their true height or normal habit of growth. Furthermore, they often have a brownish, burned look in early spring and are seldom as luxurious in growth as when seen inland. To lend variety and interest to a barrier planting or a windbreak, use several of the salt-tolerant kinds together such as Austrian, Scots, and Japanese black pine, rather than confine the planting to a single kind. Despite the convictions held by specialists regarding the merits of specific kinds for windswept locations, planting sites and other factors may favor one species more than another. The following list includes pines suitable to various parts of the country.

Aleppo pine (*P. halepensis*). This native of the Mediterranean is well suited to seashore use in areas where it is winter-hardy. Zone 6 South.

Austrian pine (*P. nigra*). Also known as black pine, this species is similar in some ways to the Japanese black pine, but with lighter green needles and slower growth. In some areas it has proved to be somewhat less tolerant of strong wind and great onslaughts of salt spray than had been expected. This plant develops dense, broad-spreading growth as it matures, making good windbreaks. Zone 4.

Bishop pine (*P. muricata*). This roundheaded pine is used on the West Coast for windbreaks and hedges. Zone 7.

Cluster pine (*P. pinaster*). Sometimes called the maritime pine, it is difficult to transplant and is best handled in the seedling stage. Ideal for sand dunes. Zone 7.

Jack pine (*P. banksiana*). Better known as scrub pine, this is a tough, rugged, lean-looking tree whose needles turn yellow in winter. One or several of these pines viewed against the sky make a fascinating silhouette. Native to the Northeast, it thrives in the poorest of sandy soils, but is less tolerant of salt spray than the Austrian and Japanese black species. Zone 2.

Japanese black pine (*P. thunbergii*). Since its introduction, this pine has proved of great value as a seaside evergreen. Rather slow-growing when young, it is easily recognized by its stiff dark green needles, 3 to 5 inches long. Strong winds may tilt it at an angle, but it is not easily blown over if set out as a small tree. By nature, the branches of the Japanese black pine become crooked as they mature, giving the tree an aspect of true oriental picturesqueness. Zone 4.

Japanese umbrella pine (*Pinus densiflora umbraculifera*). Also known as the Tanyosho pine, its low-growing branching habit gives the plant a distinctive umbrellalike form; specimens are usually dwarf in stature and grow to 10 feet or more. A variety of the Japanese red pine, it is not common. Zone 4.

Monterey pine (*P. radiata*). The flat-topped, wind-twisted specimens seen along the Monterey Peninsula on the Southern California coast are quite unlike the typical form of the tree. As a young specimen, it starts off with slender, somewhat spindly growth but develops branches after the 6th year to produce good material for hedges and windbreaks. Zone 7.

35

Taloumis

Japanese black pine takes the salt spray from both sides of this harborside garden. Junipers, mugho pine, heather and Silver Mound artemisia make appropriate ground cover. Coarse wood chips are used for a mulch.

Mugho pine (*P. mugho*). See Chapter 5.

Pitch pine (*P. rigida*). Considered a worthless tree from most points of view, nonetheless it has landscape value as a tree for sandy ground, especially dune planting. It is tough and hardy and existing specimens should be retained. Zone 2.

Sand pine (*P. clausa*). This species, found on the coastal dunes of Florida and Alabama, is smooth-barked. It is considered the toughest of the Southern pines for salt resistance. Zone 7.

Santa Cruz Island pine (*P. remorata*). Similar to the Bishop pine but a much smaller tree, an advantage for garden use. Zone 7.

Scots pine (*P. sylvestris*). A picturesque pine, with bluish green, twisted needles and orange-brown bark, it matures as a roundheaded specimen somewhat irregular in form. Notably hardy, it is an attractive short-needled type, vigorous in growth. Although it is often planted near the sea to stabilize dunes, it is not always as receptive to continuous assaults of salt spray as other kinds.

Shore pine (*P. contorta*). Black pine is another common name for this roundheaded tree, usually heavily branched and seldom more than 30 feet tall. It is native to the West Coast of the United States and has been used to stabilize the dunes of Washington and Oregon. Zone 7.

Torrey pine (*P. torreyana*). A rare species found native in two locations in California, it is a fast grower which stands the "steady surge of trade winds from a chill sea," and assumes a picturesque and interesting form. Between Del Mar and La Jolla in San Diego County, California, is a tract of land known as Torrey Pines Preserve, after John Torrey, an American botanist (1796–1873). Zone 8.

Pines are trees for sunny locations. When they are to be planted in quantity for screens and windbreaks, seedlings obtained from a forest nursery are most economical. Larger plants are best handled as balled and burlapped or container-grown specimens. It is a mistake to attempt to collect pines from the wild unless one is equipped with proper tools and unless small plants with good root systems are obtained, with soil clinging to the roots. Spring is the best time for planting followed by thorough watering and mulching. An annual feeding with evergreen fertilizer, especially in sandy soils, is advisable. Pruning of seedlings each year helps to induce dense growth and sturdy branches. Once established wind pruning will determine the appearance of the planting.

POPLAR   80′   Zones 2–5   *Populus alba*

Among the easiest trees to grow, poplars can be used to advantage to screen plantings near the sea. They have value as soil binders and for salt resistance, but the branches break easily in heavy wind. On the whole they are best considered as fillers in exposed sites. The white or silver-leaved poplar makes a pleasing effect as the leaves move in the slightest breeze showing their silvery undersurfaces. Several varieties including pyramidal and columnar forms are commonly grown.

Poplars require no special care, but should be pruned hard at planting time to induce sturdy trunks.

PRIMROSE TREE   20–40′   Zone 9   *Lagunaria patersonii*

Unusually thick evergreen leaves with gray undersurfaces and showy pink flowers resembling those of the hibiscus make the primrose tree a desirable seaside ornament or hedge plant. Pyramidal in habit and of fairly rapid growth, its chief drawback lies in the persistent seedpods which irritate the skin when handled, hence the reason for one of its common names, cow itch tree.

RED CEDAR 40–50′ Zone 1   *Juniperus virginiana*

This familiar native evergreen is found in dry, rocky soil along the entire eastern seaboard from Canada to Florida and inland to the Rocky Mountains. In every stage of its growth from youth to old age, this sturdy tree is usually columnar or narrowly pyramidal. However, when damaged by wind and weather, it often changes its shape, developing several leaders. Even when old and partly dead, the twisted trunk and branches of the red cedar are always picturesque. The glaucous foliage (needlelike and scalelike in various stages of growth); the dark blue berries, dusted with gray; and the characteristic red-brown bark which peels off in strips, are all part of the year-round interest it lends to the landscape. This evergreen makes a striking specimen, a desirable plant in groups, or it may be used as a high, informal hedge, or it can be sheared. It was once much more common in the wild, but since it makes good fence posts, the red cedar, like many of our useful native plants, is no longer so abundant in fields and pastures.

In one way or another, practically all the junipers from the low-growing ground cover types to the various shrub and tree forms are of special merit for seaside planting. (For these see Chapters 5 and 10.)

Several improved forms of red cedar are widely planted. Canaert red cedar (*J. virginiana canaertii*) is a selected kind, of compact form with notably dark green foliage and a heavy fruiting habit which makes it particularly noticeable in late fall and winter. Fountain red cedar (*J. virginiana tripartita*) is a dwarf variety, averaging 6 feet in height. The Burk red cedar is identified by its steel blue color. Keteleer red cedar (listed as *J. virginiana keteleerii*) is broader in its habit than the type and is listed by many nurserymen. Several other forms are sometimes seen in arboretums.

Common juniper and red cedar in the wild.

Taloumis

Red cedar grows naturally in poor, rocky, gravelly or sandy soils in full sun, and is of easy culture. Balled and burlapped specimens are easily moved in spring or fall. Unless one is properly equipped and experienced in the task, it is unwise to collect this tree in the wild. Roots are often embedded between stones and it is seldom easy to get a satisfactory ball of earth, essential for successful moving. However, in fields and pastures where soils are somewhat rock-free, it is possible to move plants more easily. Specimens 8 to 10 feet or taller require skill in handling and need to be carefully guyed, especially when planted in exposed areas. Small specimens, 3 to 5 feet tall, balled and burlapped, are available from nurseries and these are usually the safest size to plant. Once established, the red cedar responds readily to feeding. When planted close to the sea, the foliage sometimes burns badly from constant exposure to salt spray and this fact should be remembered when planting red cedar.

RUSSIAN OLIVE   20′   Zone 2   *Elaeagnus angustifolia*

A picturesque small tree of loose open habit, the Russian olive or oleaster is a true denizen of the seacoast. Its chief decorative asset is its silvery foliage and branchlets since the inconspicuous flowers and silvery yellow berries are of little import, except as food for birds. This loose-growing tree or big-scale shrub is effective in mixed plantings or as a specimen and is sometimes used as a tall informal hedge. The billowy, silvery effect created by the constant movement of the branches is most pleasing, especially when viewed against pines and red cedar or against the sea. In winter, the brown shredding bark is noticeable. Ideal for espaliering against fences or walls of wood or stone, the Russian olive can be adapted to give the effect of vine tracery. Although it may reach 15 to 20 feet in height, severe exposure will make it a smaller tree.

Cherry elaeagnus (*E. multiflora*) is normally much lower growing, 8 to 10 feet, with fragrant, yellow flowers, orange-red fruit, and dark green leaves with silver undersurfaces. Also small-scaled is the autumn elaeagnus (*E. umbellata*), a large shrub to 12 feet, broad spreading and noted for its abundance of fruit which changes from amber to muted red after heavy frost. From Zone 6 southward an evergreen species, the thorny elaeagnus (*E. pungens*) is widely used. The tiny white flowers that appear in October have a fragrance not unlike that of the gardenia and the fruit, which changes from brown to red, is seen in May. Several varieties with variegated foliage are widely planted in the South. Thorny elaeagnus is generally considered a shrub for poor soils and difficult situations.

All thrive in full sun or light shade and in the poorest of soils; sand or clay have little effect on them. Water them thoroughly after planting and continue until they are well established. Frequent feeding and hard pruning aid in producing dense growth. Then they can be allowed to assume whatever appearance the prevailing winds determine. Large nurseries offer container-grown plants which are easily transplanted.

A well-grown specimen of Russian olive planted along a highway, about a hundred yards from the open sea. An ideal shrub to espalier.

SPRUCE   60–80′   Zones 2–4   *Picea* genus

In the thin gravelly soil at Bar Harbor, Maine, where once a fabulous seaside garden flourished, white (*P. glauca*) and red (*P. rubens*) spruce were planted to break the wind and protect the plant treasures from storms and salt spray. For several decades these spruces have withstood the onslaught of wind and weather unleashed from Frenchman's Bay, all the while contributing to the rugged beauty of the landscape with their picturesque silhouettes. Elsewhere along the northern seacoast, native stands of spruce are seen frequently, sometimes crowding the shore. Near the sea the needles of the white spruce are bluer than when seen inland, but not as intense in color as those of the popular Colorado blue variety. Aside from forest nurseries where these trees are grown for lining out, they are not as easily available as other types of spruce which are preferred for ornamental effects. However, in choosing trees for windbreaks and screens, this factor is not of prime importance.

E. H. Wilson, the noted plant hunter, did not live long enough to see one of his favorite evergreens, the dragon spruce (*P. asperata*), attain maturity in North America. Today it is being widely planted as a seashore evergreen. The stiff bluish-green needles are noted for their dense arrangement on gracefully curved stems. The needles remain for 7 years before falling.

The Colorado blue spruce (*P. pungens kosteriana*) is widely planted because of its rich blue coloring and the ease with which it can be obtained. The Black Hills spruce, a variety of the white species, sometimes used for its slowness in growing and compact habit, and the Norway spruce (*P. abies*) are seen occasionally.

The fir (*Abies*) and the spruce are often confused because they are similar in form, in foliage, and in general aspect. When the needles of the fir drop, the leaf scars that remain are flat and circular, whereas those of the spruce are rough and stubby. Fir retains its needles much longer when cut, giving it greater value than spruce for Christmas trees. However, spruces are more adaptable in gardens than most kinds of fir, since they endure heat, dry soil, salt spray, and wind better. The showy cones of the spruce are pendulous whereas those of the fir are held erect.

Full sun and average garden soil are their simple requirements. Spruce gall and spruce mite are sometimes annoying pests and, once discovered, need to be controlled immediately lest they injure the tree's growth, which greatly detracts from the symmetry of the spruce. As with all evergreens planted by the sea, particularly in exposed sites, small specimens are easier to acclimate. Annual feedings with evergreen fertilizer are advisable.

TREE OF HEAVEN   60′   Zone 3   *Ailanthus altissima*

Of all the trees introduced to America none has become more widely established than the tree of heaven. It has many noteworthy attributes to commend it and perhaps no other deciduous tree can endure more adverse conditions and survive, making a presentable and attractive appearance. A well-grown specimen of the red-fruited form is truly distinctive. The male tree produces bloom which carries an offensive odor, so that only the female form should be encouraged. The showy, winged fruits appear in early summer, turning red as the summer progresses. It endures the heaviest of salt spray and has had its roots submerged in salt water without any permanent damage. From its early stages of growth to maturity, it is pleasing in form. Somehow it seems necessary to evaluate this common tree adequately since so many look down their noses at it. Yet "the tree that grew in Brooklyn" belongs at the top of the list of seaside trees for salt endurance. However, strong winds cause the limbs to split. Because of its rapid growth it can be used for a temporary windbreak.

Tree of heaven needs no special care except such control as will keep it from becoming a pest by self-sowing. Watch for seedlings and pull them up before they become well rooted.

Washington Hawthorn   30′   Zone 4   *Crataegus phaenopyrum*

Broadly roundheaded when mature with slender zigzag branches of thorny habit, the Washington thorn or hawthorn makes a picturesque seaside tree, free standing, in a group, or combined with Russian olive, pines, and other salt-tolerant trees and shrubs. The white flowers borne in large clusters are followed by scarlet-orange berries which blend superbly with the richly tinted autumn foliage. In spring and summer the foliage is light glossy green, resembling that of the gray birch. Unlike the English hawthorn (*C. oxycantha*) which often drops its leaves in late summer, this species is most satisfactory. The cockspur thorn (*C. crus-galli*) with its white flowers, glossy foliage which colors in autumn, and long-lasting red fruits is a rugged small tree, sometimes shrublike, that thrives near the sea. Its horizontal branching habit is all the more appealing when pruned by the wind.

Sturdy and of easy culture, give hawthorn a place in full sun or light shade. Prepare the hole for planting thoroughly and water until well established. Fireblight is occasionally a problem, best controlled by cutting off and burning all diseased parts. Cedar-apple rust, usually a problem when red cedars are found nearby, makes it advisable not to plant the hawthorn in such an area.

White Ash   100′   Zone 3   *Fraxinus americana*

A forest tree inland, weedy by nature, the white ash is tolerant of poor soils, salt air, and wind. In autumn the leaves turn yellow, changing to purplish tints before they drop. A fast grower and readily available, this native tree often meets the needs of seaside gardeners.

Full sun and ordinary soil suit it. Young specimens are obtainable from most nurseries.

Yew   2–40′   Zone 4   *Taxus genus*

Japanese yew, one of the most adaptable and rewarding of evergreens, belongs in seaside gardens. True, it is not as salt tolerant as pine and juniper, but sizable specimens of various types have been flourishing close to the sea for half a century. It is hardly a dune plant, yet it needs only the protection of a windbreak or the sheltered side of a building, a wall, or a fence to make vigorous growth. In areas where wind exposure is severe, plants tend to show the effects of winter burn if not protected. Plastic

Espaliered yews soften the white brick walls.

sprays, discussed in Chapter 20, are effective. Occasional dieback due to winter injury may occur under extreme conditions, but seldom are plants killed to the ground. Growth may not always be as luxuriant as when this plant is grown inland, but with annual feeding and a permanent mulch, Japanese yew performs most creditably in coastal gardens. While yews prefer soils of heavy texture, they can be expected to flourish in light sandy types if organic matter is added at planting time and plants are adequately mulched.

Many types and selected forms of Japanese yew are grown by nurserymen, for no other conifer lends itself to so many uses in the garden. Whether allowed to grow naturally or pruned and sheared for formal effects, this versatile evergreen can be used in a variety of ways in either sun or shade. Yews make excellent hedges, low and broad-spreading or tall-growing. For topiary effects or as untrimmed specimens, they become notable long-lived accent plants of year-round beauty. They are admirably suited for entrance and foundation plantings, as ground covers on level areas or on slopes, or combined with other conifers and broad-leaved evergreens. In autumn showy red berrylike fruits appear that further enhance the richness of the dark green foliage until they are consumed by the birds. Plants of both sexes are needed to produce fruit.

Loose-growing, untrimmed forms of Hicks yew with pliable branches are easily trained espalier fashion against walls and fences for effective tracery, as substitutes for vines. Where space is limited, they can be used to good advantage for unusual landscape effects. Unlike espaliered fruits, they require little care except for occasional pruning to retain the pattern desired.

Typical forms include the Japanese yew (*T. cuspidata*), a broad-spreading treelike shrub that grows to 30 feet or more, unless controlled. The pyramidal form called *T. cuspidata capitata* makes a handsome, cone-shaped specimen reaching 40 feet or more. However, both can be pruned annually to keep them at any desired height and width. There are many selected forms of dwarf habit available, among them the varieties *densa* and *nana*. Hicks yew (*T. media Hicksii*) which makes a columnar specimen and the Hatfield yew of broader columnar aspect, are valued for their upright growth.

Yews can be grown successfully in average, well-drained garden soil in sun or shade. Organic matter incorporated with the soil and an annual feeding with evergreen fertilizer benefit them greatly. Pruning for formal effects or to encourage dense growth is best done after new growth has developed.

Other useful trees found in coastal environments are:

ACACIA	*Acacia* genus
AMERICAN ARBOR-VITAE	*Thuja occidentalis*
AMERICAN ELM	*Ulmus americana*
BAY TREE	*Laurus nobilis*
BLACK CHERRY	*Prunus serotina*
CHINESE ELM	*Ulmus parvifolia*
ENGLISH ELM	*Ulmus procera*
FLOWERING CHERRY	*Prunus serrulata*
HORSE CHESTNUT	*Aesculus hippocastanum*
JAPANESE CEDAR	*Cryptomeria japonica*
LAUREL	*Laurocerasus* genus
MOCKERNUT HICKORY	*Carya tomentosa*
NIKKO FIR	*Abies homolepis*
OSAGE ORANGE	*Maclura pomifera*
PALMS—see Special Plant Lists, Chapter 21	
LONDON PLANE TREE	*Platanus acerifolium*
PUSSY WILLOW	*Salix discolor*
ROYAL PAULOWNIA	*Paulownia tomentosa*
RUM CHERRY—SEE BLACK CHERRY	
SASSAFRAS	*Sassafras albidum*
SIBERIAN ELM	*Ulmus pumila*
SILK TREE	*Albizzia julibrissin rosea*
SOUTHERN MAGNOLIA	*Magnolia grandiflora*
TUPELO	*Nyssa sylvatica*
VEITCH FIR	*Abies veitchi*
WILLOW	*Salix* genus

Flowering dogwood trained as an espalier.

45

Taloumis

American elms flourish in seaside areas along the New England coast.

CHAPTER FIVE

Flowering Shrubs and Evergreens

ANY of the popular flowering shrubs and small trees grown in city and suburban gardens are sufficiently vigorous to endure considerable exposure to wind and salt spray. Some are by nature highly adaptable because they are indigenous to sandy soils and a shoreline habitat. These include both native and exotic kinds, many of which are not commonly grown merely because gardeners are not aware of their adaptability. The true test of endurance for these plants is not only the effect on them of wind and salt spray and their ability to endure it, but the quality of the soil in which they are planted, its moisture holding capacity and texture, and the availability of water both at planting time and in the weeks following, as well as sufficient plant food.

Azaleas and rhododendrons are not discussed in this chapter even though they are frequently grown in seaside gardens where they can be protected from wind and salt spray and given the acid soil which they require. Likewise, many other desirable flowering shrubs are not included, since they too can be grown if given adequate protection from the elements. The prime purpose of this chapter is to evaluate and focus attention on those flowering shrubs and evergreens best suited to coastal sites.

In selecting shrubs to form a barrier for lower growing plants, those of known endurance need to be placed on the outermost rim of exposure to form a background and windbreak for those less tough. Thorough soil preparation, heavy feeding, deep mulching, guying of small trees, and frequent water at planting time and in the period following, are essential to get root systems firmly established. Planting small-sized shrubs in groups set more closely than might at first seem advisable, is good practice. Even with the best of planting conditions, there are bound to be some losses and this fact should be borne in mind when planting a seaside garden.

Shrubs with roots balled and burlapped or container-grown are generally more satisfactory for transplanting than bare-root plant material, even though they are more costly. When bare-root plant material is used, every effort must be made to keep the roots well covered during the process of planting. Tiny feeder roots, exposed to sun and wind, dry out much more rapidly than is generally realized. Keep them wrapped in moist burlap or plunge the roots into a bucket of muddy water until plants are set in the ground.

Remove broken and bruised roots as well as those of unusual length. Dig holes large enough in width and depth to accommodate them without crowding. Since subsoil in most seaside gardens is usually of poor quality, put several shovelfuls of topsoil or some form of organic matter into the hole before placing the shrub in position. See Soils, Chapter 15. Set the ball of earth at the same depth at which it grew in the nursery. Tamp soil well around the roots as the hole is filled in, adding water to eliminate air pockets, and leave a depression around each shrub for subsequent watering and to catch rain. Mulch, at least an inch or more in depth, should be spread immediately. See Mulches, Chapter 18.

Top pruning is often essential, especially if the specimen is heavily branched or if growth is tall and ungainly. Cutting back the top growth of deciduous shrubs and trees by at least one third is usually advantageous, to induce heavy root growth. Constant exposure to wind results in excessive transpiration of moisture from leaves and stems which places more than normal demands on a newly planted shrub. It is not generally realized that

Bayberry, junipers, broom and other seaside shrubs help to hold the shoreline.
Taloumis

each and every leaf gives off moisture; thus, reducing the leaf area at planting time helps to check the loss of water in a plant. Freshly planted evergreens will benefit by watering the foliage frequently as well as the roots, especially if winds are strong and temperatures are unseasonably high.

Woody plants set out bare-root in the dormant stage, particularly roses, small-sized shrubs, and hedge material benefit by hilling up the soil 6 to 8 inches after planting to prevent stems from drying out. Soil should be removed as soon as buds break along the stems. Tree trunks may be wrapped with heavy paper or burlap to reduce transpiration. These practices involve additional labor but are good insurance on windy sites.

The importance of thorough and frequent watering for newly transplanted shrubs and trees cannot be overstated, particularly in coastal gardens where soils are light and thin in texture.

Staking or guying big shrubs (and all trees) is also vital to success in establishing them in exposed areas. Care must be taken that stems are well protected from sharp edges of stakes so as not to bruise the bark. Careless handling in this respect may result in serious damage to woody stems as they are blown against stakes, particularly the rough surfaces of pipes.

Bayberry	3–9′	Zone 2	*Myrica pensylvanica*
Wax Myrtle	30′	Zone 6	*Myrica cerifera*
California Bayberry	30′	Zone 7	*Myrica californica*

If bayberry were an exotic shrub, somewhat costly and difficult to grow, the chances are that nurseries and garden centers would feature it and it would be given a choice place in gardens. Such is not often the case with native plants. Their intrinsic beauty and value are ignored because they are fairly common. Here is a sturdy shrub, disease free, effective at all seasons of the year, with pungent foliage and attractive gray berries. It can be used in many ways in seaside gardens, as a sand binder, for naturalizing, or for more formal treatment near the house.

Since Colonial days the bayberry has been the source of a fragrant wax from which attractive olive-gray candles are made. Christmas wreaths and garlands and arrangements of greens enhanced with branches of bayberry have been popular for more than a century.

The foliage of this versatile shrub is particularly appealing to flower arrangers because of its laurel-like form and good keeping qualities. The berries are popular with many kinds of birds who devour them with great relish.

The bayberry bushes found in rocky pastures and along the shoreline from Newfoundland to North Carolina are seldom more than 3 or 4 feet tall, although plants are known to grow 8 feet or more in height, often spreading equally wide. A rugged shrub that thrives in poor soils, particularly those of sandy makeup, bayberry is especially useful as a sand binder

49

Bayberry used in a seaside garden with day lilies.

for seaside gardens, or for dry banks and hillsides. Its glossy, fragrant foliage, resembling that of the bay tree, its picturesque twig habit, and the gray berries provide interest throughout the year. The leaves, that have a grayish undersurface, are nearly evergreen and cling to the stems until early spring. Plants increase by stolons, rooting deeply as they develop into sizable clumps. Shrub borders filled with rugosa roses, beach plum, sweet fern, bearberry, dwarf willow, broom, and bayberry add interest to any seaside garden.

Give bayberry full sun and poor soil, and once established it will care for itself. Like the holly and the sea buckthorn, male and female flowers are borne on separate plants, a point to remember when planting colonies of this native shrub. Stock can be increased by division of the roots. Heavy pruning of old clumps aids in renewing their vigor. It is usually a mistake to attempt to collect plants unless one is properly equipped to do a thorough job of lifting them with ample soil on their roots. Many nurseries offer collected material with good root systems, sometimes container-grown, which makes transplanting easy.

A much taller growing shrub, actually the southern form of the New England bayberry, *M. cerifera,* commonly called wax myrtle, is also referred to as bayberry and tallow shrub. It may reach 30 feet or more. Its foliage is evergreen or nearly so and the fruits are gray and waxy with a noticeable fragrance. Still another species, *M. gale,* known as sweet gale, moor or bog myrtle, is essentially a plant of peaty soils and bogs.

The California bayberry or Pacific wax myrtle (*M. californica*) is a coastal shrub or small tree. It is valued for its long life, clean evergreen foliage, and waxy purplish berries. West Coast gardeners use it for a hedge plant and it can be grown as a symmetrical small tree.

BEAUTY BUSH   6–10′   Zone 3   *Kolkwitzia amabilis*

Beauty bush, a comparative newcomer to American gardens, has become widely known in recent years. The soft pink flowers borne in graceful sprays, the clean, attractive foliage, and the curious seedpods are among its assets, together with a graceful, fountainlike habit of growth. Often this shrub becomes ungainly due to lack of pruning, but it can be cut back hard to induce new growth from the base. Unusually hardy, it endures hot, dry situations and is at its best in full sun. Because of its dense growth it makes a good windbreak. Give it ample room to develop and it will produce a most attractive specimen. Skillful pruning will keep it any desired height ranging from 4 to 10 feet.

It can be grown from seed, but cuttings from a specimen of good coloring assure one of true stock. Most nurseries and garden centers offer it.

BEACH PLUM   6′   Zone 2   *Prunus maritima*

One of the most familiar shrubs found along the coast in various parts of the Northeast, this native of the sand dunes is valued for its endurance, its showy white flowers, and its small purplish, dull red, or yellow fruits that are much prized for making jelly. In autumn, the foliage assumes orange and red tones that make a brilliant contrast when grown with beach wormwood, bayberry, broom, and other seaside plants. The landscape possibilities of the beach plum have never been as widely exploited outside of New England and certain parts of New Jersey as they might be. This rugged, long-lived shrub roots deeply in search of moisture and is seldom affected adversely by shifting sand. It deserves to be more widely grown, but is seldom featured by nurseries, and roots are offered only by a few specialists.

Plants in exposed sites average 3 feet or less in height, ideal for binding sand, and are densely branched. Effective as a specimen or in colonies with other sand dune plants, it also makes a pleasing informal hedge. When grown in loam or better than average sandy soil, plants show remarkable vigor, often developing a distinctive treelike character and a pleasing irregular form in exposed places.

On Cape Cod where the beach plum is a prime favorite, amateur and professional horticulturists have collected and selected a number of named varieties that are noteworthy for the quality and production of their fruit.

The Nanking cherry (*P. tomentosa*) makes a sizable, fast-growing, roundheaded shrub, studded with pale pink or white flowers in early spring followed by edible red fruits in June. It can be grown in sandy soils.

Like the bayberry and other native seaside plants, beach plum is not easily transplanted from the wild. It is sound practice to obtain nursery-grown stock and plant it as early in spring as possible. If the site is not ready, stock can be started in containers and set out later. Pruning to induce heavy branching, feeding, watering, and mulching pay dividends in establishing a colony. However, once plants have taken root, little care is required.

BLUEBERRY   10–12′   Zone 3   *Vaccinium corymbosum*

Blueberry bushes grow wild in the natural landscape over a large part of the eastern United States and have many attributes as desirable ornamentals. The clean, glossy foliage, dainty bell-shaped flowers, delicious blue berries, and rich autumn coloring of this picturesque twiggy shrub, total up to a high score for any plant. Blueberries grow in various kinds of acid soil, often in sandy and rocky ground, close to the coast. They endure a fair amount of shade, and they can be combined with a wide variety of native shrubs for naturalistic effects. The cultivated types that have been bred for the quality and yield of their fruit are of equal merit for landscape effects. However, the bushes often need to be covered when the fruit begins to ripen, otherwise the birds get most of the berries.

These shrubs thrive in acid soil; where there is plenty of humus, growth is usually exceptional. Even in thin soils, when fed with acid-type fertilizer, they develop into impressive shrubs. Full sun or part shade suits them and they are known to endure considerable dryness, but in dry summers the quality of the fruit is not as good. Collected stock is offered by some nurserymen, and the cultivated kinds are available from most growers and garden centers. Blueberries can often be moved successfully from the wild, but they must be dug with a ball of earth large enough to obtain a good root system. Stock is increased by cuttings.

BOG ROSEMARY   1–2′   Zone 2   *Andromeda glaucophylla*

Bog rosemary, a low-growing native shrub of the heath family, is found in peaty bogs and along the edges of ponds, both inland and near the sea, in the places where cranberries grow. It is included here because of the increasing interest in native plants. The narrow evergreen leaves are whitish on the undersurface, somewhat resembling those of the fragrant rosemary, hence the common name. However, the two plants are in no way related. It spreads by creeping rootstocks and makes a neater plant in culti-

52

Beach plum at its best along the water's edge. The fruit makes delicious jam.

vation than the specimens often found in the wild. The urn-shaped flowers that appear in May and June are pink, fading to white. A more compact form with smaller glossy foliage that turns bronze in the fall, blooms in early summer.

Grow it with other acid-loving plants in moist locations or in a bog garden, where it can increase in its natural way. For many years, it was one of the treasured natives in the great garden of the late Beatrix Farrand at Bar Harbor, Maine. Makers of wild gardens in the Northwest also enjoy growing it.

Moist acid soil, rich in humus, is needed to grow bog rosemary. It can be raised in full sun or light shade. Cutting sections of the rootstocks or layering are the simplest methods for home gardeners to use in increasing this shrub. It can be collected in the wild or it may be obtained from dealers in native plants. Plants sold as *A. polifolia* are of the species described above.

BROOM 6″–4′ Zones 5–6 *Cytisus* genus

Except along the coldest stretches of the New England seaboard, there is hardly a seaside garden on the East or the West Coast where some type

53

of broom cannot be established. Aside from its ornamental value, it is a most satisfactory soil binder on banks and slopes. Scotch broom was brought to America in Colonial times and soon established itself. In the area between Jamestown and Williamsburg in Virginia it has become naturalized and thrives like any native shrub. The same is true on Cape Cod on the south shore of Massachusetts and in the Northwest, where it grows abundantly in the wild. Gardeners who have planted it inland in heavy soils, even in protected areas, have not always been successful in establishing broom. It prefers poor sandy soil and roots itself deeply. A member of the pea family, it manufactures its own food and enriches the soil with nitrogen by means of the nodules which develop on the roots of all legumes.

Vigorous in its growth, disease free and clean of habit, it endures wind and exposure to a remarkable degree. In areas where winters are severe not all types of broom are hardy, a point to remember in selecting some of the hybrids particularly, as well as those species native to the warmer parts of Europe.

Bean's broom (*C. beanii*). Bright golden-yellow flowers on plants 1 foot or more tall, of wide-spreading habit.

Canary Island broom (*C. canariensis*). Also listed as Genista, this is a favorite pot plant of florists, but where it is hardy it grows to 6 feet or more with bright yellow flowers in great profusion and attractive pealike foliage. Easily pruned to compact form, it is highly decorative even when not in flower. Zone 6 southward.

Ground broom (*C. procumbens*). Sometimes less than 1 foot tall or a little higher, with bright yellow flowers and dense matting habit.

Kew broom (*C. kewensis*). This hybrid form, with pale yellow flowers, grows only 6 inches high and makes a plant several feet wide.

Portuguese broom (*C. albus*). Under 1 foot high, with white flowers.

Prostrate broom (*C. decumbens*). Long, slender branches, of semi-prostrate habit, make a dense mat of growth covered with bright yellow flowers in May and June.

Purple broom (*C. purpureus*). Eighteen inches in height, with purple flowers.

Scotch broom (*C. scoparius*). A vigorous shrub with wandlike, reedy stems and sparse foliage on which are borne bright yellow fragrant blossoms that move like golden streamers in every breeze. Few plants have more decorative possibilities when skillfully placed. The gracefully arching branches have solved many a flower arranger's problems. Plants may grow 8 to 10 feet tall if not pruned, but severe cutting back greatly improves the sometimes ungainly manner of growth which is typical of Scotch broom. Prune to create the effect desired, but follow the natural lines of growth. Zone 3. There are numerous hybrids, extraordinary in color combinations. All are more erect in habit than the type. Some of these are of doubtful hardiness in the northerly area of Zone 4.

> Andreanus. Yellow flowers with crimson wings.
> Burkwoodi. Venetian red and yellow.
> California. Vermilion, rose, and cream.
> Donard seedling. Pink, red, and orange.
> Dorothy Walpole. Crimson and rose.
> Lady Moore. Primrose yellow and crimson.
> Lord Lambourne. Crimson and yellow.
> Pomona. Red, rose, and yellow.
> St. Mary's. Pure white blooms.
> San Francisco. Rich velvety red.

Warminster broom (*C. praecox*). Plants that range from 3 to 5 feet tall, spreading as wide, are covered with creamy yellow fragrant flowers. This is a particularly handsome shrub when pruned hard to make a billowy mass and the blooms often last nearly a month in spring. Pruning is best done after flowering, and there is no need to shear it tight like a globe. Zone 4.

White Spanish broom (*C. multiflorus*). A large-scale shrub reaching to 10 feet with white flowers. Zone 5 southward.

Brooms need a hot sunny location in poor, dry soil, sandy or gravelly. Usually this type of situation is not too difficult a problem with many gardeners who are searching for good ground covers. Plants may be propagated easily by cuttings taken in early summer or from seed. Container-grown rooted cuttings make it easy to plant brooms at any season of the year. Large plants, because deep rooted, do not transplant satisfactorily.

CINQUEFOIL   6″–3′   Zone 2   *Potentilla* genus

The cinquefoils thrive in hot, dry situations, have clean and attractive foliage, and are ironclad in their hardiness. As tall-growing ground covers and for general ornamental use, they provide good foliage and attractive bloom during the summer months. The improved forms of this common native plant are called buttercup shrubs, an apt name for the compact masses of fernlike foliage topped with quantities of single yellow blossoms in summer.

Gold Drop is a selected form of *P. fruticosa* with bright yellow flowers that appear beginning in June. It makes a loose mound and can be used in masses in the foreground of the shrub border, in drifts among rocks as a colorful high-level ground cover, about 2 feet tall, or as a low, informal hedge. Katherine Dykes is taller, to 3 feet, of more upright habit, and can

55

The cinquefoils are desirable low growing shrubs with lacy foliage and bright yellow flower appearing in summer.

be used for accent among low carpet plants in sunny areas or in groups in a large shrub border. Jackman's Variety, a brilliant yellow, is valued for use as a low hedge because of its upright growth.

Sutter's Gold, noted for its exceptionally large blooms, is moundlike in growth. Longacre, prostrate in habit, spreads to 3 feet in diameter, is a free-flowering dwarf shrub of great beauty. Mount Everest is white-flowering, of upright habit.

Full sun and ordinary soil on the acid side are all these plants need. Feed with a complete fertilizer and water thoroughly until established. Increase is by division of the roots, or from cuttings. Many growers offer container-grown plants.

CORALBERRY	3–5′	Zone 2	*Symphoricarpos orbiculatus*
SNOWBERRY	5–6′	Zone 2	*Symphoricarpos albus laevigatus*

Coralberry and Indian currant are the common names of this widely planted, native shrub. The flowers are of little value, but the purplish-red fruits on gracefully arching stems are particularly showy in the fall. It suckers freely and makes a good soil binder, readily adaptable to slope planting.

Although the common coralberry is of clean habit, easy to grow and handle, most gardeners do not consider it particularly outstanding. However, an improved form known as Magic Berry is conspicuous for its exceptionally heavy fruiting and dense growth. The Chenault coralberry (*S. chenaulti*) has larger fruits than the type with decidedly pink coloring and is well worth growing.

The snowberry (*S. albus laevigatus*) is another native shrub, once popular in gardens. The glaucous foliage and showy clusters of large white berries borne on arching stems are unusually decorative in late summer and fall. It, too, spreads by underground roots.

All flourish in sun or shade and are not particular as to soil. Since a wide variety of shrubs flourish in full sun, here are several dependable kinds well suited to shady locations. Stock can be increased by dividing roots. Hard pruning every two to three years keeps these shrubs vigorous and tidy in appearance.

COTONEASTER	1–8′	Zones 4–6	*Cotoneaster* genus

A goodly number of shrubs from the Orient meet the demands of the seaside garden. Chief among these are the cotoneasters in a variety of shapes and sizes. Gardeners the world over are indebted to that intrepid plant hunter Ernest H. Wilson, who introduced a considerable number of species to American and English gardens nearly a half century ago. He long championed these shrubs for their beauty of form, their neat foliage, and their showy fruits. In emphasizing their versatility as desirable garden material, "Chinese" Wilson frequently pointed out that there were cotoneasters of suitable types and sizes for every climatic region of the United States. Discerning gardeners are becoming aware of this fact.

The delicate tracery of the twigs and their fanlike branching habit are notable characteristics of these sprawling shrubs. When seen protruding through the snow, or viewed in the barren winter landscape with the sun glistening on the bright berries, they become all the more appealing. For the most part, cotoneasters are broad-spreading plants of ample proportions, requiring adequate space for full development. What is more, they can be pruned with ease and kept within bounds while still retaining their graceful, fountainlike habit.

Cotoneasters are ideally suited for hot, dry situations on banks and slopes exposed to the wind. Skirting the top or base of a wall or among

Taloumis

Cotoneasters of various kinds are found in seaside gardens on both the East and West coasts. Native white and red spruce form a protective barrier for this inlet on the rocky coast of Maine.

rocks, where they can develop their broad-spreading habit and free-branching growth, they are particularly decorative. They are deep-rooted and make good soil binders. Combine the low-growing kinds with spreading junipers or use an occasional plant in a bank of pachysandra or myrtle. Cotoneasters grow well in part shade.

Cotoneasters are subject to several pests, including fire blight, scale, lace bug, and red spider, which disfigure their appearance and defoliate the plants. These troubles can be serious if not kept under control since they detract greatly from the appearance of these ornamental plants, causing dieback and defoliation. Sprays for the control of all these pests are effective, but they must be applied at the proper time. Present-day gardeners have become keenly aware of the threat of pests and diseases, and these drawbacks must be faced in selecting quantities of any given plant for landscaping. Cotoneasters are no exception in this respect.

LOW-GROWING TYPES

All the kinds mentioned here have white or pinkish flowers in June, followed by showy red fruits that add to the attractiveness of the plants in autumn. Best known of all is the rock spray cotoneaster (*C. horizontalis*).

Bearberry c. (*C. dammeri*). Distinctly flat in growth with evergreen foliage. The branches often root at the joints. This makes a most desirable ground cover because of its vigorous growth. Hardy from Zone 5, it is considered one of the good forms among the low-growing kinds.

Cranberry c. (*C. apiculata*). Seldom more than 18 inches tall, has glossy leaves, sizable fruits, and flat branching habit.

Creeping c. (*C. adpressa praecox*). A compact grower, it forms mounds a little more than 1 foot high, with wavy, glossy leaves and large red berries. Its restrained habit makes it desirable for planting in formal areas where trim, even growth is desired.

Dwarf silverleaf c. (*C. pannosa nana*). A Chinese native averaging 1 foot high, it is valued for its gray-green foliage and stiff horizontal growth. This species is not so hardy as most of the dwarfs and is suited to Zone 6 southward.

Dwarf willow leaf (*C. salicifolia herbstfüer*). Well named autumn fire, this low-growing form of the willow leaf cotoneaster is rarely over a foot in height and considerably wider, to 6 feet or more. The large clusters of red fruit are particularly showy. Hardy from Zone 5 southward.

Necklace c. (*C. decora*). Similar in habit to *C. horizontalis* with clear red fruits; the foliage is silvery gray.

Rock spray c. (*C. horizontalis*). Semievergreen in mild climates, in cold regions it sheds its leaves by early winter. The lacy twigs, red fruits, and horizontal habit of this plant make it most useful as big-scale ground or rock cover. Mature plants may grow to 3 feet high, but they usually remain a foot or so lower and can be controlled by pruning. This cotoneaster eventually spreads 8 to 10 feet or more in width—a point to remember when planting it. Hardy for Zone 4.

Small-leaved c. (*C. microphylla*). Small-leaved with rosy red fruits and long cascading branches, it makes dense growth. Foliage is about half the size of *C. horizontalis*. Zone 4.

Thyme-leaved c. (*C. microphylla thymifolia*). With narrow leaves of extremely delicate form and tiny fruits, it is a most attractive plant, compact in habit, averaging a foot in height. Hardy from Zone 4.

59

The list of tall-growing, broad-spreading kinds that follows does not include all the species and hybrid forms grown in gardens. Rather it is a selection of types readily obtainable from leading nurseries. Not all have common names.

C. dielsiana. Pink flowers, scarlet fruits, and brilliantly colored foliage make this foot shrub a most desirable object in the autumn landscape. Hardy from Zone 5.

Franchet c. (*C. francheti*). Partly evergreen with orange-red fruits, this is a big-scale plant of pleasing aspect with foliage that shows red tones in fall. 10 feet. Zone 5.

Bearberry scrambling over rocks with its roots in poor gravelly soil. An ideal ground cover for controlling erosion in sandy areas, this trailing evergreen spreads rapidly.

Taloumis

C. meyeri. Somewhat pendulous in habit with gray-green foliage, silvery on the undersurface, it bears coral pink fruits. It reaches 6 feet and is hardy from Zone 5.

C. multiflora. White hawthornlike flowers on gracefully arching branches followed by bright crimson fruits. Both contrast effectively with the blue-green foliage. 10 feet. Zone 5.

Silverleaf c. (C. pannosa). Semievergreen with silvery foliage, white flowers, and coral red fruits, it is an unusually handsome shrub needing ample space for development. Hardy from Zone 6 southward. It is especially popular on the West Coast.

Spreading c. (C. divaricata). An attractive shrub with glossy foliage and showy red fruits. It is heavily branched and makes a most attractive hedge. 6 feet. Zone 4.

Sungari Rockspray c. (C. racemiflora soongorica). A prime favorite of E. H. Wilson. Extremely hardy, it is noted for its pink berries and gray-green foliage. 7 feet. Another form, *C. racemiflora veitchi,* is valued for its showy blooms and large red fruits and is often used for big-scale hedges.

Willow leaf c. (C. salicifolia floccosa). Partially evergreen in cold climates, the wrinkled foliage is gray on the undersurface. White flowers in sizable clusters and bright red fruits. 10 feet. Zone 5.

C. wardi. An evergreen type noted for its hardiness and orange red fruits. Leaves are silvery on the underside and new growth is downy, turning a shiny brown. 8 feet. Zone 5.

Cotoneasters can be grown in any well-drained soil, even of poor quality. Full sun is best; though they can be expected to make satisfactory growth in part shade, fruiting is usually sparse. Since plants of any substantial size can seldom be moved successfully, they are offered by nurserymen in containers and are easily transplanted at any time during the growing season. These shrubs respond readily to feeding, making considerable growth each year, yet they will develop satisfactorily with little or no care. The usual method of increase is by cuttings.

COWBERRY   1′   Zone 5   *Vaccinium vitis-idaea*

An acid-soil plant of pleasing appearance when well grown in the right location, this dwarf evergreen cousin of the blueberry has small glossy leaves, pink bell-shaped flowers, and small red berries. Plants spread by underground stems, making a mass of even height, dense and pleasing in full sun, somewhat looser in appearance in the shade. There are two kinds, similar except in the size of the leaves and fruits. The mountain cranberry is the hardier of the two (*V. Vitis-Idaea minus*). Lowbush blueberry (*V. angustifolium laevifolium*) makes a most attractive ground cover in rocky,

61

Rockspray cotoneasters flank the entrance.

acid soil or where a naturalistic effect is desired. It has the added value of autumn color and its twiggy growth is of interest in winter.

Moist, acid soil in sun or shade meets the requirements of this plant. It is increased by root division and is often planted as sods sold by collectors or specialists in native plants.

DWARF WILLOW   4"–2'   Zone 2   *Salix* genus

Few gardeners are acquainted with the dwarf willows, native to the Arctic regions, that make excellent low-growing shrubs and ground covers in the colder sections of the country. For poor soils, in sunny, windswept locations, these diminutive shrubs have considerable use, but with few exceptions they are not easily obtainable. Extremely hardy, they spread by underground stems. Some have silvery foliage and make dense mats of growth only a few inches high. Others grow 1 to 2 feet tall. The dwarf willows are fascinating to grow in places where they can be used to advantage.

The dwarf Arctic willow (*Salix purpurea nana*) is being used more frequently as a dwarf hedge plant because of its adaptability to all types of soil, its ease of culture, and the rich blue-gray-green coloring of the leaves. It can be kept less than a foot high or allowed to develop naturally to 5 or 6 feet in height and an even greater width. The typical form of this plant, known as the purple osier, is several feet taller and makes a good seaside windbreak along with the goat willow, the tamarisk, and other sandy soil shrubs.

62

All of the willows are easy to root from cuttings that may be started in water or plunged into moist soil and kept moist until roots form. They grow naturally in sandy soils, rooting deeply for existence.

FIRETHORN   6–20′   Zones 4–6   *Pyracantha coccinea*

A topnotch shrub, notable primarily for its showy fruiting habit, firethorn is one of the most adaptable of ornamentals, lending itself to many uses in the garden. The small white flowers appear in clusters in May, followed by greenish berries that turn red or orange in late summer, making a splendid display until the birds get hungry. Plants are heavily clothed with small oval leaves of fine texture and the stems are distinctly spiny.

Mature plants may grow 15 to 20 feet tall, spreading as wide if allowed to. Most home gardeners prefer specimens 5 to 6 feet high, pruning to keep plants natural in appearance. Firethorn can also be used as an informal hedge, valuable for its dense growth and thorny stems that make it a useful barrier. When trained espalier fashion by selective pruning, it can be treated as a woody vine for walls and fences, providing highly decorative tracery. During severe winters the partially evergreen foliage and tip growth may burn and show signs of dieback, but such damage seldom is serious. However, this shrub is subject to scab and fire blight. Both of these diseases need to be controlled before the infestation becomes serious.

Several varieties and a number of selected forms are available. The variety *P. coccinea lalandi* has decidedly orange fruit. Government red is bright red. A yellow-fruited form, a dwarf kind known as Lowboy, and several other selected forms are available in the trade.

Average well-drained soil suits this plant which belongs in full sun for best results. Plants are not easily moved even when balled and burlapped because of the heavy, sprawling root system they develop. Consequently, nurseries and garden centers offer container-grown specimens of modest size that are easily handled at any season of the year. Once set out, they make rapid growth. Constant pruning is often necessary to keep firethorn within bounds.

FORSYTHIA   3–9′   Zone 4   *Forsythia* **genus**

Forsythias are among the commonest and most popular shrubs planted throughout a large part of the United States. There are many kinds available and some have greater merit than others. Golden bells, as they are often called, fill a variety of needs in all types of gardens. They develop rapidly into shrubs of ample size, require considerable space, and are reliably hardy and disease free. The foliage is pleasing throughout the growing year and some forms are conspicuous for their autumn coloring. The flowers, that are among the earliest to appear in spring, range from pale primrose to bright yellow.

Showy border forsythia (*F. intermedia spectabliis*), with deep yellow coloring, has been a favorite for more than half a century along with the form Primulina, much paler in value. Improved forms of recent origin include Lynwood Gold, an erect grower with deep yellow flowers closely set on sturdy stems that make a spectacular display, and Spring Glory, pale yellow in coloring, graceful in appearance, and also of heavy flowering habit. The individual blooms of Beatrix Farrand are both exceptionally large and intense in color.

For those who wish to camouflage old board fences or soften walls, the weeping forms of forsythia, especially *F. suspensa sieboldi,* can be used for espaliering. Perhaps the easiest of all shrubs to work with in this way, charming effects can be developed with dexterous use of pruning shears and large-size brads. It is also widely used for over-wall plantings to create cascades of flowers and foliage for softening harsh lines of masonry.

Dwarf forms of forsythias have considerable value as cover plants and soil binders on banks and slopes. From the New York Botanical Garden has come a dwarf kind (*F. viridissima bronxensis*) that remains about 1 foot high when fully grown. The familiar golden bells are small in size and the foliage is narrower than the type. A taller form, valued chiefly for its foliage since it is a shy bloomer, is Forsythia Arnold dwarf. The stems of this moundlike plant root easily as they come in contact with the soil. Its maximum height is 4 to 5 feet and it can be counted on to be twice as broad.

Ordinary soil in sun or partial shade is all that forsythia requires. It is drought resistant and makes a deep and heavy root system once established. Pruning after flowering requires the removal of old canes and such shortening of new growth as is necessary without detracting from the natural beauty of form of forsythia. No flowering shrub has been so badly butchered in so many gardens in the past few decades. This long-lived plant sometimes becomes tangled and overgrown through neglect, but it can be renewed by cutting growth back hard, to within a few inches of the ground. Perform the operation in spring after flowering, feed liberally with a complete fertilizer, and water it in thoroughly. Results are rewarding.

GROUNDSEL BUSH   3–12′   Zones 3–7   *Baccharis halimifolia*

The common groundsel bush, sometimes referred to as a tree, is a coarse species with white thistlelike fruits and leathery, coarse-toothed, resinous foliage that turns bronze in autumn. Among the toughest of our seaside plants, it is native from New England to Texas and is commonly found in brackish marshes, where it grows 6 to 8 feet tall.

An evergreen kind, *B. pilularis,* known as dwarf baccharis and dwarf chaparral broom, a denizen of the dunes, is valued as a sand binder on the West Coast where it is native. Usually it grows about a foot tall in cultivation and may spread 8 to 10 feet wide. Another species (*B. viminea*), known as mule-foot, is somewhat taller with willowlike leaves.

These plants thrive in full sun under ordinary sandy soil conditions in exposed places. They can be increased from cuttings or, in the case of the groundsel bush, from seed. Many native plants are not offered in the trade because of limited demand and must be collected from the wild or propagated by those desiring to use them.

HYDRANGEA 3–20′ Zones 4–5   *Hydrangea genus*

Seaside gardeners need to take a thoughtful look at this group of shrubs and consider all their merits. Hydrangeas are free from serious pests and they are of easy culture. They are well suited to seaside gardens not only because of their vigor and their long-lasting flowers, but especially for their lavish color in summer when blooming shrubs are scarce. There are hardy kinds for sun and shade, a climbing form for use on walls, ledges, and banks, as well as tender types, sometimes grown in tubs, or in the open ground with protection in cold climates. All have rather coarse foliage and big-scale flowers. Yet, when given a suitable setting among evergreens and deciduous shrubs, hydrangeas have notable landscape value.

The much maligned peegee hydrangea (*H. paniculata grandiflora*) is usually put in the wrong places, and often badly trimmed. Commonplace because it has been overplanted for a half century or more, it is actually a particularly striking summer-flowering shrub when allowed to dominate the setting of a large border. The flowers, creamy white at first, change to bronzy pink with age and the foliage takes on rich autumn tints as fall approaches. Hardy and long-lived, this big-scale shrub has the aspect of a small tree, making a fountainlike mass 8 to 20 feet tall, and often spreading as wide. However, it can be kept much smaller by skillful pruning.

Hydrangeas are the glory of summer gardens, especially near the ocean.
Taloumis

The oak-leaved hydrangea (*H. quercifolia*), found in the wild from Georgia to Florida, is well suited to shady plantings but flourishes in full sun as well. It blooms freely late in summer and its showy panicles that open creamy white, changing to rose pink and purple, are notably long-lasting. Although the foliage, shaped like a large oak leaf, is rather coarse, it becomes a notable accent plant as it turns orange, gold, and bronze in autumn. Extremely hardy and slow growing, this clean, sturdy shrub seldom grows more than 4 to 5 feet tall. Grouped with evergreens and flowering shrubs of more delicate foliage, it lends distinction to summer and autumn gardens.

Hills of Snow (*H. arborescens grandiflora*) is another native averaging 3 feet in height, often planted on banks and slopes among ferns in shady parts of the home grounds. It is valued for its creamy white blossoms in early summer borne on long stems. It was formerly more popular than it is in present-day gardens. It thrives in sun as well, blooms on new wood, and is best cut back hard each spring to encourage dense growth. Thus winter dieback which often occurs in severe winters is no disadvantage.

FRENCH HYDRANGEA

The double-flowered hydrangeas grown by florists for the spring trade are hybrids of *H. macrophylla,* native to Japan where they have been improved and cultivated for centuries. E. H. Wilson found this species growing wild along the shores of Japan nearly 50 years ago. Thus it is not surprising that these showy plants are so much at home near the sea. They have been long cherished in coastal gardens in the British Isles and on the Continent, where dozens of varieties are grown. Frequently referred to as French hydrangeas since many varieties were developed in France, they are also called hortensias. Many have proved hardy in sheltered locations even in the colder sections of the U.S. Northeast. However, all require protection where winter temperatures drop below zero for extended periods. The fact that even in severe weather temperatures usually remain higher along the coast than inland should encourage more gardeners to experiment with these showy ornamentals more extensively. In Europe, the double bell-like forms are known in the trade as mopheads in contrast to those with flat, platelike blooms that are called lacecaps.

When severe dieback occurs, plants produce little or no bloom the following season, since flower buds are formed at the tips of the previous season's growth. However, by skillful pruning, by mulching heavily after the ground freezes, and wrapping plants with burlap, roofing paper, or similar protection, the plants survive for long periods and make spectacular displays of bloom from midsummer to early autumn. In coastal gardens from Cape Cod south, where they have proved hardy with little or no protection, they are featured in dooryards and sometimes in extensive plantings. For porch and terrace use, they are particularly effective when

Hills-of-snow hydrangea, ferns and violets flourish on this shady slope.

planted in tubs and other large containers. With the present enthusiasm for container gardening, French hydrangeas are attracting well-deserved attention.

Varieties include red, pink, white, and blue flowering forms. However, true pink or red varieties change to blue when grown in acid soil. This fact should be borne in mind when selecting varieties and planning color schemes. Furthermore, the quality and intensity of true blue varieties is governed by the degree of soil acidity. Since pale or sickly blues are seldom desirable, acidity can be increased easily and quickly by applying a scant handful of acid-type fertilizer around each plant and watering it in. Alum and aluminum sulfate are sometimes used for this purpose. These procedures are also used to obtain a rich blue with pink varieties. When pink varieties are grown in acid soil areas and good quality pink flowers are desired, lime must be added to the soil. The presence of lime in acid soil makes the aluminum insoluble, thus preventing a change to blue.

Domotoi. Blooms often measure 10 to 12 inches across and are notably long lasting. Starting with soft green they develop into globe-shaped masses of pure pink in alkaline soil. In acid soils, the color changes to light blue. Plants average 2 to 3 feet in height and width.

Parsival. This is a low-growing variety valued for its free-flowering habit. The degree of acidity in the soil determines the depth of the blue flower color.

Veitchi. The flat flowers of this species have a fringe of white petals surrounding turquoise blue centers. In mild climates this plant makes a stand of 6 to 8 feet in height, but remains much lower where winters are severe. Like so many of these showy types, it is well adapted to part shade as well as full sun.

LACECAP HYBRIDS

Varieties with lacecap blooms are those with flat, platelike flower heads. The central mass of fertile flowers is surrounded by a circle of large-petaled, sterile, ray flowers giving the effect of a lacy cap.

Blue Wave. This hybrid varies from blue to pink with the central or fertile petals retaining a purplish blue cast. It is ideal for partial shade since the color is usually richer than when grown in full sun.

Bretschneideri. This shaggy hydrangea, a native of China, has whitish flat heads which become deep blue in acid soil. Plants range from 4 to 8 feet, depending on the climate in which they are grown.

Mariesi. This is a long-time favorite with those who have grown it. The flowers are usually rosy pink, but where soils are strongly acid the color is a rich blue. Among the newest of plant introductions is a form with variegated foliage. Here, indeed, is a handsome summer-flowering shrub for dramatic effects in part shade. Plants average 3 feet in height, and the introducer claims that it has survived severe winters in the colder sections of New England with no protection.

Serrata, Grayswood. In Japan this species is known as Tea of Heaven. Plants average 3 feet tall with attractive bright green foliage and distinctive flat heads of bloom. The color ranges from blue with white centers as the flowers open, to pink and finally crimson tones as they age.

Since blooms are produced on year-old wood, pruning must be done thoughtfully. Immediately after flowering, remove dead blooms and stems, cutting back to sturdy new growth. Also remove any weak stems and undesirable growth to improve the appearance of the plant. New basal shoots are the source of next year's flowers. In the colder parts of the Northeast, some gardeners avoid all pruning except the removal of flower heads until spring. If heavy pruning is resorted to late in the growing season, followed by heavy watering and feeding, new growth developing may not have sufficient time to harden before winter, with the result that flower buds are likely to be killed.

Well-drained garden soil suits the various kinds of hydrangeas. The macrophylla varieties respond to periodic feeding and require considerable water in dry weather, and particularly when flower buds are opening. They retain their color better and longer when grown in part shade. Winter protection as previously discussed should not be neglected. If tubbed specimens are stored in frostproof cellars during the winter they require only enough water to keep them from drying out. Where winters are mild, they can be stored in the open in a protected place. All types can be propagated from cuttings.

INKBERRY   2–10′   Zone 3   *Ilex glabra*

Inkberry deserves attention separately from its holly relatives since this native, broad-leaved evergreen is extremely hardy and adaptable to seashore conditions from Massachusetts to Florida. In the wild, it develops into a thicket because of its habit of spreading by stolons or underground stems. Companion plants found with it include American holly, several viburnums, blueberries, sweet pepperbush, and others. Gallberry is a familiar common name in the South in reference to the bitter flavor of the fruits. At first glance, inkberry might be taken for a form of evergreen willow because of its loose, open habit, but actually it is the toughest member of the genus Ilex. (See also Holly, Chapter 4 and Japanese holly which follows.) It can be used in sun or shade, trimmed to make a low hedge, a specimen, or allowed to assume its natural, somewhat irregular willowy form.

The flowers are of little consequence and the shiny black berries are only outstanding when seen against a light background. Rather, it is the glossy, leathery, evergreen foliage that is the chief asset of this plant. Although it may reach 10 feet if allowed to grow unpruned, annual hard cutting produces a much more satisfactory and useful shrub, ranging from 2 to 6 feet tall. It combines well with bayberry, sweet fern, wild roses, mugho pine, sweet pepperbush, blueberries, and other sturdy seaside shrubs for use in bank plantings and shrub borders.

Despite a preference for moist soil and swampy areas in its native haunts, inkberry grows well in acid soil under average conditions. Stock may be increased by cuttings.

JAPANESE HOLLY   1–3′   Zone 5   *Ilex crenata* varieties

During the past few decades, Japanese hollies have become exceedingly popular, and they can be used to good advantage in sheltered areas in seaside gardens. However, they cannot be expected to endure salt spray and exposure to the same extent as inkberry, which is separately described. Because of their dwarf habit, their compact growth, their rich evergreen foliage, and their distinctive forms, they fit a variety of uses on the home grounds. Since they differ considerably in appearance, in foliage, and in the color and size of their fruits from the red-berried hollies, they are treated separately.

The original form of Japanese holly (*I. crenata*), introduced a century ago, develops into a sizable shrub 18 to 20 feet high and wide at maturity, but such specimens are rarely seen. Rather it is the selected dwarf forms that fit the needs of present-day landscaping. These are kept at the desired size by pruning and shearing. Slow-growing and compact, the smooth, leathery, boxlike foliage of Japanese holly is one of its most rewarding features. Neither the tiny white flowers nor the black berries are of particular significance.

Stokes Variety, Green Cushion, Green Island, and others like *I. crenata nummularis, I. c. microphylla,* and the Kingsville holly are typical of the improved forms available. Because of their moderate rate of growth, their pleasing texture and moundlike habit, they rank high as desirable plants for landscaping. Then, too, they are excellent substitutes for boxwood where that is not hardy and minimum maintenance is essential.

Japanese holly needs fertile soil on the acid side with plenty of peat moss or leaf mold incorporated. Balled and burlapped or container-grown specimens are easily handled. They can be set out at any time during the growing season. Plants can be increased by cuttings.

| JAPANESE QUINCE | 1–3′ | Zone 4 | *Chaenomeles lagenaria japonica* |
| FLOWERING QUINCE | 6′ | Zone 4 | *Chaenomeles lagenaria* |

For generations quince bushes were synonymous with dooryard plantings along much of the Atlantic seaboard and inland as well. Sometimes seen as hedge plants but more frequently as great specimens, together with lilacs, wisteria, and strawberry shrub, they seemed to belong near the front door or by the side entrance to the house. Flowers were bright red or orange and these big shrubs often outgrew the space provided for them, reaching 6 feet in height and often spreading twice as wide. Furthermore, their spiny stems made them difficult to prune.

The new dwarf forms, 1 to 4 feet tall, valued for their dense, twiggy growth, are somewhat sprawling in habit, with glossy foliage and bright flowers, ranging from white to deepest red. The spiny stems give them value for checking traffic where it is not wanted. These shrubs sucker as they develop and make suitable cover plants and soil binders for slopes and level areas where this type of growth is needed. The Alpine flowering quince is usually less than 1 foot tall, with bright orange flowers in spring. Knaphill and Rowellane are hybrids of recent introduction, reaching 2 feet or more, with flowers in the bright red range. Named varieties in varying shades of pink are becoming increasingly popular.

Ordinary garden soil and full sun suit the flowering quinces. They are easily propagated by root division or by pulling the suckers apart.

| JUNIPERS | 1–2′ | Zones 2–5 | *Juniperus* genus |

On steep slopes in full sun where grass is difficult to maintain because soil tends to be dry and erosion threatens, few plants are more adaptable

Spreading junipers, heather, thyme, dwarf yew and other low-growing shrubs link this contemporary house with its surroundings.

and desirable than low-growing junipers. Horizontal in habit, evergreen, and soft in texture, these prostrate types are attractive throughout the year. As the branches spread they root, making a wavy carpet. Creeping junipers are often the answer to problems created by the construction of split-level houses, particularly in areas of rolling terrain. Also, when used in masses to link several changes of level on home grounds, they are more effective than grass because of their height, color, texture, and mode of growth.

Most widely planted is the creeping juniper (*J. horizontalis*), which makes a dense mat of gray-green needlelike foliage. For color and variety the blue-gray Waukegan juniper (*J. horizontalis douglasi*) makes a pleasing companion plant. For stronger blue-green color, you can use the blue creeping juniper (*J. horizontalis glauca*), a slower and more compact grower. Another variety in wide use is the Andorra juniper, valued for its delicate texture and rich purple color during autumn and winter.

The Sargent juniper (*J. chinensis sargentii*) is of more billowy habit and somewhat taller as it matures. It is grayish green and somewhat bolder in habit than the common creeping types.

71

The Japanese garden juniper (*J. procumbens*) is darker in color, dense, and rather upright in habit, and about 2 feet tall when mature.

The common juniper of rocky soils in upland pastures, listed as *J. communis depressa,* is a wide-spreading plant which may eventually grow 3 feet tall, but usually is lower. Gray-green and silvery in texture, it is especially desirable where there is space to accommodate it in naturalistic plantings. Bluish fruits add interest in autumn and winter. Of more compact habit, the mountain form (*J. communis saxatilis*) makes broad patches slightly under 2 feet in height.

For sandy banks and slopes, the shore juniper (*J. conferta*), a Japanese native, is a real asset, especially close to the sea, since it is not harmed by salt spray. Bright green shoots grow somewhat upright from low, spreading branches. Plants are 1 foot or less in height and spread 8 to 10 feet across, hugging the ground.

Regardless of how poor the soil is or appears to be, junipers will prosper with proper soil preparation. Assuming that the slope has been raked and graded, dig holes wide and deep enough to accommodate equal parts of garden soil and peat moss thoroughly mixed with a handful of acid-soil fertilizer. Water thoroughly and leave a slight depression around each plant to catch water. Additional water will be needed twice a week until the plants are established. Rooted cuttings from flats, potted plants, or balled and burlapped specimens may be used.

Leucothoe   3–6'   Zone 5   *Leucothoe catesbaei*

One of the most graceful and decorative of all our broad-leaved evergreens, leucothoe is a truly outstanding, low-growing, native shrub. The arching habit of its branches, the lustrous quality of its foliage which has few rivals among garden plants, and the waxy white lily of the valley type flowers, borne in clusters on the underside of the leaves, are other assets. This is a plant of year-round beauty and of particular value in winter because of the bronzy tones of the foliage. It can reach a height of 6 feet, but is not often seen that tall in the Northeast. There winter has a way of pruning it by killing back the growth, but it breaks from the base readily and is greatly benefited by pruning. Flower arrangers usually keep their plants in prime condition, with the result that its underground stems spread out, making it a most effective ground cover. It is especially effective when planted with rhododendrons, azaleas, and other acid-loving plants. A variegated form with highly colored foliage in shades of red and creamy yellow has been introduced in recent years. It is decidedly showy and surprisingly hardy.

Good garden soil, on the acid side, rich in humus, is needed to grow leucothoe successfully. It grows in sun or shade, but is less apt to suffer winter damage in shady locations. A mulch of peat moss and pine needles or oak-leaf compost benefits it greatly, since it is shallow rooted. It can be increased by dividing the roots or by cuttings.

72

The common purple and white lilacs are garden heirlooms along the Eastern seaboard and inland as well. They seem to be most suitably placed when they appear to be growing out of the foundation of an old house. Today, the preference is for the French hybrids, both single and double varieties notable for their large florets and flower clusters and their rich coloring—purple, pink, red, and white.

Beginners and experienced gardeners are often puzzled because lilacs are slow to flower. The common white and purple forms may require seven or eight years before bloom appears in quantity. However, grafted specimens of the French hybrids usually flower much sooner.

Lilacs should be pruned after flowering and the flower heads removed. Bloom is produced on the previous season's wood, and this fact should be borne in mind if it becomes necessary to do a drastic job of pruning to improve the shape of a plant. Suckers at the base of lilacs often present a problem. If too many are allowed to develop, blooms on older branches will be lessened, since some of the plant food derived from the soil is absorbed by the suckers developing at the base. Grafted plants of the French hybrids often produce suckers, and these should be cut out as soon as noticed. Some dealers offer plants grown on their own roots and these are preferred.

Mildew, scale, and an occasional borer are the pests common to lilacs. Mildew, which causes an unsightly grayish cast on the leaves, is more prevalent during wet summers, but causes no serious harm. Sulfur dust or Mildex can be used as a means of control.

Scale, when prevalent, can be most annoying. It appears like a crust on stems and spreads rapidly if not checked. Badly infected branches should be cut out and burned. A miscible oil spray applied before the buds break in spring is the usual control. Borers, easily recognized by the piles of sawdust on the ground in early summer, can be wormed out with wire. Then plug holes with borer paste or soap.

All lilacs need time to become well established and the plants do best in full sun. Well-drained garden soil free of competition from the roots of trees and other shrubs is also essential. Lilacs persist in considerable shade, making an abundance of suckers but few blooms. Since they prefer sweet or alkaline soil, a generous sprinkling of ground limestone applied every two years is essential.

MOUNTAIN ANDROMEDA   3–6′   Zone 4   *Pieris floribunda*

One of our truly notable broad-leaved evergreens, the mountain andromeda is native in mountainous areas from Virginia to Georgia and is often referred to as mountain fetter-bush. Mature plants range in height from 3 to 6 feet, but are easily kept lower by pruning. Because of its moderate rate of growth and its broad-spreading habit, it makes an ideal dwarf shrub or ground cover, best suited to a place protected from the wind.

In its typical form mugho pine is broad-spreading and dense in growth, making a useful windbreak of year 'round beauty.

The showy spikes of white bloom are held upright and appear in early spring. Conspicuous flower buds add to its winter beauty. Particularly useful for combining with rhododendrons and azaleas and other broad-leaved evergreens, it makes a tasteful underplanting for dogwood, sourwood, and other high-branched trees. For accent among carpeting plants, the laurel-like foliage offers a dramatic contrast.

Well-drained, acid soil with plenty of organic matter produces good growth. It can be grown in sun or shade. Stock is increased by cuttings and occasionally in home gardens by layering of the lower stems. Side branches close to the soil can be induced to root by pinning them down.

MUGHO PINE   3–4'   Zone 2   *Pinus mugo mughus*

Pines are important in home gardens but most of them are trees, described in Chapter 4. However, the mugho pine fits the category of shrubs and a most useful and desirable ornamental it is. Actually, this plant in its typical form is a small tree reaching 25 feet when mature and is known as the Swiss mountain pine. It is the variety *P. mugo mughus* that is truly dwarf, and there are several other distinct forms, valued for their slow-growing, compact habit. To be fairly sure of getting the true dwarf forms when purchasing them in a nursery or garden center, select those with the smallest needles. A row of seedling mugho pines lined out in almost any nursery will show considerable variation. Yet, even by selecting those plants that show the slowest rate of growth, you cannot be certain of acquiring dwarf forms. True dwarfness of habit is best perpetuated when the plants are propagated by cuttings, a rather slow process. Even when grown from seed, it takes 10 years or more to obtain a shapely, compact plant, which is accomplished by shearing annually. These sun-loving evergreens are excellent for dry situations among rocks or on slopes. Use them in drifts for billowy ground cover effect and allow enough space for the full development of each plant.

Well-drained gritty soil suits these plants and a sunny location is best for the kind of rugged growth they make. By cutting back the new growth halfway each year in early summer, you can keep specimens low and compact. They can be grown in limestone soils.

The dwarf form of mugho pine makes an excellent ground cover in full sun.
Taloumis

OLEANDER   20′   Zone 7   *Nerium oleander*

Gardeners in the Northeast must be content to grow oleanders in tubs since they are not hardy. From Zone 7 southward, they are treated as big-scale shrubs or as small trees, flourishing in the open in hot, dry locations. The showy blooms produced in summer range from white through red, and may be single or double, according to the variety. The smooth, narrow evergreen foliage of leathery texture borne on graceful branches is attractive at all seasons, as is the sturdy upright growth of this native of southern Europe. Sometimes called rosebay, the oleander has been cultivated for centuries in gardens or as a tub plant in the warmer parts of the Old World where impressive specimens are commonly seen. The juice of the leaves, stems, and fruit is poisonous, a point to bear in mind where children are concerned. A species known as sweet oleander (*N. indicum*) averages 8 feet in height with pink or white blooms of marked fragrance.

Whether grown in tubs or in the ground, oleanders are best suited to full sun, and even intense heat and wind do not affect them. Average garden soil suits them, but as with most plants, periodic feeding pays dividends, as well as more frequent watering when flower buds are forming. Constant pruning improves the appearance of the plants and constant pinching keeps them to the desired height. Flowers are produced on new wood, a point to remember when pruning.

OREGON HOLLY-GRAPE   1–3′   Zone 4   *Mahonia aquifola*

Like drooping leucothoe, this broad-leaved evergreen is often kept low by the effects of the winter sun. It is a spectacular plant in many ways, effective for accent use because of its striking yellow flowers followed by showy clusters of blue fruits in early summer, and its bold, glossy, deeply cut foliage. This native of the Northwest increases by underground stolons and spreads fairly rapidly once established. Dr. Donald Wyman of the Arnold Arboretum reminds us that it was introduced to East Coast gardens by the Lewis and Clark expedition. Although it is a tough, sturdy plant, the foliage often burns badly in winter. Thus, in areas where frost penetrates the soil deeply it is best suited to shady locations. Plants reach 2 to 3 feet in height as they develop, but in the colder sections of the country they are often less than 2 feet tall. A lower growing form, *M. repens,* is a good low-cover plant, less than 1 foot tall. It is similar in appearance, but the foliage lacks the luster of the taller form.

Well-drained soil in full sun or part shade suits this decorative shrub. Pruning to keep it vigorous and to eliminate winter burn serves to make growth dense. It is easily increased by division of the stolons, which root as they spread.

RED CHOKEBERRY   8′   Zone 2   *Aronia arbutifolia*

This shrub is known to every youngster who has roamed the fields and pastures in early autumn and sampled the harmless looking red berries that appear in clusters on good-sized bushes. They resemble small cherries but are bitter and highly astringent leaving one's mouth and lips puckery. Yet the Indians used to make jelly from them. Plants reach 8 feet in height but can be kept lower by pruning, and the foliage, grayish on the under-surface, contributes its show of brilliant red color to the autumn landscape. It is native from Massachusetts to Florida. An improved form, *A. arbuti-folia brilliantissima,* is valued for its exceptionally bright fruits. Because of its sturdy growth and easy culture, and its ability to thrive along the coast as well as inland, it is worth considering for shrub borders.

Not particular as to soil, red chokeberry can be grown in full sun or part shade and is of easy culture. It is particularly desirable for use among native plantings.

Red Osier Dogwood   7′   Zone 2   *Cornus stolonifera*

Red osier dogwood and the yellow-twigged form are native shrubs of more than ordinary value especially for moist soil or low, boggy areas. Yet they can be expected to do well even in ordinary soil. White flowers in flat clusters, white fruits in late summer, and bright red or golden yellow twigs in winter according to the type planted make this shrub a distinct asset in the landscape. Allow it plenty of room in which to develop for this is a shrub of generous proportions to 7 feet in height and spreading much wider when left to itself. It is a good soil binder because of its heavy root system and habit of increasing in size by underground stems. The color of the twigs, especially when the sun shines on them, greatly enlivens the winter landscape.

There is a dwarf form (*C. stonifera kelseyi*) averaging 2 feet in height. The Siberian dogwood (*C. siberica alba*) is somewhat similar with several forms including a variety with variegated leaves. One called Coral Beauty, with pale blue berries and brilliant winter twig color, grows 4 to 5 feet tall.

Plants are offered by most nurserymen and require no special care. Additional plants can be obtained from cuttings.

Saint-John's-wort   18″   Zones 4–6   *Hypericum* genus

The Saint-John's-worts are showy, low-growing shrubs found native in various parts of the United States and Europe. They have soft, light green foliage and thrive in full sun, but make a good display in a fair amount of shade. Showy yellow tassel-like blooms appear over a long period in summer, and plants require no special soil or attention. Nurserymen on both sides of the Atlantic have turned their attention to these showy plants in recent years, and several improved forms have been featured in cata-logs. Some kinds are known to rock-garden enthusiasts and others are collected by those who grow dwarf shrubs. The Saint-John's-worts make good ground covers of varying heights and are most adaptable as well as decorative, but some of them cannot be counted on for hardiness in areas of prolonged subzero temperatures without benefit of snow cover.

A species native to the Blue Ridge Mountain region, *H. bucklei,* less than 1 foot tall, bears its yellow tassels in June. One plant makes a mat of soft foliage a yard wide, and, while not evergreen, is most desirable. *H. calycinum,* listed in many catalogs, grows 1 foot to 18 inches tall and spreads by underground stems, making a mat of glaucous foliage which is evergreen, or partially so, depending on the winter temperature.

A taller growing species, *H. moserianum,* reaches 2 feet in height and is known as goldflower. Even when it dies back to the ground, it makes rapid new growth and blooms freely in July and August. A creeping form, *H. repens,* is a low-growing kind, 6 to 8 inches tall, with showy bloom in early summer. The new variety Sungold, patented in recent years, grows 1½ to 2 feet tall and spreads twice as wide, with an abundance of golden-yellow flowers throughout the summer. Hidcote grows nearly twice as tall in moderate climates and, even where it dies back to the ground, it flowers freely in the current season's growth.

Well suited to sandy soils in full sun or light shade, plants are listed by many nurseries throughout the country. Container-grown plants are easy to plant at any season of the year. Stock may be increased by cuttings, segments of the rooted stems, division, or seed, according to the types grown.

SALT TREE   5–7′   Zone 3   *Halimodendron halodendron*

A curious shrub from Turkestan brought to the U.S. after the American Revolution, this member of the pea family has spiny stems and silky blue-green foliage. Purplish pealike flowers appear in early summer, followed by seedpods of brownish yellow. Its common name, salt tree, a direct translation from the scientific term, reveals its native habitat. It is actually a moderate-sized shrub.

It can be increased from seed or cuttings and, once planted, requires no special care.

SEA BUCKTHORN   30′   Zone 4   *Hippophae rhamnoides*

All too little known and seldom planted, the sea buckthorn is one of the most decorative of all the big-scale shrubs suited to seaside gardens. Mature specimens may become treelike in habit, attaining a height of 30 feet, but in exposed areas it usually grows 8 to 12 feet tall. This sturdy shrub, native to various parts of Europe and Asia, is widely grown in coastal gardens throughout the British Isles. The genus name, *Hippophae,* is of Greek origin and means spiny plant.

Related to the Russian olive, sea buckthorn is a spiny stemmed shrub with gray-green, willowlike leaves that are distinctly silvery on the underside, especially in spring and early summer. Small yellowish flowers are borne in clusters in early spring before the leaves appear. The foliage makes a pleasing contrast with the orange or orange-yellow fruits that appear in short clusters in autumn. From a distance, the heavily fruited stems give the appearance of a richly colored yellow-berried holly minus its evergreen foliage. Curiously enough, birds dislike the fruits because of their bitterness, a characteristic which gives this shrub significant winter value, since the berries remain on the branches throughout most of the winter. However, they give off an unpleasant odor and are not suited for use indoors.

This shrub can be expected to thrive in the driest of sandy soils, even in sand dunes, and requires no special care. It is a very typical denizen of the seaside, able to endure wind, salt spray, and exposure. Use it to make a solid impenetrable hedge or plant it in masses to create a coppice growth, or in a wide shrub border with bayberries, rugosa roses, and other woody plants of contrasting foliage and texture.

Another species, *H. salicifolia,* native to the Himalaya region, grows to 50 feet when mature but is suited only to warm climates. Its foliage is somewhat broader than *H. rhamnoides,* with dull green coloring and yellowish fruits.

Sea buckthorn makes dense shrubby growth spreading by underground stems which makes propagation by layering an easy means of increase. It can also be raised from seed. Like the hollies, this shrub produces staminate and pistillate flowers on separate plants. Thus, to insure the production of fruit, specimens of both sexes must be set out in colonies, one male to every five or six female plants. In setting out plants, it is important to give them adequate water and mulching until they are well established.

SHADBUSH   15–20′   Zone 3   *Amelanchier canadensis*

A sturdy native treelike shrub for windbreaks and use where its height and spread are needed, shadbush is native to the eastern coast of North America and assumes the stature of a tree inland. Clouds of white flowers appear in early spring followed by dark red fruits, hence the common name Juneberry. Serviceberry and shadblow are other popular names. The leaves and stems are grayish and the reddish buds add color to the winter landscape. It is found in swamps, along streams and salt water inlets, and in exposed areas along the coast. There are several other species found in the wild that are sometimes used in naturalized plantings. The apple serviceberry (*A. grandiflora*), a hybrid of two native species, is valued for its large flowers, showy fruits, and autumn color.

Like many of our native plants, it is offered only by large nurseries. Of easy culture, it needs no special care once planted.

SPICEBUSH   8–15′   Zone 2   *Lindera benzoin*

Spicebush is one of our native shrubs that found a place in gardens in Colonial times because of the pleasant aromatic qualities of its flowers, foliage, and twigs. In fact, a fragrant tea was brewed from the twigs. During the Civil War the berries were dried and used as a substitute for allspice.

The yellow flowers are borne in tight clusters in early spring, and plants of both sexes are needed to produce the red fruits that show to good advantage after the leaves, having changed to golden yellow, drop to the ground. A useful shrub for mixed borders where naturalistic effects are sought, it is sturdy and long-lived.

Average garden soil in sun or shade is sufficient for spicebush, but it can endure considerable moisture. Plants can be increased by cuttings.

SUMAC   3–30′   Zones 2–4   *Rhus* genus

Sumacs are so ordinary that most people have little regard for them. Yet they thrive in hot, dry places under the most difficult conditions, enduring wind and salt spray, and often fill a need in seaside gardens, especially when naturalistic effects are sought. Among the familiar native kinds are the shining sumac, the staghorn, and smooth sumac. These range in height from 15 to 30 feet when mature. Because of their rapid growth, they are good for achieving screening effects quickly. When found growing naturally, they can be thinned to allow for the introduction of other big-scale shrubs and trees in order to lend variety to the textured effect and general appearance of a planting. Indeed, the showy fruits and colorful autumn foliage as well as the picturesque growth of these woody plants are not to be underestimated.

One variety, the fragrant sumac, a harmless cousin of poison ivy, is a wide-spreading, low shrub with aromatic foliage sometimes used to cover banks or as an underplanting for shrubs and trees. At first glance, because of the similarity of the foliage, it might be mistaken for the ubiquitous poison ivy, except that the leaves of that objectionable plant are distinctly glossy. Fragrant sumac makes a good soil binder where a native

Sumac, Scots pine, and rugosa roses are taking hold in this wild planting where daffodils carpet the ground in the spring.

Taloumis

Summersweet, a favorite seaside shrub.

plant is needed and keeps a most pleasing appearance throughout the year. In autumn, the foliage turns brilliant yellow and scarlet. When used on dry banks, interplanted with native spreading junipers, it makes a pleasing combination. Hard pruning induces dense growth, and individual specimens of this native shrub that have been pruned heavily are decidedly ornamental. Where an evergreen winter effect is not important, it can be used widely since it requires practically no maintenance. Tiny yellow flowers appear in spring, followed by red fruits. The maximum height of fragrant sumac is 3 feet.

Ordinary soil, even of poor, gravelly texture, suits all the sumacs and they grow well in sun or shade. Increase is by division of the roots. The fragrant sumac can also be grown from cuttings.

SUMMER SWEET 9′ Zone 3 *Clethra alnifolia*

Summer sweet and sweet pepperbush are popular names for this summer-flowering shrub that is found native along the entire Eastern seaboard. It is easily recognized by its showy spikes of fragrant white flowers in late

81

July, followed by clusters of small black seeds resembling peppercorns; hence the name sweet pepperbush. These are decorative for dried arrangements. The foliage takes on yellow and orange coloring in autumn. A true denizen of the seacoast, it is often found close to the shore in great masses growing with the seaside rose and other wildings. It spreads by underground stems and makes a dense mass of roots, giving it value as a soil binder. While it endures dry soil, it is sometimes found in moist places. Although it grows to 8 or 9 feet, it can be kept much lower by pruning. There is also a pink-flowering variety 4 to 5 feet and a Japanese species (*C. barbinervis*) that blooms a little earlier and grows much taller.

Summer sweet can be grown in ordinary garden soil, but the better the soil, the more luxurious will be the growth. Plants are available from many nurseries. Clumps can be divided to increase stock since the underground stems develop roots as they spread.

Sweet Fern   3–5′   Zone 2   *Comptonia peregrina*

Shrubs with fragrant foliage are scarce, but sweet fern is one of them—distinctly aromatic and most pleasing to the nose. Shrubby fern and sweet bush are other common names of this shrub, familiar to earlier generations when boys used to gather the leaves and dry them as substitutes for tobacco. The fernlike foliage is delicately cut and most attractive, but the flowers and fruits are of minor significance. It makes a pleasing companion for low-growing native junipers, the seaside rose, bayberries, and rugosa roses. Sweet fern spreads by underground roots, giving it prime value as a soil binder. Well suited to dry locations and poor, gravelly soils, it deserves more attention from seaside gardeners.

Some nurserymen offer clumps collected from the wild, usually as fair-sized sods, but plants that have been lined out in nursery rows for a year or two are more satisfactory. Losses with plants collected from the wild are apt to be considerable, particularly when the roots are cut severely, hence the need for lining out. However, once established, sweet fern requires no special care and is of permanent value in any seaside planting. As with many native plants, hard pruning greatly improves its appearance. Feeding with a complete fertilizer, after the plants are established, encourages vigorous new growth. Old plantings also benefit from this kind of attention.

Tamarisk   6–25′   Zones 2–3   *Tamarix* genus

Long known for its tolerance of salt spray and its ability to grow in sandy soils, the tamarisk along with the goat willow have stood the test of time as favorite seaside trees. Lacy and delicate in appearance, the scale-like foliage is loosely distributed on graceful wandlike branches, and the fluffy flowers that appear in summer in long, airy racemes are notably decorative. Generally considered the toughest and hardiest of all, *T. pentandra* develops as a small tree to 15 feet or more by hard pruning.

82

Sweet fern, one of the most useful native shrubs for hot, dry situations.

The Odessa tamarisk (*T. odessana*), native to the Caspian Sea, with pale pink blooms and an improved form known as Summer Glow with bright rose-colored flowers, are shrubby forms, 6 to 8 feet in height. These two kinds need to be pruned hard in early spring to produce dense masses since they bloom on wood of the current year's growth. In Florida and the Gulf region, the salt tree (*T. apylla*) flourishes as a windbreak and makes a pleasing ornamental as well, since the foliage is persistent. It grows to 25 feet or more in height. *T. parviflora* blooms in late spring and may grow 12 to 15 feet tall unless cut back hard. Prune after flowering, since the pink flowers appear on the wood produced the previous season.

These shrubs or small trees flourish in sandy soils in full sun and require no special care except for hard pruning at planting time and periodically as needed to produce dense growth for the base.

83

Viburnum carlcephalum is valued for its fragrant flowers and clean foliage.

Viburnum   6–30′   Zones 2–7   *Viburnum* genus

Viburnums are sturdy shrubs, valued for their vigor and hardiness. They are notably decorative in flower and fruiting habit and the foliage of most kinds remains clean and attractive throughout the growing year. For the most part, they are big-scale plants which lend themselves admirably to mixed borders and screen plantings, as informal hedges, and as specimens.

Some kinds can endure considerably more exposure than others, particularly wind and salt spray. Among them is arrowwood (*V. dentatum*), 12 to 15 feet tall with white flowers, blue fruits, and foliage which turns glossy red in autumn. Most adaptable and not particular as to soil, a position in sun or shade suits it. Withe rod (*V. cassinoides*) which is equally sturdy, contributes a similar display of beauty, but the fruits are much more interesting since they range from green through yellow, red, and black, as they ripen. A shrub of moderate height, it grows about 6 feet tall.

An evergreen form, not hardy in the Northeast, known as laurustinus (*V. tinus*) is widely grown from Delaware south. The dark green foliage

The double-file viburnum becomes a big-scale shrub of distinct horizontal branching habit and requires ample space to develop.

and reddish flower buds that open waxy white, make a handsome effect. The flowers appear in late autumn and, when winters are mild, continue until early spring, followed by black fruits. This is a favorite seaside shrub in the South and in the British Isles as well. An improved form, *V. tinus lucidum,* is superior to the type. All of these are tried and true shrubs, ideal for quick-growing windbreaks.

One of the best known of all the viburnums is the European cranberry bush (*V. opulus*) which grows to 10 feet or more. The white, flat flowers borne in May are followed by clusters of red fruits in autumn. There is also a handsome yellow fruiting form. Even more showy in every way is the doublefile viburnum (*V. tomentosum mariesi*) with a distinctly horizontal branching habit. The flat white flower heads, red coloring of the foliage in autumn, and brilliant red fruit add to its value. Plants average 6 to 7 feet, often spreading as wide to make decidedly spectacular specimens. This shrub is much more desirable than the snowballs we grow commonly.

The tea viburnum (*V. setigerum*) is a loose, open-growing shrub of

Arrowwood and other viburnums are excellent shrubs for seaside plantings.

picturesque habit to 12 feet with a spectacular fruiting habit. The orange-fruited form is preferred by many. The Wright viburnum (*V. wrighti*), a native of Japan, ranges from 4 to 6 feet in height, making a broad, compact mass of rich green foliage in summer which changes to crimson in autumn when the fruit clusters turn red. This is an exceptionally good shrub of moderate height for the small garden.

Two of recent introduction are prized for their fragrant flowers. The Burkwood viburnum, a shrub of medium size, 5 to 6 feet, carries showy heads of pink buds which open to a waxy white in early spring. Glossy foliage clothes the stems all summer and in autumn the leaves assume the warm tones of the season. A superb shrub, it makes a worthy replacement for the fragrant or mayflower viburnum once popular, but subject to both insects and disease which make it unsightly. *V. carlcephalum,* the so-called fragrant snowball, was aptly named by an American nurseryman. This patented plant was developed in England, the result of crossing two popular species. Plants may grow to 7 feet, but may be kept lower if desired. The fragrant white flower clusters often measure 5 to 6 inches across, and the sturdy foliage contributes its share of color in the fall.

Somewhat taller, to 8 or 9 feet, the linden viburnum is a shrub of merit, valued for its clean foliage that colors in autumn and its red or yellow fruit, according to the kind chosen. Among the truly big-scale kinds are the wayfaring tree (*V. lantana*) which tolerates dry conditions, and the Siebold viburnum (*V. sieboldi*) which grows to 25 feet if not cut back. In flowers, foliage, autumn color, and fruiting, both are distinctive and can be used to good advantage where they have room to develop.

Given adequate preparation of soil at planting time and average care, the viburnums can be counted on to make a creditable appearance over a period of years. The only pruning required is the removal of branches to retain a pleasing form. Most nurseries and garden centers offer them. All can be propagated from cuttings.

Other shrubs both native and exotic that can be utilized in a variety of ways in seaside gardens are listed here. Many are widely known and commonly seen in gardens while a few are less familiar, but all are

Purple-leaved barberry makes a striking combination with the silvery-gray foliage of artemisia albula which spreads rapidly if not checked.

Taloumis

adaptable to soils of poor quality and light texture and can endure varying degrees of exposure.

ADAM'S NEEDLE	*Yucca filamentosa*
ALTHEA	*Hibiscus syriacus*
AMERICAN ELDER	*Sambucus canadensis*
AMUR PRIVET	*Ligustrum amurense*
ANTHONY WATERER SPIREA	*Spirea bumalda var.*
BARBERRY	*Berberis* genus
BLUEBEARD	*Caryopertis clandonensis*
BUCKTHORN	*Rhamnus* genus
BUSH CLOVER	*Lespedeza* genus
BUSH HONEYSUCKLE	*Lonicera* genus
BUTTERFLY BUSH	*Buddleia* genus
CAROLINA ALLSPICE	*Calycanthus floridus*
DARWIN BARBERRY	*Berberis darwini*
EUONYMUS—see Chapter 10	
GOAT WILLOW	*Salix caprea*
HEBE	*Hebe* genus
JAPANESE AUCUBA	*Aucuba japonica*
JAPANESE BARBERRY	*Berberis thunbergi*
JAPANESE PITTISPORUM—see Chapter 4	
MIRROR PLANT	*Coprosma baueri*
NANDINA	*Nandina domestica*
NATAL PLUM	*Carissa grandiflora*
PRIVET	*Ligustrum* genus
ROSE OF SHARON—see Althea	
ROSES—see Chapter 6	
ROSEMARY—see Chapter 8	
SILKY DOGWOOD	*Cornus amomum*
SPIREA	*Spirea* genus
SWEET BAY	*Magnolia virginiana*
VANHOUTTE SPIREA	*Spirea vanhouttei*
VIRGINIA WILLOW	*Itea virginica*
WEIGELA	*Weigela hybrids*
WILLOW	*Salix* genus
WINGED SPINDLE TREE	*Euonymus alata*
YEDDO HAWTHORN	*Raphiolepsis umbellata*

CHAPTER SIX

Roses by the Sea

N nearly every land that borders on the sea, some type of rose flourishes either in the wild or cultivated state. The species of wild roses and their hybrids endure wind and salt spray with ease, but the cultivated types need protection from excessive exposure. Everblooming kinds like the hybrid teas, the floribundas, the grandifloras, and those climbers that repeat are particularly satisfying since they bloom on, even after hard frosts have blackened the flowers in inland gardens.

Since many books devoted to rose culture are easily available, there is little point in discussing the relative merits of varieties of these types. Rather, attention is focused on the various species of wild roses and their hybrids which deserve to be more widely planted. They are all too little known and grown. Yet they are notable for their vigor, hardiness, easy culture and maintenance, and disease resistance. Rose enthusiasts refer to them as shrub roses and the list that follows is representative of the kinds that can be used to advantage in gardens by the sea.

Austrian copper. The copper-red single flowers are yellow on the underside. Requires little pruning, makes an attractive plant, and thrives in poor soil. 6 to 8 feet.

Fruehlingsmorgen. A single rose with large cherry-blossom pink flowers that appear early in rosetime. 5 to 7 feet.

Fruehling's Gold. A sweetly scented yellow cup-shaped Scottish rose that thrives in light soil. 3 to 5 feet.

Harison's Yellow. An old-time favorite with double golden-yellow blooms, vigorous, trouble free, and long-lived. 6 to 8 feet.

Hugonis. An impressive plant with pale yellow blossoms at tulip time, delicate foliage, and spiny stems. Does well in poor soil. 8 feet.

Hybrid Musk Roses. These include several varieties of bushy habit producing blooms in pyramidal trusses. Of medium habit and dense growth. 3 to 5 feet.

Mabelle Stearns. A most remarkable rose with superb blossoms of peach pink produced from rosetime to frost. It averages 2 feet in height and spreads more than twice as wide.

Moyesii Hybrids. These hybrids of an interesting Chinese species have exceptionally large bottle-shaped hips. Varieties include white, pink, yellow, and red flowering kinds. 6 to 8 feet.

Rosa virginiana (*lucida*). Often called the seaside rose, this native species is listed here to call attention to our native roses, which thrive in poor soil and are persistent.

Sparrieshoop. A perpetual flowering shrub rose that can be trained as a pillar if desired. Superb single pink flowers in clusters on long stems. Does best when kept about 5 feet tall.

Stanwell Perpetual White. Both the foliage and white flowers of this Scottish rose are delightfully fragrant. Blooms from June to autumn. 3 feet.

York and Lancaster. This famous rose recalls the War of the Roses. The semidouble blooms may be white or pink, or white marked with pink. The richer the soil, the better the plant and the blooms. 6 feet.

TRAILING ROSES

CREEPING RUGOSA ROSE	1″	Zone 4	*Rosa rugosa alba*
MEMORIAL ROSE	1″	Zone 5	*Rosa wichuraiana*
TRAILING HYBRID ROSES	1″	Zone 5	*Rosa hybrids*

Roses used as ground covers have special merit in gardens along the coast. Attractive foliage, colorful and often fragrant bloom (sometimes everblooming), showy fruits with some kinds, and vigorous growth are among their assets. Then, too, the fact that they are thorny provides protection from trespassing along boundaries, a point not to be overlooked in some areas. Certain of our large-flowered climbing roses, not generally thought of as suited to trailing, have been adapted for use on banks and slopes to create striking landscape effects. In regions of extremely low winter temperatures, a number of climbers are brought into abundant bloom only by growing them on the ground.

Trailing roses are best suited to properties where they can sprawl over large areas. There are two distinct groups for general ground-cover use: the ramblers and the trailing, or creeping, varieties. Scrambling over ledges or rocky areas, mass-planted on slopes or steep banks within the grounds or along boundaries, flanking steps to various levels—these are typical ways to use both the ramblers and the trailing varieties.

Floribunda roses are valued for their free-flowering habit.

The rambler roses, of which Dorothy Perkins and Crimson Rambler are the two best known, have lost favor with gardeners because they are subject to mildew in most gardens.

Best known of the trailing roses are the Max Graf and the Memorial Rose. These have been widely used as ground covers for nearly a half century. During the past two decades, the late W. D. Brownell of Little Compton, Rhode Island, developed many notable trailing or creeping varieties that have become popular wherever roses are grown. They are noted for their vigor, the excellence of their color, and their hardiness. To see them is to want to find a place for them. Many are included in the following list.

Apricot Glow. Fragrant, double apricot-pink flowers in June. This trailer is valued for its bloom, its glossy foliage, and its vigor.

Carpet of Gold. One of many outstanding climbers developed by the Brownells. Shiny, vigorous foliage with double yellow, fragrant blossoms in clusters.

Cherokee Rose. A single white fragrant rose, borne on sturdy evergreen growth, it is the state flower of Georgia. Tender in the North, it is seen frequently in Florida, in the deep South, and on the West Coast.

Creeping Everbloom. A double 4-inch red hybrid-tea-type rose, it is free-flowering, recurrent in its bloom, and fragrant.

Crimson Shower. A recently introduced hybrid of the rugged Memorial Rose with clusters of clear crimson bloom from July to late summer.

Everblooming Yellow Climber. This is another of Mr. Brownell's valuable roses. The semidouble yellow blossoms are fragrant and can be counted on for repeat bloom.

Golden Glow. Large bright yellow blooms with tea fragrance in June and July, and leathery foliage, are the notable features of this variety.

Little Compton Creeper. Single, bright wild-rose-pink flowers in loose clusters, this is a superb variety with glossy foliage and colorful vermilion fruits in autumn. Not quite so flat as some others, it grows at a slight angle, making a memorable display.

Climbing roses, although frequently trained on fences, trellises, and arbors are equally effective scrambling over stone walls, and ledges.

Taloumis

Max Graf rose makes an attractive ground cover.

Max Graf. Single pink flowers with showy golden stamens, it has the rugged rugosa-type foliage which indicates its hybrid origin. Unlike most roses that thrive in full sun, it tolerates considerable shade, is completely hardy, and a vigorous grower. It is one of the oldest and most widely planted roses for ground-cover use.

Memorial Rose. This is actually *Rosa wichuraiana,* a species native to the Orient. The single white, fragrant blossoms, accentuated by showy yellow stamens, appear in early summer. Canes root when covered with soil, making it a valuable bank cover.

Mermaid. Visitors to rose gardens are often intrigued when they see the handsome single rose Mermaid growing on banks, holding its superb large single flowers, often measuring 5 to 6 inches across, against a mass of glossy foliage that makes a very handsome display.

Pink Cherokee. Fragrant, single, deep pink blossoms appear all summer on this rampant grower that is a favorite in the South. A tender rose, it is not suited to cold climates.

Red Cherokee (Ramona). This is a sport of the Pink Cherokee with all-summer light crimson flowers that fade to a softer pink and are fragrant.

Rosa rugosa repens alba. This creeping form of the rugosa rose is not grown too widely, but it deserves considerable attention from gardeners faced with the problem of ground covers in poor, sandy soils by the seashore or elsewhere. The white flowers are followed by showy red hips.

White Banksia. This is the Lady Banks rose of the South, also widely grown in California. A rampant grower with large clusters of tiny flowers, it has the fragrance of violets. There are single and double forms, and a yellow variety.

Plant these trailing types as you would any rose, by digging a generous hole and preparing the soil with plenty of plant food and good garden soil. Water thoroughly and give them a temporary mound of soil until the roots are set. On steep inclines, it is good practice to provide a pocket of soil around each plant to catch water and a mulch to keep the soil from washing out of the roots. They require little care aside from occasional pruning to remove canes that tend to grow upright and those that extend themselves beyond the limits set for them. Weeding and general maintenance can be reduced considerably by mulching the soil with a heavy application of straw, salt hay, or mulching paper. Plants can be planted bare-root in spring or fall, or from containers at any time during the growing season.

Rugosa Rose   4–6′   Zone 3   *Rosa rugosa*

Of all the seaside shrubs that endure salt spray and wind and thrive in poor soil, few can rival the rugosa rose. In Japan, this native of the Orient is known as the sea tomato. Since its introduction to America more than a century ago, it has been used extensively as a seashore shrub and, in many of our coastal areas, has become widely naturalized. Glossy, leathery textured and heavily wrinkled, the foliage turns a rich orange in autumn. At that time its showy blooms and its equally colorful red fruits make it all the more valuable as an ornamental plant.

Because the rugosa rose spreads by underground stems, making dense growth, it is an excellent soil binder. Although some varieties reach 6 feet in height at maturity, others average only 3 to 4 feet. Furthermore, all of the hybrids can be kept lower than their normal height by pruning, which induces density and compactness of habit. However, mature bushes in broad masses allowed to reach their maximum height afford considerable protection to lower growing plants.

Blooms may be single or double, ranging from pure white to reddish purple, and appear from June until hard frost. The large, bright red fruits are ornamental throughout the growing year and the combination of flowers and showy red hips adds to the appearance and interest of this rugged shrub. The hips are the source of a flavorsome jam rich in vitamins.

94

The rugosa rose, noted for its richly-textured foliage, free-blooming habit and showy red fruits, is an indispensable seaside shrub.

Rugosa roses may be combined with bayberry, sweet fern, dusty miller, mugho pine, creeping juniper, and other shrubs to create irregular drifts of richly textured foliage. For binding sandy soil on slopes or level ground, combinations of plants such as these are both practical and highly ornamental. And not many shrubs are more appealing when used as specimens, among boulders, or along stone walls. From a landscape standpoint, this sturdy rose makes an ideal informal hedge, impenetrable because of its spiny stems, and highly ornamental in appearance. It can be trimmed to give a tailored effect if desired but is at its best when pruned to improve the form of the individual plants and allowed to grow in its typical billowy form. Groups of rugosa roses are often used to advantage to soften the corners of houses and other structures, or as entrance plantings. Occasional pruning keeps them within bounds. Foliage texture is an integral part of plant composition and no rose contributes more conspicuously to this facet of garden art than the so-called Japanese brier.

Hybrids of the rugosa rose are numerous. Among them are:

Agnes. Double pale yellow, fragrant; a most desirable variety. 6 feet.

Alba. Single white. 6 feet.

Albo-plena. Double white. 6 feet.

Belle Poitevine. Semidouble, deep pink. 4 feet.

Blanc Double de Coubert. Semidouble, fragrant white. 5 feet.

Conrad Ferdinand Meyer. Large, double pink; can be trained as a climber. 6 to 8 feet.

Dr. Eckener. Semidouble, copper rose. Blooms with all the beauty and appeal of hybrid teas. 8 feet.

Flamingo. This hybrid with tea rose blood is a single rose of flamingo pink with pointed buds borne in clusters that flower freely, becoming deeper in color in cool weather. Gray-green foliage. 5 feet.

George Will. Deep pink bloom in clusters. 3 feet.

F. J. Grootendurst. Clusters of bright red, double, fringed flowers, borne in pyramidal clusters; this is an outstanding seaside shrub often referred to as the carnation rose. 4 feet.

Frau Dagmar Hartopp. A recent introduction with silvery pink blooms. Valued for its dwarf habit and attractive appearance. 18 to 24 inches.

Max Graf. See trailing roses.

Pink Grootendurst. Pink fringed flowers in large clusters, creating a handsome effect. 4 feet.

Plena. Double fuchsia purple flowers.

Repens alba. See trailing roses.

Rosea. Persian rose, single.

Sarah Van Fleet. Rose-pink, fragrant blooms on a big-scale plant to 7 feet or more.

Schneezwerg. Semidouble, fragrant white flowers borne in profusion throughout the growing season. From midsummer on, the blossoms and showy red fruits add materially to its decorative effect. Ideal for foreground planting since it grows only 2½ feet tall.

Sir Thomas Lipton. Semidouble, fragrant white flowers. 4 feet.

Stella Polaris. Single white blooms of good size. 4 feet.

Vanguard. A spectacular big-scale plant, when mature with glossy foliage and long-stemmed orange-salmon blooms. It can be handled as a climber or a specimen shrub. 8 feet.

Wasagaming. Double rose-pink, fragrant. 3 feet.

The rugosa rose requires no special soil, but planting with the usual care given any shrub gets it off to a good start. Ample feeding pays dividends. It blooms most freely in full sun but can be grown in partial shade. Old canes need to be removed to keep the plants vigorous. Increase is by division of the roots, which spread rapidly. Plants are obtainable bare-root in early spring and in the fall. Some nurseries offer it container-grown so that it can be planted throughout the growing season.

Since named varieties of rugosa roses are not available at all nurseries and garden centers, it is often necessary to order them in advance from rose specialists so that they can be planted in early spring or late fall.

PLANTING, PRUNING, MAINTENANCE

Roses are essentially plants for sunny locations, but they perform well in light shade provided they have no competition from invading tree or shrub roots. In planting roses, choose a well-drained site and dig a hole twice as wide and deep as the span of the roots. Roses send their roots deep into the soil, hence the need for deep preparation. In the bottom of the hole place a generous shovelful of organic matter, which may be moist peat moss, chopped sod, compost, or well-rotted cow manure. These are humus builders to aid the plant in developing its feeding roots. Add two or three handfuls of dried cow manure or one handful of a complete fertilizer. Mix these ingredients thoroughly with topsoil and other material in the hole.

Unwrap the rose plant, removing it from the moist fiber material surrounding the roots. Cut off any damaged roots and set the plant in the hole, holding it in position with one hand while soil is filled in around the roots with the other. As the hole is filled, stamp the soil with your feet to eliminate air pockets.

In placing the plant, set the knot or graft union at least an inch below the surface of the bed. Water thoroughly and "hill up" or mound the soil around the stem to a height of eight inches. This practice keeps the stems and buds from drying out until the roots are established. Scatter the mound after the buds break into leaf.

Once planted, prune back all damaged stems to live wood and shorten unusually long canes to 10 inches. If a number of roses are packed in one bundle, protect the roots from drying out by covering them with moist burlap until they are ready for planting. Better still, place them in a bucket of muddy water.

Pruning. Types that produce bloom on new wood (hybrid teas, floribundas, and grandifloras) usually need hard pruning in early spring. Use sharp shears and make clean cuts. Remove all dead and bruised canes, cutting back to live wood. Allow about $\frac{1}{2}$ inch of stem to remain above the top bud on each cane. Then shape plants for evenness of height and leave an open center for good air circulation, removing canes that rub against

97

one another. Some gardeners cut back growth to within 6 inches of the ground (low pruning). Others prefer to start the season with plants a foot or more in height (high pruning), depending on the amount of winter injury that has occurred.

Climbers, with the exception of ramblers, bloom on year-old wood. In spring remove only dead and bruised canes and shorten those requiring it. Additional pruning is best done after flowering, removing only such amounts of old wood as necessary for the appearance of the plants and shortening canes to keep them within bounds.

Ramblers are pruned after flowering, taking out to the base of the plant all canes that have flowered.

Other types of roses need only such pruning as the general shape of the plants require, and the removal of deadwood.

Feeding. Assuming that the soil has been carefully prepared prior to planting time, newly set roses require no feeding until early summer after the first splash of bloom has faded. Use a complete fertilizer, scattering it lightly around each plant without touching stems or foliage. Work it in with a small hoe and water thoroughly. Established plants are fed in the same way, twice and often three times during the growing season. Give the first application after pruning in early spring, the second just before first flowering, and the third 6 to 8 weeks later. Feeding after August 1 encourages new growth which frequently does not mature before winter, resulting in winterkill.

Mulching. Mulching roses in early spring reduces maintenance for the entire growing season and conserves moisture. Buckwheat hulls, peat moss, and other materials are desirable. See Chapter 18.

AUTUMN CARE

Fall is often the best season of the year for hybrid tea roses, particularly from the point of view of color. The floribunda and grandiflora hybrids also perform well at this time. True, they are a joy in June when their vigorous young growth unfolds and blossoms are numerous, but hot weather makes them short-lived. Usually bloom in July and August is not of top quality, and Japanese beetles make short work of buds and flowers. However, with the approach of autumn these groups of roses regain their vigor and can be counted on to flower until hard frost. A rose in November is the choicest and most welcome of all.

Avoid Pruning. Fall is a season to give rose bushes special care. It is far better to obtain all the bloom possible on new growth. After heavy frost, tall and unruly growth can be removed along with any of the canes that might interfere with hilling-up of the soil around plants for winter.

Check on Blackspot. If blackspot or any other disease has been a nuisance, gather up all infected foliage and burn it. This practice prevents

98

spores from hibernating in the soil or mulch and infecting next year's growth.

Avoid Late Feeding. Some home gardeners make the mistake of feeding roses in late August or early September. This is poor practice, for late feeding induces soft new growth which is bound to be winterkilled.

Tie Climbers. Most climbing roses produce an abundance of new growth from the base of the plant during summer and early autumn. New canes often protrude, taking up space and sometimes becoming a nuisance when they catch in clothing. Tie them to their supports and prune out excess growth that cannot be tied back without breaking it.

Cut Sucker Growth. Sometimes rose bushes that have shown poor growth during the summer produce several vigorous shoots from the base at this time of year. Examine these rapidly growing canes carefully, since they may be developing from the understock on which the rose is grafted. First note the point of union, usually a rough knob on the main stem near or below the soil surface. Shoots that develop below the graft should be cut off at the ground.

Fall Planting. Container-grown roses of all kinds can be planted safely until the ground freezes. At this time of year, garden centers and nurseries offer surplus stock at reduced prices. Often it is possible to obtain bushes at moderate prices.

From mid-October on, rose growers ship roses bare-root for fall planting. These plants are approaching dormancy and should be planted as soon as they arrive. However, they must be hilled up with soil before the first hard frost.

Some gardeners make a practice of ordering new roses each fall, burying them in trenches so they can be planted as soon as the soil is workable in spring. This is sound practice for the colder parts of New England, especially with the hybrid tea varieties.

Winter Protection. Deep snow is the ideal protective blanket for roses, but when it is of an uncertain quantity, hybrid teas and grandifloras need protection. Beware of old stable manure and leaves, since they cause more harm than good. Hilling up soil around each plant in late fall before a hard freeze gives protection to those portions of the canes that are covered. A cover of evergreen boughs over hilled up roses helps to keep the ground frozen, and shades exposed canes. The soil must be removed as soon as possible after the ground thaws in spring.

CONTROLLING ROSE PESTS

Specialists who recommend spraying or dusting roses at ten-day intervals with an all-purpose mixture of fungicides and insecticides are approaching the problem of control from the preventive angle. It is much more practical to protect roses and keep them growing vigorously than to attempt to combat insects and diseases once they have made headway. Pests that attack roses fall into several classifications. There are sucking insects, such as aphids, that take the life out of young growth, various kinds of chewing insects, such as beetles and rose chafers; and diseases like blackspot, mildew, canker, and rust. Under normal conditions no gardener should expect to be visited by all these pests, but there are seasons when some are more abundant than others.

Aphids. These are legion in variety and are familiar even to most beginners. They collect on buds and young growth, often in great numbers, ranging in color from green to red and black. Damage consists of sapping the strength of new growth and some kinds transmit diseases. Control them with a contact spray such as Black Leaf 40, Lindane, or any of the all-purpose sprays.

Blackspot. When serious, this fungus can be most discouraging since it causes plants to be defoliated and in any case badly disfigures foliage and the general appearance of the plant. Spores are carried through the winter in the soil or in lesions on the canes. Some gardeners are seldom troubled seriously. However, this disease does thrive in moist, humid weather, and often appears spontaneously. It can be caused by watering roses in the late afternoon so that foliage remains wet overnight. Mulching is a great help, since it prevents the spores from being washed onto the leaves in rainy weather. Dust or spray with Ferbam or an all-purpose rose preparation. Many gardeners prefer dusting for the control of blackspot.

Borers. The larvae of the rose sawfly bores holes in the canes causing dieback, a condition common nearly everywhere that roses are grown. Cut off and burn damaged canes.

Brown Canker. Causes purplish spots on the canes and lives through winter, causing growths on the stems and, later, on the foliage. Control is best achieved by cutting and burning all infected parts. Since the spores thrive in moist winter conditions, roses should be mulched with a material that dries quickly. Old manure used to mulch roses seems to develop conditions that encourage the development of canker.

Japanese Beetles. These are widespread pests, especially partial to roses, and the damage they do needs neither description nor elaboration. Handpicking destroys not only them but their progeny. The most effective control is to spray all turf areas in early spring to kill the grubs before they emerge. See discussion in Chapter 20, under lawn pests.

Leafhoppers. They are well named, since they hop about taking the sap from the lower surfaces of the leaves, disfiguring them with a whitish mottled effect. Control with contact sprays as described above.

100

Mildew. Attacks many kinds of plants, causing a thin grayish coating to appear on leaves and stems. It thrives in humid weather when air circulation is poor and temperature changes are sudden. The old-fashioned rambler roses are particularly subject to mildew and gardens where roses are grown in quantity can be kept much healthier if ramblers are eliminated. Dust with Ferbam or Captan.

Red Spider. Is so tiny in size as to be invisible to the naked eye, but its damage is evident by a cobwebby effect on the underside of the foliage. This tiny pest is a mite which can be dispersed with a strong spray of water or a miticide, such as aramite. All-purpose rose sprays are effective.

Rose Chafer. This is actually a fancy name for the rose bug which can be controlled by handpicking or an all-purpose spray.

Rose Midge. A midsummer pest that lays eggs on the foliage and buds, causing them to be distorted in appearance. Destroy infected parts, and use an all-purpose spray.

Rust. Produces orange spots on the undersides of the leaves and causes the upper surfaces to become yellowish. Destroy all infected parts and spray with sulfur.

Thrips. These are also tiny in size and discolor flower buds, damaging them permanently. Since they work their way inside the blossoms, they are hard to reach. With badly infested plants, all buds and blossoms should be cut off and burned. Spray plants thoroughly with an all-purpose rose spray.

CHAPTER SEVEN

Heath and Heather

F all the plants brought across the sea during the past 300 years, few have more romantic associations with the everyday life of bygone days or conjure up more nostalgic memories than heather. Those who have walked the moors in the British Isles or on the Continent and picked their own nosegays of heather and gorse in the August sunshine have a very special kind of fondness for this plant of the wasteland. Curiously enough, this little shrub, steeped in sentiment and tradition, does not always take kindly to cultivation in some parts of our country.

Are the heaths and the heathers actually difficult to grow? They flourish in unexpected places in apparent neglect or at least with a minimum of care, and the soil is usually of poor quality. Yet many gardeners are bewildered when their beloved plants die, sometimes the first winter after planting—and they give up. One large patch of heather known to this writer was started 40 years ago on a windswept bank, a hundred yards from the sea. Over the years it has developed and spread extensively, growing in the pockets of a great outcropping ledge. The soil is acid, gritty, and thin in texture, produces a rather poor stand of sod, and gives no indication of any notable degree of fertility. The seeds of the original clumps may have been carried by the wind; new plants often appear in unexpected places on the property. No attempt has been made to coddle these great drifts of heather and the sod has been allowed to grow between them as it does in the wild on the moors across the sea.

This is apparently nature's way. Unfortunately, it takes most of us a lifetime to learn the simple lessons of ecology, the science of the home environment of plants. In few situations faced by gardeners is it more important to understand the basic requirements of the plants we grow than when we are gardening by the sea. Success with heath and heather offers a truly great challenge and the measure of success achieved can most surely be attributed to an understanding of the principles of ecology.

Heath and heather, catmint, snow-in-summer, thyme and other seaside perennials and shrubs have been used to advantage in this Cape Cod garden.

HEATH	4–15″	Zone 5	*Erica* genera
IRISH HEATH	18″	Zone 5	*Daboecia cantabrica*
SPIKE HEATH	6″	Zone 5	*Bruckenthalia spiculifolia*
HEATHER	6–24″	Zone 4	*Calluna* genera

When and where they flourish, these low-growing evergreen shrubs are a joy at almost any season of the year. In the Northwest so many kinds are cultivated that gardeners enjoy bloom from some species or variety every month of the year. In the Northeast severe winters make this pleasure impossible, but even on Cape Cod some of the winter-flowering kinds blossom freely in protected places during mild spells. In various parts of New England heather (*Calluna*) has become naturalized to some extent, often near the coast.

Unlike many ground covers that are planted in the shade, the heaths and the heathers are essentially for open spaces exposed to full sun and wind. Use them in large irregular groups, often with several kinds planted together, for continuity of bloom. Often, settings for houses on slopes can be greatly enhanced with a heather lawn, interspersed with weathered rocks. In fact, for hot, dry situations, where the soil is known to be poor, this kind of cover, ranging in height from 4 inches to 1 foot or more, is decidedly picturesque and more suitable than grass. Companion plants for use with them include sand myrtle with its dark green foliage; thyme, with its flat matting effect; and blue fescue and thrift, with their grassy texture. Sheets of heather blending into the dark glossy green of bearberry make a dramatic contrast on a slope or on fairly level areas. These are excellent landscape materials for broad sweeping carpets. In small gardens, treat them as a unit of the planting rather than spotted here and there.

The heaths (species and varieties of *Erica*) have needlelike leaves, sometimes with a bluish cast, while others are yellow-green. These include winter-blooming kinds as well as spring and summer-flowering types. Related kinds include the spike heath (*Bruckenthalia spiculifolia*), with pink flowers in early summer on plants 1 foot high, and Irish heath (*Davoecia cantabrica*), with dainty white, purple, or pink bell-like flowers borne in graceful spikes from summer to early fall.

Actually, these miniature matting shrubs are not difficult to grow if their soil requirements are met and the right site is chosen for them. Peaty, sandy soil on a slight slope is the kind of place they like and where they show to best advantage. It also assures good drainage, vital to their permanence. Naturally rocky areas or those where weathered rocks are introduced add to the naturalized effect of the setting. Full sun or high shade that gives filtered sunlight in the heat of summer results in good bloom. They will grow in a fair amount of shade but bloom is usually sparse.

Erica carnea (**Spring Heath**). Widely grown for its early spring bloom (February to May, according to locality). Plants are a foot high or less. Varieties include:

A well-developed specimen of heather, container-grown, easy to transplant.

King George. Rosy crimson blooms. This variety received an award of merit from the Royal Horticultural Society.

Ruby Glow. Rich ruby color.

Springwood White. Of dwarf trailing habit with white flowers and light green foliage, it rates high.

Springwood Pink. An equally good pink-flowering form; like its white companion, this carpeting form is only 3 or 4 inches high.

Vivelli. Carmine-red bells with red-toned foliage in autumn.

E. ciliaris (**Fringed or Dorset Heath**). Tender in the colder regions of the Northeast, yet it usually sends new growth from the ground. The grayish pink bells appear in September, but there are several varieties that bloom a month earlier.

E. cinerea (**Twisted Heath**). These are summer-flowering kinds, considered quite drought-resistant when established.

105

Atrorubens. Domelike in form, slender arching stems, with deep-red bells in July and August.

C. D. Eason. Bright rich red flowers, conspicuous in summer.

Golden Drop. Yellowish foliage that changes to russet and red in winter. Pink flowers appear in summer.

Violacea. More upright than the variety mentioned above, bearing large spikes of bold purple.

E. darleyensis (**Darley or Winter Heath**). A vigorous grower, big-scale in its habit, to 2 feet or more, this mound-shaped plant bears pinkish lilac bloom through the winter months in mild climates and early spring in the Northeast.

E. Tetralix (**Bell-Flowered or Cross-Leaved Heath**). Downy gray foliage and flowers of waxy texture add to the charm of this species.

Alba mollis. White bells borne aloft on stiff, twiggy branches in profusion through the summer months.

George Fraser. The pale pink flowers and bluish foliage are most attractive.

E. vagans (**Cornish Heath**). Plants range from 1 to 2 feet in height, according to variety, with showy bloom in fluffy whorls in summer.

Alba minor. A dwarf white form.

Lyonesse. A white-flowered variety of merit.

Mrs. D. F. Maxwell. An upright grower with dark green foliage and long spikes of vivid pink bloom, it performs from early summer to autumn.

St. Keverne. Clear pink flowers appear in clusters at the tips of the stems and it blooms for a long period in late summer.

In contrast, the heathers (species and varieties of *Calluna*) have scale-like overlapping leaves that give them the appearance of miniature junipers. There are distinct yellow-leaved kinds and bronzy tipped forms, as well as the typical soft greens. Some take on bronzy or purplish tones in early winter as the temperature drops. Flowers appear in loose sprays and may be white, pink, lavender, or purple. Heather is known as ling in Scotland. To find a sprig of white heather is considered good luck and, if carried or worn, assures a safe return to the place whence it came.

Calluna vulgaris. Plants vary in height from 4 inches to 2 feet or more, according to variety. The dwarf forms, those of medium height, and the tall growers—when grouped in broad masses on a slight slope or sandy knoll—are enchanting.

Alba Rigida. Dwarf and spreading in habit, with white flowers.

Alporti. Tall, upright grower, deep crimson on a fuzzy leaved plant.

Aurea. Coppery foliage in dwarf mounds with pink flowers.

Camla. Of low, spreading habit, the flowers are double light pink.

County Wicklow. Bright pink flowers on a dwarf plant.

Cuprea. Golden-yellow foliage that turns bronzy in autumn.

Foxii Nana. One of the smallest of all, forming a tight cushion with tiny spikes of purple bells.

Hammondii. A tall grower, noted for its sturdy habit, with white flowers.

J. B. Hamilton. Less than 1 foot tall, of compact habit, with arching stems of bright pink flowers beginning in early summer.

Johnson's Variety. Lavender bloom in late fall.

H. E. Beale. Double silvery pink on long stems, it rates among the best, and reaches 2 feet or more when in flower.

Kuphaldti. A dwarf plant of twisted growth only a few inches tall, with pinkish lavender bloom.

Mair's White. A late-blooming variety with large spikes of white flowers.

Mrs. Ronald H. Gray. A true dwarf with carpets of lavender bloom and emerald-green foliage.

Nana compacta. Dainty mosslike growth and lavender-pink bloom.

Searlei. A late-flowering white of low habit.

Tib. A foot or more tall with red-purple bloom from early summer to late autumn.

Winter damage is a prime factor to consider in growing heath and heather. During severe winters it can be serious, causing the stems to split. When this condition occurs, plants must be cut back hard in early spring to encourage new growth from the base. Frequently plants suffer badly from wind- and sunburn during mild winters when snow is not sufficient. In fact, open winters take their toll of even the sturdiest of plants and sometimes finish them. A practical way to handle this problem with heath and heather is to provide cover with evergreen boughs, well anchored so that they will not be blown about by the wind. This task is something of a nuisance but it is well worth the effort, and is particularly advisable for newly planted colonies. Heavy shearing of damaged specimens in *early* spring, followed by a feeding of evergreen fertilizer watered in thoroughly, will encourage new growth and restore the plants to their former vigor. In

Genereux

Cherry laurel, heather, Japanese yew, inkberry and other seaside shrubs.

fact, an annual spring shearing is sound practice to induce new growth from the base and keep the plants from becoming leggy.

Early spring is the ideal time to set out the heaths and the heathers. Rooted cuttings from pots or field-grown clumps are offered by most specialists and nurserymen. If rooted cuttings from flats are used, protect the delicate roots from drying out. Whenever possible, prepare soil in the autumn and leave it in a rough state through winter. A mixture of equal parts of well-rotted cow manure or compost and peat moss (obtained from local bogs) added to the existing sandy soil supplies the organic matter needed by the roots. Soil preparation should be at least 1 foot deep. If done in the spring, allow a few weeks for the soil to settle before planting. Good drainage at all times is essential. Thorough watering is needed after planting and attention to this chore is essential for the first year. While these hardy shrubs can endure considerable drought, they may need thorough soaking occasionally in extremely dry spells, unless your soil has abundant organic material.

Plants may be increased by dividing established clumps in spring, by layering, and by cuttings. Of these methods, layering is the easiest for most home gardeners. Heaths growing in large masses tend to layer naturally as the lower branches trail or come in contact with the soil. Layering can be encouraged by mounding soil over the lower stems and pinning them down or by placing a stone on a branch to hold it close to the soil. Another method is to heap soil up around the crown of the plant to induce stems to produce roots. These rooted portions can be cut from the mother plant and set out where they can be given care until they are large enough for permanent planting. Some gardeners keep them in a cold frame the first winter, as with rooted cuttings. It is a mistake to put young plants in permanent places in full sun unless they can be give frequent watering.

Cuttings of half-ripened wood made in late July usually root in 4 to 5 weeks in a covered frame or propagating case. Strip the foliage from the lower portion of the stem, being careful not to injure the thin bark. Insert in sandy peat and keep moist until roots are well formed. Then transplant to a cold frame for the first winter.

CHAPTER EIGHT

Rosemary

ᴘERHAPS no other denizen of the seaside holds a warmer place in the hearts of gardeners than rosemary and surely no fragrant herb is linked more intimately with history, literature, tradition, and everyday life. As St. Thomas More reminds us, this pungent leaved herb is sacred to remembrance and friendship and (according to John Gerard, noted seventeenth-century herbalist), "a remedie against the stuffing of the heade, that cometh through the coldness of the braine, if a garland thereof be put about the heade." Greek students used to twine rosemary in their hair when studying for examinations; to them it was literally, not symbolically, an aid to memory, and it "comforteth the cold, weake and feeble braine in a most wonderfull manner." For possessing these and numerous other virtues, rosemary deserves a chapter by itself. In fact, the literature on this amazing plant is so voluminous that a fascinating book could be written about it.

Because it is not hardy in the Northeast, it is treated as a tender plant, set out each year in early spring, and allowed to grow in a sunny spot until hard frost. As a container-grown specimen, it frequently graces terraces, walks, and even window boxes, and in winter it is a delight as a houseplant in a sunny window.

Long associated with Christmas, sprigs of rosemary find their way into wreaths, garlands, and kissing balls. Skilled cooks still use the leaves, fresh or dried, to flavor fish, meats, and other dishes. It is literally the herb of herbs as attested in the writings of ancient and modern recorders of the virtues of plants.

Native to the bleak, windswept headlands of the Mediterranean coast, it flourishes within reach of the salt sea spray. As Minnie Watson Kamm reminds us in *Old-time Herbs for Northern Gardens:* "The plant that delights in the spray of the sea was translated into Latin *ros marinus,* ros meaning dew, thence corrupted to *ros maris,* and in early Christian times rosemarie or rosemary, thus becoming associated with the Virgin Mary purely out of a fancied resemblance in the name.

"It has enjoyed a reputation among peoples of various climes for almost three thousand years and has run the gamut of economic uses; for seasoning food, in medicine, in perfumes, as a strewing herb, in the brewing of beverages, as a 'bee-alluring plant,' as incense, as a symbol at weddings and funerals, and even as an ingredient in the embalming of the dead."

Like lavender it is a small shrub, but the two are easily distinguished since the leaves of lavender are felty gray, and the plants are low-growing to 18 inches in height and compact in habit. The grayish green rugose leaves of rosemary, an inch or more in length, are narrow and revolute, with a whitened feltlike surface on the underside. They tend to point upward on the stem to resist drought. As with many drought-resisting plants, the foliage is strangely aromatic, an attribute that makes it unappealing to animals. It is nature's way of perpetuating plants in dry climates; otherwise, they would be exterminated by hungry animals.

The stems of rosemary are square in cross section when young, averaging 2 feet or more in height in cold climates. In Greece, Italy, Spain, and France and the coastal islands where conditions are ideal for its growth, this fragrant bush attains a height of 5 to 6 feet, spreading as wide, and rambling over ruins and garden walls in the greatest profusion and luxuriance. South of Washington, D.C., in California and in the Northwest, plants reach considerable size.

Flowers may appear in early spring, in late summer, at Christmas or later, and are usually bluish lavender in color, tubular and not too showy, occurring in small clusters at the nodes. Tradition has it that the flowers were originally white but were changed to blue when the Virgin Mary once spread her cloak to dry on a rosemary bush during the flight into Egypt. Selected forms are noted for their rich blue coloring.

On the Island of Majorca rosemary grows as thickly as heather with flowers of "every shade of blue from palest skim-milk to deepest ultramarine." John Evelyn, writing in the seventeenth century, spoke of flowers "credibly reported to give their scent above thirty leagues off, at sea, upon the coast of Spain."

Great, broad, spreading masses of rosemary still flourish amid the ruins of the Parthenon, green reminders of an era when the Greeks used both rosemary and lavender to crown their virgins before sacrifice on the altar; later, they used the stems and leaves of both as incense to their living sacrifices. The Romans considered rosemary a most desirable hedge for their formalized gardens because it was easily trimmed. Pliny described it thus in his *Natural History:* "The garden avenue is bordered with box, and where that is decayed, with rosemary, for the box, wherever sheltered by the buildings, grows plentifully, but where it lies open and exposed to

Rosemary at the Temple of Zeus, Athens, Greece.

the weather and sprays from the sea, though at some distance from the latter, it quite withers up." Rosemary is of prime use in such locations.

Wreaths of rosemary adorned the foreheads of youths and maidens at festivals in Rome, as mentioned by Ovid in the "Story of Cyllarus and Hylonome":

> *And (she) took especial pride to sleek*
> *Her lightsome locks of hair;*
> *With rosemary she wreathed them.*

Among the Egyptians rosemary had a place in gardens and the Arabs at Algiers and Morocco prized it as a border for their rose gardens, clipped into low flat-topped hedges. It is believed that it was first taken to Britain by the Romans, and grew in the south of England as well as it had in Rome, and has been flourishing there ever since. North of the Alps, its introduction was furthered by a "Kapitulare" of Charles the Great, A.D. 812, who ordered the rosmarinus to be planted in the Royal Gardens. Then too, it was part of the precious overland cargo transported by the great trading companies, the Hanseatic League, the Easterlings, the Staple of Calais, and others. Returning travelers and Crusaders also took the plant home with them.

During the Dark Ages, various monastic orders grew rosemary in their kitchen gardens and medicinal plots, and it appears frequently in extant lists of useful plants. Mention is made of it in the eleventh-century *Herball of Apuleius* and the *Leech Book of Bald.*

It is believed that the plant was reintroduced to England at the time of the Norman Conquest when William and his followers took with them many of their favorite flowering and medicinal herbs, including hens-and-chickens which found a home in the thatch roofs. Dodoens (1579) reminds us that gardeners maintained it only with great diligence, for it was not hardy in exposed places.

This plant treasure was first cultivated in the gardens of the nobility and it was several centuries before it was grown in the cottage gardens of the lowly. Barnaby Googe, in his delightful book of husbandry published in 1578, reminds us of its use in topiary work: "sette by women for their pleasure, to grow in sundry proportions, as in the fashion of a cart, a peacock, or such things as they fancy." But by the eighteenth century the plant had fallen from grace and become commonplace, as William Shenstone tells us in *The Schoolmistress:*

> *And here (is) trim rosemarine, that whilom crown'd*
> *The dainty garden of the proudest peer,*
> *Ere, driven from its envy'd site, it found*
> *A sacred shelter for its branches here.*

In the heyday of Queen Elizabeth's reign, rosemary became the object of symbolism in a romantic way that gave it rank with the lily and the rose, as revealed in this widely quoted sentiment:

> *Rosemary is for remembrance,*
> *between us daie and night,*
> *Wishing that I might always have,*
> *you present in my sight.*
>
> —Clement Robinson
> *A Handefull of Pleasant Delites* (1584).

Indeed the language of flowers was lofty and eloquent centuries before the Victorian era—Rosemary has long been a favorite name for girls.

Shakespeare attests its popularity on several occasions. Ophelia offered a sprig to her brother, saying: "There's rosemary; that's for remembrance; pray you, love, remember." (*Hamlet,* Act IV, Sc. 5.) Perdita in *The Winter's Tale* (Act IV, Sc. 4) expressed her sentiments thus when she offered herbs to her guests:

> *For you there's rosemary and rue; these keep*
> *Seeming and savor all the winter long:*
> *Grace and remembrance be to you both.*

113

Because it symbolized fidelity among lovers, it had an important place among decorations at weddings, and was carried by the attendants. Its use in the ceremony is referred to in an old ballad, *The Bride's Good-morrow:*

> *Young men and maidens do ready stand*
> *With sweet rosemary in their hand,*
> *A perfect token of your virgin's life.*

It is told that when Anne of Cleves arrived at Greenwich as the bride of Henry VIII, she wore in her hair a coronet of gold and precious stones filled with branches of rosemary. At a country wedding in Kenilworth where Queen Elizabeth was present, "each wight had a branch of broom tied on his left arm for rosemary was scant there." In Germany and other countries, brides used to wear sprigs of rosemary in their hair and carried it in their bouquets as well. The foliage was gilded for weddings, along with bay leaves, as the poet Herrick relates in *Hesperides:*

> *This done we'll draw lots*
> *Who shall buy and gild*
> *The baies and rosemary.*

However, a preacher named Roger Hackett delivered a sermon in 1607 admonishing those who thus desecrate the natural foliage: "Smell sweet, O ye flowers, in your native sweetness: be not gilded with the idel arts of man." At wedding feasts, a sprig of the plant was put into the wine and dedicated with special good wishes for the bride's happiness.

In *Flowers and Their Histories,* Alice M. Coats writes: "It seems to have been almost universally used in funeral ceremonies and there are many references to it; one of the most curious examples being that of a soldier shot for mutiny in 1649, whose body was adorned with bunches of rosemary, one half of each being stained with blood. In France it was the custom to put a branch of rosemary in the hands of the dead, and grue-some stories are told 'that when the coffins have been opened after several years, the plant was found to have vegetated so much, that the leaves have covered the corpse.' The custom of throwing sprigs of rosemary into the grave persisted in England till the nineteenth century."

Robert Herrick summed it up thus:

> *Grown for two ends, it matters not at all,*
> *Be't for my bridall or my buriall.*

Again Shakespeare in *Romeo and Juliet* (Act IV, Sc. 5) reminds us of the age-old custom. "Dry up your tears," says Friar Lawrence to the mourners at Juliet's bier:

> *and stick your rosemary*
> *On this fair corpse; and, as the custom is,*
> *In all her best array bear her to church.*

114

Rosemary thrives in hot, dry places, but is not hardy north of Washington, D.C.

This old custom of adorning corpses with rosemary and the carrying of sprigs by mourners was deeply rooted in practical usage, since the plant was considered a powerful disinfectant. The practice actually began in the time when pestilences were widespread. It was the custom for people to carry a sprig of rosemary in their hands as they walked about the village or town and to hold it up to their mouths as they talked. Little wonder, then, that branches of it were laid in the coffins of the dead "against the morbid effusions of the corpse" and carried by the mourners as protection against these "effusions."

The prostrate rosemary (left) lends itself to the art of bonsai. Plant at right is the typical form of this fragrant-leaved shrub.

As a medicinal plant, rosemary was held in high repute. Both the Greeks and the Romans used it for pleurisy and colds, extracting the oily juice and mixing it in honey. It was considered a cure for gout, for forms of paralysis, fistulas, gangrene, and the like. The distilled oil found its way into salves, sweet washing waters, and perfumes. In the days before modern deodorants, it was compounded with other herbs and spices into a pomander worn at the waist. Later the distilled oil was used with that of other herbs, carried in a tiny vial for the same purpose, and both doctors and clergy carried these aromatics to ward off diseases when they visited the sick. It is still used in making certain kinds of soap, hair oil, mouth washes, and medicines, and as a flavoring for cordials. For centuries housewives have laid it among their woolens as protection from moths.

Its uses in the culinary world are legion. The chopped leaves, fresh or dried, added to cream cheese make a delicious sandwich. For flavoring fish, beef, sausage, and as a garnish for pork, it still finds favor. In soups, stuffings, jelly, and as a tea, rosemary imparts a warm piny taste, described as penetrating, lingering, and unusual. For those who have not used it, it should be said that a pinch goes a long way.

Rosemary was brought to America before 1620 by Captain John Mason, who planted it in Newfoundland. John Josselyn, who visited at

Salem, Plymouth, and other settlements in New England in 1638 and again in 1660, reported: "It is no plant for this country." Settlers in Williamsburg, Virginia, and elsewhere in the South were more fortunate since rosemary survived the winter, and those in northern climates soon learned to treat it as a tender plant.

The common rosemary is *Rosmarinus officinalis* but there are many varieties available in England and on the Continent that are seldom if ever seen in America. Christine Kelway, noted English gardener, writes of them in *Seaside Gardening:*

"A distinctive rosemary is the narrow-leaved *R. o. angustifolius* Corsican Blue. Its green needle leaves are far narrower than the type, giving the whole plant a feathery look. It makes a large bush 4 feet high and as much through and has very bright-blue flowers. Miss Jessup's Upright may or may not be the same as *R. o. pyramidalis,* but this useful rosemary has an erect fastigiate habit and is a very vigorous grower, making it extremely good for windy positions close to the sea. A delightful newcomer to our garden is the distinctive Tuscan Blue, with leaves of the brightest green of all and a close bushy habit that is most attractive. It should have the sunniest, driest spot to encourage it to show its deep sky-blue flowers, as it is not as free-flowering as most rosemaries. Primley Blue and Severn Sea are two others worth growing, both having bright-blue flowers. Majorca Pink is an exciting colour break in soft lilac-pink, a distinct change from the lavenders and blues. The branches are tall and stiff with narrow leaves. It is reputed to be slightly more tender than some others, but it is hardy enough by the sea."

On the West Coast, the dwarf rosemary (*R. officinalis prostratus*) is used extensively as a ground cover. In cold climates it is grown as a highly decorative form of bonsai in containers since it is by nature irregular in habit and is easily pruned and trained. This carpeting form of rosemary as seen in California gardens makes a billowy mass for banks, planting, or on level ground in the bright sun. Its dark green texture and soft blue flowers are most refined in appearance, and when combined with gray foliage it is all the more striking. Ideal places to use it are along paths and steps or in containers where it can be enjoyed at close range and crushed at will.

Those gardeners who have grown rosemary in cold climates and have seen it flourish from spring to hard frost regret its lack of hardiness, for it is a superb landscape plant. Allowed to grow naturally with a minimum of pruning, it is rather loose in habit and broadly columnar. Pruned to make a specimen it can be grown in pyramidal form. When sheared as a hedge, it provides pleasing texture. Sometimes the branches are procumbent, creating a softening effect against walls and other architectural features in the garden. All these results can be achieved when rosemary is grown in containers. In the warmer sections of the country where this plant is hardy,

117

it deserves to be more widely planted since the possibilities for decorative effects are limitless.

Full sun and a light, well-drained soil on the alkaline side suit rosemary best, but it will grow well in light shade. In soils known to be acid, sprinkle ground limestone around the plants and dig it in. Plants grown in containers respond to periodic feeding with a complete fertilizer.

Propagation is by cuttings, seed, and simple layering. Many commercial growers increase their stock from cuttings, but the home gardener usually finds it easier to pin down side shoots of young growth which soon take root. Plants grown from seed make surprisingly rapid growth in a single season.

Often quoted is the old adage, "Where rosemary flourishes, the mistress rules." Yet no man in his right senses would think of cutting down a flourishing bush, for a hundred other old-time sayings would flash through his head while committing the act—and all to no avail. Even the soothsayers had their way of balancing the scales with immortal words. Beware to him

> *Who passeth by the rosemary*
> *And careth not to take a spray*
> *For women's love no care hath he*
> *Nor shall he, though he live for aye.*

Taloumis

Rosemary makes an excellent plant for containers in sunny locations.

CHAPTER NINE

Useful Ornamental Vines

VINES have a multitude of uses in gardens along coastal areas. The ways in which they can be used effectively depend not only on the kinds and types of support on which they can be displayed, but also the protection from wind afforded such kinds as the showy clematis. Fences, arbors, trellises, pergolas, cedar posts, and other suitable supports need to be of sturdy construction and firmly set in cement to withstand heavy wind and seasonal storms. For the most part, most hardy climbing plants can withstand considerable buffeting of wind and salt spray without permanent damage. Frequently they can be utilized to create desired background effects where shrubs cannot be used because of the space they require.

Striking cascading effects can be achieved with showy flowering types of vines to enhance the appearance of outcropping rocks or ledges. Those of rapid growth, suitable for camouflaging fences and retaining walls, may be allowed to spill over on the ground of adjoining areas for cover. Then, too, vines are sometimes desirable for softening the appearance of walls of brick, stone, and stucco houses.

Vines make ideal ground covers in large areas where they have ample room to develop. Their prime value is that of growing rapid cover for banks and slopes where steep grades make upkeep a problem. Many climbing plants are sturdy, deep-rooted types adapted to wind and exposure, requiring little care. In addition, they have merit in stabilizing soil to prevent erosion. A number of vines spread by underground roots or produce roots along their stems, making them valuable as soil binders. Evergreen kinds such as bearberry, myrtle, English ivy, and euonymus are among the most desirable of ground covers.

Showy bloom as well as decorative foliage are other assets of climbing plants. The colorful flowers of such vines as the large-flowered clematis, honeysuckles, morning glories, the climbing hydrangea, tripterigium, and

119

others, add materially to their value. Fragrance is another asset of jasmine, clematis, roses, and nasturtiums. The trailing roses make the most spectacular display of all, and many varieties do double duty with showy hips in the fall. Ornamental fruits of striking color are characteristic of bearberry, clematis, bittersweet, porcelain ampelopsis, and others.

However, not all vines described in this chapter are satisfactory for the small seaside garden. Those that climb by tendrils and trailing stems usually prove to be a nuisance, since they encroach on shrubs and trees, creating a tangled mass of growth. This fact needs to be carefully considered before planting any of the more vigorous kinds listed below. Others, like Hall's honeysuckle, are so rampant that they become pests unless carefully restrained. Despite the appeal of its showy fruits in autumn, bittersweet may turn out to be more of a detriment than an asset. Then, too, large areas covered with rapid-growing vines make ideal seedbeds for weedy trees and shrubs, not to mention a host of troublesome weeds.

The following list is typical of the kinds of vines suitable for use where space and appropriate settings are available. It is a good plan when selecting climbing plants to evaluate the advantages and disadvantages of each, as well as the care required to keep them in bounds. Annual kinds are desirable for the summer place because they create colorful effects in a single season.

AKEBIA   15–20′   Zone 4   *Akebia quinata*

Attractive because of its refined foliage, five-leaf akebia is valued for its rampant growth to provide screening on trellises, fences, and arbors, and it makes a useful cover plant in the right place. Grow it on banks and slopes or let it scramble over rocks or place it where there is room for it to spread without becoming a nuisance. Because of its vigorous growth, it is not suitable for use in limited areas anywhere in a small garden, unless cut back frequently. The five-parted leaves are semievergreen and of delicate texture. Curious purple flowers that appear in clusters in late spring, although not showy, add a note of interest.

Akebia thrives in sun or partial shade and can stand windy exposures. Reliably hardy, except in the coldest parts of the country, it grows best in good garden soil.

BEACH PEA. See Chapter 11.

BEARBERRY. See Chapter 5.

BITTERSWEET   10–20′   Zone 2   *Celastrus scandens*

This native vine, much admired for its colorful fruit, can cause woe to any gardener who plants it without knowledge of its persistence, vigor, and deep-rooting habits. In the right place, it can serve as good cover for

120

The various kinds of hybrid clematis flourish in seaside gardens.

rocky areas, rough ground, or on banks or slopes where erosion is a problem. It is effective on sturdy fences where quick cover is needed. Its top
growth can be kept in bounds by frequent heavy pruning. Otherwise, it
forms a tangled growth and its ropelike stems twine around shrubs and
trees, often killing them.

It grows in almost any kind of soil and is hardy in the coldest parts
of the country. For fruit, plants of both sexes are needed. Seeds germinate
readily and this weedy habit of bittersweet must be noted also. Once
planted, it is not an easy plant to eradicate.

Genereux

Fruits of the bittersweet wintercreeper are unusually decorative.

Boston Ivy. See Virginia creeper.

Carolina Jasmine   10–20′   Zone 6   *Gelsemium sempervirens*

The fragrant yellow blooms of Carolina jasmine, borne in clusters early in the season, and the neat evergreen foliage, are offset somewhat by its rather ragged appearance. But, used on banks or wherever cover is needed, the rangy habit is not readily noticeable, and hard pruning after flowering induces dense growth. It is hardy from Virginia south.

This vine is at home in sun or shade and is not partial as to soil, although it makes its best growth in good garden soil.

Wherever there is a fence, a trellis, an arbor, a post, or a wall that affords sun at least half the day, a spot can be found for one or more varieties of clematis. They can be trained on wire or formal trellises for architectural effects, or allowed to clamber at will. As they reach out for the sun, the leaf stems entwine themselves around whatever support they can find. The silky seedpods are highly decorative in late summer and autumn.

Even for those who are limited to pots and boxes, the large-flowered hybrids make excellent pot plants, provided they are given support in the form of heavy stakes of wood or wire, or an ornamental trellis on which to display their beauty.

Clematis hybrids combined with climbing roses make charming color combinations, especially when pale pink, white, or yellow roses are used with the various blue, purple, and mauve varieties. Cedar posts planted with several varieties of clematis provide dramatic accents in perennial and shrub plantings. For camouflaging tree stumps, unsightly fences of wood or wire, or allowed to scramble over stone walls, the various kinds of clematis are admirably adapted.

Ernest H. Wilson introduced the rosy red blooms of pink anemone clematis (*C. montana rubens*) to American gardens from the Orient. This and the paler pink colored species, anemone clematis (*C. montana*), are rampant growers with abundant clusters of bloom in May, with flowers measuring 1½ to 2½ inches across. These bloom on year-old wood and require pruning after the current season's bloom. They are vigorous growers, often reaching 15 feet or more in a single season.

Native species include the scarlet clematis (*C. texensis*) with scarlet urn-shaped flowers that appear in great profusion in early summer, continuing till fall. It is a sturdy vine 6 to 10 feet long that grows in dry soil. A notable hybrid is Duchess of Albany, bright pink with brown and white markings. The marsh clematis (*C. crispa*), sometimes called the blue jasmine or bluebell, is native from Virginia south. Actually a more or less shrubby vine 8 or 9 feet, it produces its bloom on the growth of the previous season. For naturalistic plantings there is virgin's bower (*C. virginiana*), native over a wide area in the Northeast. Small white flowers in clusters followed by silky seedpods make it conspicuous in the late summer landscape.

Among the large-flowered hybrids that produce their big splash of bloom in June followed by occasional flowers in midsummer and often a good display in early fall, is the striking variety Nelly Moser. Distinct purplish red bars give a lush tone to the warm mauve blooms. W. E. Gladstone, in lilac with a lighter center, and William Kennett, a profuse lavender, are also notable.

To most gardeners, clematis is typified in the rich purple of Jackman clematis (*C. jackmani*), which rates high for its vigorous habit, summer flowering, and striking color. There are many outstanding varieties including Comtesse de Bouchaud, carmine rose; Gipsy Queen, rich purple; Mme. Edouard Andre, deep red; Star of India, an unusual reddish purple; and Mrs. Cholmondeley (pronounced Chumley), lavender-blue. In addition, there is a white hybrid, Snow White. These forms can be cut back hard each year in early spring to induce an abundance of growth from the base. Flowers are produced on the wood of the current season.

In the dark red and violet range, we find the President with showy white centers to accentuate its velvety tone. For sheer contrast in color and spectacular size, Henryi is a warm white form well worth growing. It rates as the largest flowering of them all.

Two double forms of established popularity are the lovely Duchess of Edinburgh and the bluish lavender Belle of Woking. Both of these flower on old wood and should not be pruned until after bloom has finished. Then remove only such growth as is necessary to improve the shape of the plant, as well as any dead stems that may exist.

An old favorite, Mme. Baron Veillard, produces superbly shaped lilac-rose flowers. It should be noted that the color is more intense in cool weather and the autumn crop of bloom is often richer than that produced early in summer. As the summer season continues, we find other topnotch kinds making their appearance. Huldine is noted for its medium-sized flowers of pearly white marked on the reverse with mauve-pink bars.

The favorite of autumn gardens is the sweet autumn clematis (*C. paniculata*), with its abundance of lacy white bloom followed by silky seedpods that are worth cutting and drying for winter bouquets.

Most kinds flower on new wood (except as noted) so that serious winterkill does not affect the current season's bloom. Except for the removal of deadwood, little pruning is necessary until the plants are well established, usually after the second year. Then they can be cut back to a foot in early spring, before growth starts.

Clematis flourishes in fertile, well-drained soil with a moist root run. The roots and lower stems prefer shade with top growth in the sun for at least half the day. Prepare the location with care. Dig a generous hole, 18 inches deep and 6 to 8 inches wide, and fill it with a mixture of the best available topsoil and humus. Either compost or thoroughly moistened peat moss will suffice. To this mixture add a generous handful of a complete fertilizer and (where soil is acid) one of ground limestone for each plant. These ingredients need to be thoroughly incorporated with the soil.

In setting out plants, whether dormant or pot grown, place them so that the crown is two inches below the soil level. This practice allows for additional growth to develop below the surface and also provides insurance in the event the top growth is killed back by wilt. It is claimed that shallow planting is a cause of wilt. When the crown is set below soil level and wilt

Hybrid clematis Crimson Star, everblooming honeysuckle, white astilbe, dusty miller, boxwood and a wide variety of hardy perennials lend color and texture to this summer seaside garden.

occurs, new shoots often develop below the infected area. All diseased parts should be removed and burned and the soil should be treated thoroughly with a fungicide like Ferbam. This practice is recommended also if replacements are required.

After planting, tie the stem to a stake as well as to some suitable support on which the vines can climb. A collar of hardware wire placed around the stem at ground level protects it from bruising. All reputable growers sell clematis with a stake attached to the stem for a definite purpose. The weakest part of the clematis vine is the stem itself, and when bruised it can easily be infected by insects or disease.

Clematis is no more demanding in its fertilizer requirements than other flowering plants. It will persist with considerable neglect, but responds readily to feeding. When plant food is scattered around the plants, it should be watered in so as not to damage the basal stems. Where soils are known to be strongly acid, annual applications of ground limestone are desirable.

The easiest way to provide a moist root run for clematis is to mulch plants with peat moss, buckwheat hulls, marsh hay, or any convenient material available. At least an inch of peat moss or buckwheat hulls is needed to retain soil moisture. Since the roots spread considerably once plants are established, mulch an area at least two feet in diameter around

Climbing hydrangea, a sturdy, woody vine for coastal gardens.

Taloumis

the stem of each plant. Organic fertilizers and dried animal manures incorporated with mulching materials make plant food available as plants are watered or rain supplies the needed moisture.

CLIMBING HYDRANGEA   30′   Zone 4   *Hydrangea peteolaris*

Where there is space and a rocky slope needs cover, or an outcropping of rock or a ledge requires softening, this vigorous summer-flowering vine may well be the answer. When planted near a brick, stone, or cement wall, climbing hydrangea eventually takes over and spreads widely, making a richly textured bank of foliage and flowers. In winter, the tracery of twigs and stems has considerable appeal. Although slow in getting established, it makes rapid growth, branching freely as it matures. The large glossy leaves are useful for creating bold effects and the panicles of white bloom in early summer followed by the seed capsules are decidedly ornamental. Its ability to cling to hard surfaces by means of aerial rootlets is a point in its favor.

Climbing hydrangea needs only good garden soil and a sunny or partially shaded location. It is extremely hardy, drought resistant, and relatively free of serious pests. Container-grown plants are easy to handle.

ENGLISH IVY   4–10″   Zones 4–5   *Hedera helix*

Enduring in its beauty indoors and out, English ivy is as well suited for climbing walls, fences, rocks, and other types of support as it is utilized as a green carpet or ground cover. When trained espalier fashion on stone or stucco walls, the distinctive pattern of the leaves shows to good advantage. The less common forms grown in containers are often featured on terraces and patios. This beloved plant has a multitude of uses.

It ranks with pachysandra and myrtle as one of the most versatile ground covers in gardens here and abroad. The typical form of English ivy, so common everywhere, with its long, trailing stems, is ideal for northern or western exposures on banks, slopes, or level ground where other plants are not easy to establish and an evergreen cover is desired.

Ivy has been widely hybridized so that there are many selected forms grown in various parts of the country, some hardier than others. The ideal ivy is a type that can endure wind and winter sun without burning and can be grown in practically any type of soil. To most people, ivy is ivy, so long as it has the typical leaf and grows, but there are major differences. Baltic ivy (*H. Helix baltica*) has generally proved to be quite hardy even under difficult conditions and is widely planted, but during severe winters in the Northeast it does not always prove itself.

The following list includes some of the varieties offered by growers. A few have been widely tested for hardiness and have proved satisfactory in selected areas. Some listed here may be duplicates, since the naming of varieties seems to have been rather haphazard. Location of an ivy planting

English ivy used extensively as a ground cover.

as to winter sun and general exposure usually reveals that some tender kinds can be grown in sheltered parts of the grounds even though they are not accepted by some gardeners as being partially or reliably hardy. This kind of experimenting is half the fun of gardening.

Arrowleaf (*sagittifolia*). Dull foliage, small in size.

Baltic (*baltica*). A refined form of the type with smaller glossy leaves, generally claimed to be one of the hardiest of all.

Bulgaria. A hardy sport from the St. Louis area.

Bunchleaf (*conglomerata*). Slow-growing and stiff branches with crimped leaves closely set, it is hardy to zero.

Caenwoodiana. Small leaf, distinctly lobed, dainty.

Cavendishi. Creamy white margins give it distinction.

Crimean (*taurica*). Bright green with narrower leaves.

Finger Leaf (*digitata*). Large, wide foliage with 5 to 7 lobes.

Foot Leaf (*pedata*). Long, narrow middle lobes with white veining that accentuates the dark color of the foliage.

Glacier. A selected form hardy north to New Jersey.

Gold Leaf (*aureo-variegata*). Yellow margins make it striking.

Hagenburger's Variegated. Long-leaved variegated form that has proved hardy to New Jersey; widely planted on the West Coast.

Heart Leaved (*helix cordata*). The almost black-green foliage assumes bronzy purple coloring in the fall.

Irish (*hibernica*). Lighter green than the typical English ivy and usually larger, with short lobes, it is not so hardy as the species.

Marbled (*marmorata*). Similar to Irish ivy with yellowish white markings.

Pittsburgh. Branches free from the leaf axils. Excellent for tailored treatment.

Poets' (*poetica*). Wavy bright yellow-green foliage.

Purpurea. Leaves turn bronze-purple in winter.

Rumania. This sport, and Bulgaria introduced by Dr. Edgar Anderson of the Missouri Botanic Garden, proved hardy there.

Silver Leaf (*argenteo-variegata*). Silvery white, variegated.

Stardust (*H. helix baltica var.*). A silvery variegated Baltic form.

Thorndale. This selection developed in Chicago has proved hardy without protection.

Tree (*arborescens*). This form results when climbing forms reach the top of a support. The leaves are distinctly different from the rest of the plant, being almost without lobes. Green flowers appear, followed by dark fruits. When this growth is propagated, the resulting plants do not climb, but make small bushes.

Twisted (*tortuosa*). Leaves are almost entirely curly.

Ivy is easy to root from cuttings, or one may use trailing stems with roots. Some gardeners prefer to use hairpins or other means to peg down long trailers so that they will form roots. Wherever roots develop, pieces can be cut from the main plant and started anew. This is one of the great joys of growing ivy and one of the reasons for its widespread popularity and also for the fact that it can increase its ground-covering capacity with great rapidity.

Most forms of English ivy are hardly suited to full sun, and this point should be borne in mind when planting it. Other plants can be used in sunny locations.

HALL'S HONEYSUCKLE. (See Chapter 9.)

Everblooming honeysuckle softens the lines of the fence.

HONEYSUCKLE   10–30′   Zones 3–4   *Lonicera* genus

Climbing forms of honeysuckle contribute generously to the summer color pageant and are valued for their rapid growth and hardiness. Since they withstand dry conditions and wind, they fit admirably into the planting schemes of coastal gardens. Best known of all is the trumpet honeysuckle *L. sempervirens,* native from Connecticut to Florida and west to Texas. It climbs by means of wiry stems and although the foliage is not impressive, the bright orange to coral tubular blooms are spectacular. These are borne in clusters and make an impressive show through the summer months. There are varieties with red and yellow blooms as well.

The everblooming honeysuckle *L. heckrotti,* which loses its leaves in winter, is outstanding for fragrant blooms of reddish purple and yellow. Sweet or Italian honeysuckle (*L. caprifolium*), with blue-green foliage and yellowish white fragrant flowers tinged with purple, is a late spring blooming kind followed by orange-red berries in autumn. The Tellmann honeysuckle is similar in many ways to the common trumpet type. There are other species as well and a number of improved forms. All the climbing honeysuckles make good ground covers for large areas in hot, dry situations, particularly slopes and banks. (See also Hall's honeysuckle, Chapter 9.)

Average garden soil suits these vines which thrive in sun or part shade, and they require no special care. Constant pruning keeps them within bounds and encourages new growth from the base. Plants can be increased by cuttings.

JASMINE. (See Carolina Jasmine, Star Jasmine, and Winter Jasmine, herein.)

KUDZU VINE   3′   Zone 6   *Pueraria thunbergiana*

For difficult places where sun, wind, and generally poor growing conditions prevail, kudzu vine makes a heavy foliage mass and rapid cover. It serves as a soil binder because of its habit of developing vigorous underground stems that travel rapidly. The purple flower spikes are not always seen because of the large, coarse, beanlike foliage. Well suited to warm climates, kudzu vine is used in the South and Southwest. In the Northeast, it is hardy to New York City but dies back to the ground in winter.

PASSIONFLOWER   30′   Zones 6–8   *Passiflora* genus

Some kinds of passionflower are hardier in sheltered locations than is generally believed, and reports appear continually telling of vines that have survived cold winters in various parts of the country. Most species are of tropical origin and are widely grown in the South and on the West Coast. For generations the curious blooms have fascinated people everywhere as much as they did the Spanish missionary who discovered this plant in Brazil in the seventeenth century. The intricate flower structure containing the symbolism of the Crucifixion has distinct appeal.

These vines thrive in full sun, tolerating considerable wind and exposure and are often seen in gardens bordering the coast in the South, the Northwest, and in California. They are rampant growers, often reaching 30 feet or more in a single season. Flowers may be white, pinkish, blue, red, or yellow, according to the species grown. In the colder sections of the country, plants are often set out in late spring and treated as annuals. They are sometimes grown in large pots and trained on trellises for terrace and patio.

Passionflower flourishes in well-drained, sandy loam, responds readily to feeding, and requires no special care. Hard pruning is essential to keep most kinds within bounds and, in small gardens, training is necessary to prevent too dense growth. When allowed to grow at random, the twining stems scramble over large areas, festooning trees and shrubs and often creating an impenetrable mass. Increase is from seed or cuttings.

PORCELAIN AMPELOPSIS   3–20′   Zone 3   *Ampelopsis brevipedunculata*

Like Virginia creeper and Boston ivy, this sturdy vine is a plant of many uses. It is tough, hardy, and vigorous and has the added advantage of showy blue fruits in autumn. Less rampant than the others mentioned, it is particularly useful for poor soils as a ground cover as well as a screen on trellises, arbors, and walls. Since it climbs by twisting tendrils, it needs the kind of support that allows it to fasten itself. The showy fruits, borne in clusters, change from lilac to yellow-green to bright blue when mature, a pleasing contrast to the bright green grapelike foliage.

Well-suited to coastal conditions, it tolerates wind and drought and can be grown in sun or shade. Porcelain ampelopsis thrives in all types of soil and can be grown in all parts of the United States. Hard pruning and thinning in early spring benefits this vine. Stock can be increased by cuttings.

ROSE. (See Chapter 6.)

SILVER-LACE VINE   3–30′   Zone 3   *Polygonum aubertii*

In late summer and fall, the silver-lace vine presents a memorable display when the delicate masses of fragrant white flowers make their appearance. It is a rampant grower covering large areas in a single season, by means of twining stems. Actually, the leaves are not particularly attractive but the vine is valued highly for its bloom which creates billowy effects for a month or more. It is particularly striking when allowed to cascade over walls, rocks, and high fences. A good plant for hot, sunny locations, it endures wind and exposure with ease and is extremely hardy and disease-resistant as well.

Not particular as to soil, silver-lace vine is a deeply rooted woody plant that requires no special care or attention except for constant hard pruning to keep it within bounds. This treatment is often necessary each fall or early spring, except in places where the vine is needed to cover extensive areas quickly. Plants are easily started from cuttings.

STAR JASMINE   10′   Zone 7   *Trachelospermum jasminoides*

Also known as Confederate jasmine, this glossy leaved evergreen vine is cherished for its fragrant white flowers, borne in loose clusters in late spring and summer. Cultivated as a greenhouse plant in the North, it is hardy from North Carolina southward and is widely grown in the Southwest and in California. It makes a most desirable ground cover for sun or shade. Pruning or pinching the twining stems induces dense growth to form a richly textured green carpet that serves admirably as a setting for the sweetly scented blooms. Star jasmine can be grown in sun or shade in good garden soil.

TRIPTERYGIUM   10–15′   Zone 3   *Tripterygium regeli*

This is an uncommon and seldom planted vine from the Orient, related, curiously enough, to bittersweet. It is included here not only for its showy, fragrant, creamy flowers borne in trusses, 18 inches or more in length in early summer, but also for its tolerance of wind and its way of flourishing in seaside gardens. Brown spotted stems, bright green oval leaves, and greenish white winged fruits are other features of this moderate growing vine. It needs the support of a trellis or wire to keep it climbing. For many years it was one of the highlights at Reef Point Gardens at Bar Harbor, Maine.

Tripterygium can be grown in a wide variety of soils and responds readily to moisture, which is essential to good flowering. Prune annually in spring for appearance and increased vigor. Increase is by cuttings or from seed. Unfortunately, this plant is seldom offered in the trade.

TRUMPET VINE   3–30′   Zone 3   *Campsis radicans*

Wherever it grows, the trumpet vine usually makes a creditable display of bloom from midsummer to early autumn. It is native from Pennsylvania south, and has been cultivated in the Northeast and along the Pacific Coast for decades as a notable garden item. The trumpet-shaped flowers borne in showy clusters may be red, orange, or yellow, according to variety, and are prime favorites with hummingbirds. Trumpet vine is long-lived, easy to grow, but slow to leaf out in spring. It becomes awkward and leggy at the base as it reaches up, spreading its branches far and wide as it travels. Yet, despite its ungainly appearance at various seasons including winter, it is greatly enjoyed for its superb flowers. The compound foliage is rather coarse but decorative. Given a place on high fences, tree stumps, and walls, it makes a handsome summer canopy and thrives with a minimum of care. Because it tolerates wind readily, it is most useful in coastal gardens.

Essentially a plant for sunny locations, the trumpet vine endures soils of more than average moistness but will grow almost anywhere. Pruning to keep it within bounds is a spring chore and constant pinching back of new growth keeps it neat in appearance. Since it becomes woody, producing heavy growth, trumpet vine needs a sturdy support. Stock can be increased by cuttings.

VIRGINIA CREEPER   50′   Zone 3   *Parthenocissus quinquefolia*

A vine of many uses with ornamental foliage that colors brilliantly in autumn, Virginia creeper, also known as woodbine, is one of the relatively few climbing plants that can be expected to thrive almost anywhere, with little or no care. In every stage of its development, it has eye appeal. Useful for screening and softening walls and fences, it accomplishes its task quickly. It clings best to rough surfaces by means of rootlike holdfasts and also makes a good ground cover. The five-parted leaves are purplish in spring, changing to dull green in summer, and terminating in a brilliant display of red. Clusters of deep blue fruits appear in the fall.

Other species include Boston ivy (*P. tricuspidata*) with large grape-like leaves, of glossy texture; they turn yellow, orange, and scarlet in autumn and bear bluish black fruits. A widely known variety, miniature Boston ivy (*P. tricuspidata lowi*), is valued for its small foliage, less than an inch in length, that changes color with the seasons and makes delicate tracery wherever used. This is a vine of refined habit, less rampant than the species. A new miniature type known as Beverly Brooks (a selection of *P. tricuspidata veitchi*) is recommended as a replacement for the typical

Taloumis

Woodbine, also known as Virginia creeper, and sumac are among the toughest of our native seaside plants for hot, dry situations.

form because of its smaller leaf and less rampant growth. It is completely self-clinging. The various forms of Boston ivy are useful, big-scale ground covers on banks, slopes, and steep, rocky areas.

Although these vines grow best in moist soils, they soon take hold in almost any type of soil, sending their roots deep. They endure sun, dryness, and wind, are reliably hardy, and can be grown successfully in shade as well. All are propagated by cuttings or bits that root readily with soil contact.

WEEPING FORSYTHIA. (See Chapter 5.)

WINTER JASMINE   15'   Zone 5   *Jasminum nudiflorum*

Often more a trailing shrub than a vine, winter jasmine makes a good tall-growing ground cover for slopes and banks, since the arching stems root as they touch the soil. Clean foliage, dense fountainlike masses of green twigs that are pleasing in winter, as well as cheery yellow flowers in early spring, make it a most desirable plant for informal use. Flower buds are often damaged or blasted in cold temperatures, but the plant persists with vigor.

Give it well-drained soil in full sun or light shade. Frequent pruning keeps it tidy.

WINTERCREEPER   1–20'   Zone 4   *Euonymus fortunei*

The evergreen forms of euonymus known as wintercreepers are excellent climbers and ground covers as well. Extremely hardy and vigorous, they maintain a fresh, attractive appearance throughout the year. Unfortunately, they are subject to scale insects, which require considerable spraying to eradicate. If neglected, these scaly pests spread rapidly, causing plants to lose their foliage and eventually die. Apparently, euonymus scale is more inclined to affect plants on walls in hot, dry locations than when grown as a cover plant. When present, scale spreads to other plants such as pachysandra, English ivy, and bittersweet.

Ways in which the various types of wintercreeper can be used are many. Its deep-rooting habit makes it a good soil binder. For covering banks and slopes, for clothing rocky areas, under shrubs and trees, and as a lawn substitute in the shade, it is most valuable. It responds to shearing and clipping for tailored effects. On stucco, brick and stone walls, and on tree trunks, it clings readily by means of aerial roots, known as holdfasts, creating a richly textured surface.

The common wintercreeper (*E. fortunei*), sometimes referred to as *E. radicans,* is the toughest and most vigorous of evergreen vines. There are many varieties, since it tends to produce variations in foliage, known as sports. Some are valued for their colorful fruits, others for variegated foliage or deeper color in autumn. These include:

Argenteo-marginatus. A silver-leaved sport.

Acutus. A widely used form for ground cover because of its small foliage; also a good climber.

Carrierei. Glossy foliage and showy fruits make this form useful for ground cover where height is needed. If allowed, it forms a sprawling shrub but can be controlled by pruning to stay low enough for ground-cover use.

Colorata. An excellent ground cover, it turns purplish red in autumn, changing to a deeper tone as winter approaches.

135

Gracilis. White, yellow, and pink coloring in the foliage. The variety Silver Queen is similar.

Minimus. Miniature leaved wintercreepers include Kew, with ¼-inch leaves, smallest of all and slow in habit. It makes delicate tracery on rocks and walls.

Vegetus. Highly decorative with rounded, leathery leaves and showy fruits resembling bittersweet, only smaller.

Any well-drained soil is satisfactory for this sturdy evergreen that thrives in sun or shade. Propagation is by division, pieces of the rooted stems, or by cuttings, that root easily in sand and peat.

WISTERIA   25′   Zone 4   *Wisteria sinensis*

The popularity of wisteria, its vigor, and the attractive bloom it produces, are common knowledge to most gardeners. It requires only determination and a pair of sharp pruning shears to keep it within bounds so that even on a small place it can be planted to advantage on a fence, a trellis, or a pergola. Sometimes it is allowed to scramble over a ledge. However, it is a mistake to allow wisteria to grow too close to wooden structures, since the twining stems quickly work their way under clapboards and exterior trim or between the slats on blinds, often causing considerable damage. By hard pruning, it can be kept to a single upright stem and grown in tree or shrub form. This treatment is often satisfactory in small gardens.

Two distinct species are grown in gardens: Japanese wisteria (*W. floribunda*) with pendulous racemes of bloom ranging from 1 to 3 feet, Chinese wisteria with much shorter racemes, 7 to 12 inches in length, which is far more common. However, considering that the Japanese species with its extremely long blossoms needs a special kind of setting to show itself to full advantage, Chinese wisteria is generally more adaptable in the average garden. Tree and even shrubby forms of wisteria are sometimes effective, but they require considerable pruning to maintain these forms.

Despite its easy cultural requirements, wisteria is sometimes sparse in its bloom, to the great disappointment of those who plant it. "What can I do to make my wisteria bloom?" is a question with a familiar ring. Top pruning—cutting back new growth hard and continuously from late spring until midsummer—sometimes helps to induce flower buds, or root pruning may bring the desired results. A trench a foot or more in depth is dug around the base of the plant, 2 to 3 feet from the trunk (depending on its size). Use a sharp spade, plunging it into soil to sever as many roots as possible. Superphosphate is commonly used to increase flowering of certain woody plants. A generous handful dug in around a small trunk, or 2 to 3 pounds for each diameter inch of trunk on an old wisteria plant, is the usual method. Superphosphate is best applied immediately after normal bloomtime, since flower buds develop in early summer. In some in-

Wintercreeper softens the framework of an old grape arbor, lending interest at all seasons of the year.

Chinese wisteria, a row of plantain-lilies and a specimen of Japanese holly soften the classic lines of this screened porch.

stances, there are plants that apparently do not respond to any of these treatments.

Wisteria is long-lived, deep-rooted, and dependably hardy. Yet, during severe winters, flower buds of the Chinese wisteria are sometimes damaged, especially in the northerly parts of Zone 4. Full sun or part shade suits it, but when planted in shady areas flowers are seldom produced freely. Many growers offer container-grown specimens that have compact root systems, and usually these plants have produced a few blooms. Selected colors of either kind are frequently grafted plants; therefore, any growth appearing below the graft union must be cut out together with shoots from the base of grafted plants. Where sand is predominant, add several shovelfuls of humus in preparing the hole; otherwise, average garden soil is sufficient. Feed sparingly with a low nitrogen fertilizer like 5–10–10 until its bloom habit has been determined. Even then, do not overfeed unless an abundance of foliage is preferred to flowers.

ANNUAL VINES

BLACK-EYED SUSAN VINE   6'   *Thunbergia alata*

This bright-flowered vine has possibilities for much greater use in gardens for temporary ground and bank cover. It is a perennial, native to South Africa, but is generally treated as an annual in cold climates. By nature a trailer, it makes a pleasing carpet in sunny places with cheery blooms in white, yellow, and orange, accentuated with dark centers.

Black-eyed Susan vine grows best in rich garden soil but does well under average garden conditions.

CANARY-BIRD FLOWER   10'   *Tropaeolum peregrinum*

A curious and delicate climber, noted for its deeply lobed leaves and dainty yellow fringed flowers, with greenish spurs, it is sometimes grown to amuse children. Suited to hot, dry situations, it thrives in poor soil. Since it is not transplanted easily, sow seed in the open ground after danger of frost has passed.

CARDINAL CLIMBER   *Quamoclit sloteri*

Dark green fernlike foliage and scarlet trumpet-shaped flowers with white throats make this hybrid vine desirable where temporary effects are needed with climbers. Since it is not transplanted easily, sow the seed in the open ground after danger of frost has passed. To aid germination, soak the seed overnight before planting. It requires no special attention and can be used in sun or part shade.

CUP-AND-SAUCER VINE   10–20'   *Cobaea scandens*

Sometimes called cathedral bells, the blooms resemble those of Canterbury bells and are violet or purplish in color. There is also a white form.

Where the autumn season is long, the plum-shaped fruits will mature. In warm climates, from lower Delaware south, it is a perennial. A fast grower, cup-and-saucer vine endures wind and dryness and is well suited to coastal conditions. Actually, this climber is satisfactory in nearly all sections of the country. Each compound leaf has a spirally formed tendril that helps the plant to anchor itself.

A native of Mexico, it grows best in a warm, sunny spot and responds to feeding. For a head start, seed may be sown in pots indoors, a practice essential for bloom where fall frosts come early. Since the seed rots easily if the soil is unduly moist, it is best to press it into the soil sideways with the top barely covered.

HYACINTH BEAN   20'   *Dolichos lablab*

A fast grower with large, coarse, beanlike foliage and showy spikes of slightly fragrant, purple or white flowers, often 6 inches long, this is one of the easiest annual vines to grow. The blooms are desirable for cutting since they last well, and purplish beans follow in autumn. Actually a perennial in warm climates, it makes a most satisfactory annual.

Ordinary soil and full sun suit the hyacinth bean. Seed may be planted in the open ground where the vine is to grow after danger of frost has passed, or indoors in pots for an early start. The seedlings are not easily transplanted.

MORNING GLORY   10–15'   *Ipomoea purpurea*

Most popular of all the annual vines, it is useful wherever climbing plants are needed. It also makes a good temporary cover for banks and slopes. Flowers may be white, pink, blue, purple, or red, according to the variety planted. Heavenly Blue is the prime favorite. Morning glories make delightful cascading effects as well as dense growth, and on trellises, arbors, and fences they lend themselves as colorful summer drapery.

Seeds have a hard coating and need to be soaked for a day before planting. When started from seed, plant where the vines are to be used, since this annual does not transplant easily. Plants in pots can be purchased from many local growers. Morning glories flower best when grown in poor soil, in a sunny location.

NASTURTIUM   5–6'   *Tropaeolum majus*

A familiar annual vine for hot, dry places, it prefers poor, sandy soil for abundant bloom and has long been a favorite seashore flower. Fragrant blooms in a variety of colors, soft green foliage, plus a rapid-trailing habit make it a most useful ground cover for banks, the tops of walls, or rocky areas. However, it tends to become something of a pest in warm climates because of the ease with which it reseeds. Both double and single flowering kinds are popular. Trained on supports, nasturtiums make effective plants for pots and boxes on porches and terraces.

Best planted where it is to grow, it can be started from seed, or seedlings are sometimes planted in pots for transfer to the open ground. Despite its vigor and ease of culture, it is notably sensitive to cold weather and cannot be planted until all danger of frost has passed.

SCARLET RUNNER BEAN   10′   *Phaseolus coccineus*

An old-time favorite that makes a spectacular display in summer, this ornamental bean is well worth growing. The typical form bears spikes of bright scarlet, pea-shaped flowers and there is a white variety as well as one called Butterfly with distinctive white wings and standards of salmon brown. Foliage is beanlike, light green, and most attractive. Scarlet runner makes an effective temporary screen or it can be used on fences. The large purple pods filled with sizable beans are favorites with those who enjoy eating various types of beans.

Sow the seed in the open ground where plants are to grow, after frost danger has passed. Scarlet runner flowers heavily in fertile soil and is benefited by feeding.

CHAPTER TEN

Ground Covers

$\mathcal{G}$ROUND COVERS have special merit in seaside gardens as stabilizers of soil. These low-growing plants that increase by underground stems (stolons) and are by nature trailing in habit, are also of prime value for checking erosion. They improve the texture and humus content of soil as they gather falling leaves among their stems and crowns. This decaying vegetable matter is gradually incorporated with the soil. As they grow and spread, they form mats or carpets on the surface of the soil. Some produce roots along their stems, and this serves to keep them flat and hold the soil. Others spread by trailing stems in a procumbent manner so as to create a slightly wavy or billowy effect, without forming roots unless induced. The manner in which these plants develop roots and the depth to which they penetrate the soil determine their value as soil binders.

The most desirable of all ground covers is grass. Yet there are places where grass does not grow easily and where it cannot be cared for satisfactorily. Then, too, the time required and the cost involved to maintain a high-grade lawn are often considerable. The need for continuous fertilizing, spraying for insects and pests, and frequent cutting can add up, in terms of both man-hours and dollars, to a sizable total. Furthermore, in shady areas where gardeners often struggle to keep grass growing, more time and energy are spent than the plot is worth. The answer is ground covers.

When not covered with grass, exposed ground needs to be planted, to prevent erosion and to keep it from becoming infested with weeds. Ground covers fulfill a variety of other needs on the home grounds, in which their practical value is easily recognized. The following are typical situations in which they can be used.

Binding Sandy Soils. Plants that tolerate salt spray—like bearberry, rugosa rose, shore juniper, beach wormwood, and many others—are invaluable for holding sandy soil in seaside plantings and inland.

Concealing Exposed Tree Roots. This problem often plagues gardeners, especially if large trees are a part of or adjoin a lawn area. Grass is neither easy to cut nor easy to maintain. Exposed roots are a hazard. Cover plants solve both problems.

Carpeting Shady Areas under Trees and Shrubs. Matting plants or taller kinds are needed for soil cover, as well as to provide a pleasing setting for the trees or shrubs.

Clothing Rocky Uneven Land. Where roughness is desired but needs cover, outcroppings of rock can become a distinctive feature of the grounds when planted with a variety of ground-cover, crevice, and rock plants.

Covering Slopes and Banks. Erosion is the chief problem in both sun and shade. Most slopes and banks are not suited to grass from the point of easy maintenance. Steep grades often require deep-rooted low-growing plants to hold the soil and to tie them in with the over-all planting scheme.

Underplanting Trees and Shrubs to Keep Down Weeds. Soil under high-branching plants can be a nuisance to keep attractive unless some suitable cover is provided. Ferns of various kinds are often suitable.

Taloumis

Periwinkle and ferns surround two delightful garden ornaments.

143

Settings for Lilies and Other Bulbous Plants. Lilies grow best when they have shade over their roots. The contrasting foliage of ground-cover plants provides a setting and acts as a foil for lilies and other kinds of flowering bulbs.

Reducing Weeds Among Perennials. Cover planting has proved to be most satisfactory where large-scale perennials such as peonies, hardy asters, chrysanthemums, poppies, iris, day lilies, and the like are grown in large groups of a single kind. Evergreen candytuft, Silver Mound artemisia, snow-in-summer, barrenwort, and similar plants are suitable.

Solving Problems in Wet Soils. Some creeping plants are by nature adapted to boggy conditions where they thrive on hummocks. Others prefer moist, heavy soil. Ferns, forget-me-nots, primroses, violets, foam flower, dwarf willow, and others are well suited.

Ground covers in their diverse forms lend a finished appearance to shrub and perennial plantings, thereby eliminating sharp edges between beds and grass areas. Large surfaces of bare ground are not particularly pleasing, since the soil tends to cake and crust. Unless the beds are mulched with peat moss or some other suitable material, or a dust mulch is maintained, weeds appear that require cultivation to eradicate. A drift or mass of silvery gray, green, or blue-green foliage is preferable to a weedy tangle between clumps of perennials or groups of shrubs.

These versatile creepers and carpeters have value in the over-all landscape picture for linking the various units of a planting on the home grounds, so that one flows into the other. The transition between a lawn and the trees and shrubs that enclose it can be enhanced by the use of a medium-sized cover. Small shrub groupings can also be softened with ground covers. Plants of varying sizes and shapes within a unit can be linked or tied together with one or more kinds of carpet plants. This is particularly true in foundation plantings.

Evergreen ground covers are especially valuable for their year-round color and interest. They become eye-catchers in plantings that can be viewed from windows, driveways, and roads adjoining one's property. They are equally important in approach plantings, corner groupings, strips along walks, and other areas adjacent to the house—be it the front door, the service entrance, or the rear driveway. Blankets or sheets of cover plants are the simple and easy solution to tasteful landscaping. They seem to belong in these locations.

The selected group of ground covers in this chapter is but a sampling of the many useful kinds that can be planted to advantage on the home grounds. See also Vines, Chapter 9.

ARTEMISIA, SILVER MOUND   4–12″   Zone 3   *Artemisia schmidtiana*

A clump of silver mound artemisia sparkling with dew in the early morning sunlight is a memorable sight and no low-growing perennial is

Taloumis

Artemisia Silver Mound is one of the hardiest and handsomest of seaside perennials. In early morning, drops of dew rest on the segments of the silvery foliage.

better suited to the seaside. It grows with great vigor in full sun and poor soil and makes handsome mounds of silvery, finely cut foliage that is eye-catching all season long. Frequently used as a specimen plant in small rock gardens or as an edging for wide borders, it shows off to equally good advantage as a ground cover in rocky areas or on slight slopes. A tall-growing type, a foot or more in height, and the dwarf *A. schmidtiana nana,* are both desirable. In fact, the latter is often desired for its low growth. Other species of this hardy and vigorous tribe of perennials include fringed wormwood (*A. frigida*), 15 to 18 inches tall, and the rather weedy Roman wormwood (*A. pontica*), 10 to 12 inches high, common in old gardens. All have inconspicuous yellow flowers, but the great charm of these plants is their foliage and the ease with which they grow. Every garden needs silvery foliage for accent. This group of artemisias has many uses, especially for massed foliage effects. See also beach wormwood, in this chapter.

Division of clumps is the way to increase stock. Artemisias spread rapidly and are easy to divide at any time during the growing season. If silver mound gets shoddy with too much rain, causing the mounds to open, cut it back and watch it quickly send up new growth.

Here is a plant for rocky areas and particularly deep pockets in ledges where there is sufficient soil for it to form large mounds of richly textured foliage. Another common name for it is bishop's-hat in reference to the curious form of the flower, which resembles a biretta. This native of Japan spreads by creeping rhizomes, making a tightly arranged mass of roots that often need to be cut separately. The foliage is equally dense in habit.

E. grandiflorum, which is most commonly grown, has heart-shaped leaves suspended on stiff, wiry stems. Red tones show in the new foliage in spring and bronzy red coloring enhances its appearance in autumn, lasting into winter and even into a second spring where winters are mild. The delicately formed, spurred flowers that appear in loose sprays during May may be white, yellow, pink, or violet, according to variety.

E. alpinum rubrum is more dwarf in habit, with compound leaves and rich red blooms.

Bright yellow flowers with red for contrast are typical of *E. pinnatum.* A number of hybrid forms appear under various names.

The better the soil in humus content, the better the growth of this little charmer. It thrives in acid soil, which can be improved with peat moss and leaf mold. Shady locations are preferable where summers are hot, but it does well in sun where soil is deep and moist. Easy to increase by division after flowering or in early fall, heavy clumps may need to be cut apart with a sharp knife. Since it is reliably hardy and easy to grow, most gardeners never have too much of it.

BEACH WORMWOOD   18–24"   Zone 2   *Artemisia stelleriana*

Silvery gray and almost white in bright sunlight, this creeping perennial of the sand dunes has many common names, among them beach wormwood and dusty miller. The leaves, which resemble those of a small oak, are soft and silky and look as though they were cut from fine cloth. It spreads by creeping stems and thrives in hot, dry, sandy soils. Heavy wet soil will finish it in short order.

Tolerant of salt spray and rugged, it makes an ideal soil cover for seaside gardens, aiding in the control of erosion. Used with dwarf forms of *Rosa rugosa,* it makes a striking contrast. Or it may be blended with the straplike foliage of day lilies, the coarse olive-green of bayberries, or the needlelike foliage of the shore juniper and the dark green cut-leaved sweet fern. In hardy borders used in drifts with various kinds of perennials and annuals, beach wormwood is of special value for it accentuates the brightness of the pinks, the blues, and the yellow tones. (For other artemisias, see silver mound artemisia and wormwood.)

Propagated by root division or by cuttings, beach wormwood requires little or no care; it needs only a hot, dry location and light soil of poor quality. To thicken the growth, cut it back hard in early spring after the growth has started.

BEARBERRY	12″	Zone 2	*Arctostaphylos uva-ursi*
HOOKER MANZANITA	18″	Zone 7	*A. hookeri*
LAUREL HILL MANZANITA	6″	Zone 7	*A. franciscana*

One of the most desirable of all our native ground covers for seaside gardens is bearberry or kinnikinnick, as the Indians have called it for centuries. This trailing evergreen shrub is widely distributed along the seacoast over a large part of the United States. It is at home in dry, sandy, or rocky acid soil, where it makes long, trailing mats of rich, leathery foliage showing bronzy tones in autumn. It is not uncommon for a single trailing stem to extend several yards from the base of a clump. The white bell-shaped flowers, borne in clusters on dark red stems during May and June, are followed by attractive red fruits in autumn.

Ideal as a ground cover and soil binder for sunny banks and slopes or sprawling over rocks in hot, dry, sandy locations, it is being widely used in these situations in gardens and along highways throughout the country both near the sea and inland. Because it is slow to propagate and difficult to transplant, except when container-grown, the common bearberry is not as widely known or appreciated as it deserves to be.

Other species native to the West Coast, commonly referred to as manzanitas (little apples), range from small trailing forms to small trees. These are the most familiar shrubs of the California chaparral belt, hardy from Zone 7 southward. To the California Indians the fruits were considered the little apples of God, since they furnished an important source of food in the form of dried meal served as porridge. Laurel Hill manzanita (*A. franciscana*) has gray-green foliage, grows about 6 inches high, and creeps at a rapid rate. Hooker manzanita (*A. hookeri*) is taller growing, 18 inches to 2 feet in height, and makes a neat mound of shiny foliage several yards wide. Both have pink flowers in early spring, followed by "little apples." These plants layer naturally as they creep. For sandy banks and slopes and general ground-cover use on the West Coast, these native plants are of prime importance and value.

For success in planting, the bearberry and the manzanita must be handled with care because of the sensitive root systems. Prepare the area to be planted with a mixture of acid peat moss and sandy loam and use nursery-grown stock from containers. Few gardeners are ever successful in transplanting clumps from the wild unless they are carefully handled in large mats or clumps and moved with a generous ball of native soil. This method of handling is best done in early spring; some gardeners have been known to move sods of bearberry before the frost has left the soil. Frequent watering, shading from wind, and mulching are necessary to establish these plants in exposed areas, but it is worth all the effort involved.

Nurserymen who propagate them from cuttings offer small potted or container-grown plants, which are easy to handle throughout the growing season. Two- or three-year rooted cuttings are not impressive to look at and may not even appear to be worth the price asked, but once established they make surprisingly rapid growth. Usually by the second year after planting, the trailing stems extend over a considerable area. Space 2 feet apart each way. Feeding in late spring with evergreen fertilizer brings good results.

BLUE FESCUE 6–8" Zone 3 *Festuca ovina glauca*

Ornamental grasses have a special kind of appeal in gardens by the sea where the color of the blades, the flower spikes and growth habit of the plant show to good advantage against sand. Blue fescue is a fascinating plant that grows in tufts, making a striking appearance when used to make a patterned ground cover. The name fescue brings to mind other kinds of grasses well suited to shade, and all of these shade-loving grasses have the characteristic of growing in tufts or bunches. However, few are so pronounced in their tufting habit as the blue fescue, which thrives in the sun as well. It must have perfect drainage and dry soil. This fescue had a vogue among rock-garden enthusiasts some 30 years ago, but presently it is not widely known in the Northeast. West Coast gardeners, on the other hand, use it in block plantings, alternating it with brick and stone patterns, using various plants in masses with it for contrast and also as a ground cover under trees.

Easy to increase by dividing the clumps, it benefits from occasional shearing. It takes heat and plenty of it, but will grow in light shade.

BUGLEWEED 4–12" Zone 4 *Ajuga* species

In some ways bugleweed is well named for it is a rapid-growing ground cover which can become weedy. Yet it is a good soil binder, but requires average moisture and cannot be grown in pure sand. It is widely used in shade as a substitute for grass, both on flat areas and on slopes. For carpeting under shrubs and trees, in strip plantings, among rocks, on terraces, or between stone crevices, it is one of the easiest of all ground covers to grow. The blue, pink, and white forms grouped together make a colorful display. However, it does not stand any great amount of foot traffic. Except in naturally dry soils, this plant flourishes with little care. It is ideal for shade or partial shade, or in sunny locations where there is more than average soil moisture.

Common bugle (*A. reptans*) is the most rapid grower of all. The rosettes of glossy foliage lie flat on the ground and it spreads by creeping stems from 3 to 10 inches or more in length. Some kinds do not produce runners, and their ability to cover is not so rapid. Sturdy, upright flower spikes, 3 to 6 inches tall, bloom in May and June. Blue is the predominant color but there are pink- and white-flowering kinds and several have bronze, variegated, or mottled foliage. Many kinds are listed by growers because of the great demand for this plant. Some are selections of recognized forms and others are of hybrid origin. The following list of species and varieties probably contains some duplicates, but this is the way they are sold.

Ajuga reptans. Common bugle.

Alba. Light green foliage and white flowers.

Atropurpurea. Bronze leaves with blue spikes.

Bronze Beauty. A selection with large bronzy-and-blue flowers.

Multicolor. Spotted and variegated yellow, brown, and red with blue flowers.

Rainbow. Similar to multicolor and may be identical.

Silver Beauty. Green and white foliage, not a rampant grower.

Variegata conspicua. Creamy white markings and blue flowers.

A. genevensis. Geneva or Alpine Bugle. This species tends to make broad mats, does not spread so rapidly, being without runners.

Brockbanki. Dwarf habit, with deep blue flower spikes.

Metallica crispa. Dark bronze foliage with a metallic quality, crisped edges, blue flowers.

Rosy Spires. Bright green foliage with showy pink flowers.

A. pyramidalis. An improved form with bottle green foliage and larger flower spikes than those listed above.

Easy to increase, the smallest piece with roots will take hold. It can be set out at any time during the growing season, since it requires only ordinary soil and routine care in transplanting. Ground covers for shade are not too numerous, and this is one of the most useful and least expensive because of its rapid method of increase. *Ajuga* has a shallow rooting system and shows the effects of prolonged dry spells in thin soils, but responds quickly to watering.

CINQUEFOIL. See Chapter 5.

COTONEASTER. See Chapter 5.

DAY LILY. See Chapter 11.

DWARF ROSEMARY. See Chapter 8.

ENGLISH IVY. See Chapter 9.

Lavender cotton, with its yellow, button-like flowers, thyme, pachysandra, catmint, lavender, mullein, and a host of other perennials thrive in this coastal garden.

EVERGREEN CANDYTUFT. See Chapter 11.

FLEECEFLOWER 1' **Zone 5** *Polygonum*

Fleeceflower is an appealing common name for *Polygonum reynoutria,* a comparative newcomer among perennials. To many gardeners, the mention of polygonum brings to mind the deep-rooted Mexican bamboo, one of the worst pests ever to invade the home grounds. The Reynoutria fleeceflower (*P. reynoutria*), also called dwarf lace plant, averages 1 foot in height, with rather coarse foliage. However, the red stems and creamy flowers are most pleasing, and it has proved to be a useful ground cover in both sun and shade, thriving where other plants, including most ground covers, are not happy. Hence it is recommended as a soil binder for difficult situations.

It spreads by underground stems that root as they grow, and the smallest segment will produce a new plant. Its invasive habits must be remembered when choosing a place to use it, but it can be most useful where needed.

FOAM FLOWER   1'   Zone 4   *Tiarella cordifolia*

One of the loveliest and daintiest native carpeting plants found in moist woodlands from Nova Scotia to Georgia and Alabama and westward to Michigan is appropriately named foam flower for its feathery spikes of bloom that appear in early spring well above the foliage. This native perennial adapts itself easily to cultivation. Dark green maplelike leaves sometimes marked with brown make an even, soft-textured mass throughout the growing season. Here is a shade-loving plant for moist places which can be used as mixed cover with other native and exotic plants such as blue phlox, bloodroot, and primroses, or in drifts by itself.

It requires little attention, grows in average garden soil, and spreads moderately to carpet a given area. Root division in spring or fall is the way to increase stock.

GOLD DUST   1'   Zone 4   *Alyssum saxatile*

This old favorite is generally thought of as a rock garden plant. Yet its gray-toned, durable foliage and showy heads of yellow bloom, plus its ability to make a large sprawling mass, make it a desirable ground cover. Well suited to rocky areas where cover is a problem, it is at its best in full sun and gritty soil. The common kind with brilliant yellow flowers in April and May is known as Gold Dust, Basket-of-Gold, and Golden Tuft. There is a double-flower variety, a popular pale yellow kind (*A. saxatile citrinum*), and a recent introduction called Dudley Neville which is more dwarf than the type and has pleasing sulfur-yellow blooms. Another species, about 1 foot tall, with wiry, woody stems, listed as *A. argenteum,* is distinguished by its small silvery leaves and large flat heads of yellow bloom in summer.

Start with young plants from pots or rooted cuttings, or all of these types can be raised from seed. Alyssum has a taproot and is almost impossible to move successfully, once it is established in a planting. Full sun, ordinary soil, and good drainage are all it needs. Clip off the flower heads after bloom has passed and shear the plants hard to promote growth and an abundance of new foliage that keeps its neat appearance all summer.

GOUTWEED   8″   Zone 3   *Aegopodium podograria variegatum*

Both the botanical and the common names of this hardy perennial will discourage many gardeners from planting it. To some who have had experience with it, it is one of the worst of weeds and a "cussed" nuisance. Yet others find it desirable for carpeting areas under such trees as maples, where cover of any kind is difficult to maintain, or for planting on banks and other bare areas. The plain green form of goutweed is not much planted. However, the variegated form, with its attractive green and white leaves produced on creeping rootstocks, makes a most effective mottled carpet, especially in shade. Flat white carrotlike flowers appear in June. Goutweed grows anywhere it can take root, in sun or shade. Despite its bad reputation, it can be kept within bounds by most gardeners who choose to use it.

The smallest bit of its creeping root will start a new plant, and it can be moved at any time during the growing season. Usually, where it is used for ground cover, it can be kept under control more easily in poor soil. The first hard frost kills the foliage.

HALL'S HONEYSUCKLE   18–24″   Zone 5   *Lonicera japonica halliana*

The most widely used vine for covering banks and slopes in many parts of the country, both inland and by the sea, it can also be the meanest of pests to eradicate. It has clean foliage and delightfully fragrant flowers and will grow anywhere in any kind of soil, including poor sandy types. On the other hand, it makes a tangled mat of growth and twines itself around shrubs and trees. In many areas it is disliked because birds drop seeds of poison ivy, which thrives in its dense growth. When neglected, it can become a breeding place for various kinds of weed trees and, because it is so resistant to the elements and is often allowed to grow without pruning or restraining, has rightfully earned the name of pest. Unless very carefully restrained, Hall's honeysuckle is not suited to the small home grounds or to any restricted area. When it is cut back annually and kept in check, it is most attractive. Where there is ample room for it to spread, its value lies in its ability to make quick cover and bind soils on slopes and banks. It is also a very inexpensive plant to use.

Any type of soil suits it, in sun or shade. It is increased by division of the roots.

HEATH, HEATHER. See Chapter 7.

HOUSELEEK   1–3″   Zone 4   *Sempervivum tectorum*

Wind, salt spray, and drought have little effect on the common houseleek or sempervivum (*S. tectorum*), which has been growing in American gardens for 300 years. Tradition has it that William the Conqueror brought the houseleek to England and it has had a variety of medicinal uses in the past. A curious plant, with rosettes of fleshy leaves, it gathers its young

152

around it in a cushion or mat, hence the common name, hen and chickens. It fills the seams of rocks with ease and is sometimes used along rocky paths and outcroppings, but always in the sun. When planted in the shade, it loses its vigor, becoming soft and loose in growth. On dry slopes as a ground cover, especially where soil is poor and gritty, it flourishes and crowds out most weeds. If interplanted with sedums, especially such weedy kinds as *Sedum acre,* it is soon crowded. Best left to itself, or planted with other varieties (of which there are quantities), it makes a flat uneven cover of crisp texture and color, depending on the kinds used. There are numerous species and varieties, some with webby filaments giving a cobweb effect and others with rich reddish leaves.

Houseleeks are ideal rock cover in sunny places, for they fit so compactly into the space at hand as to belong where they are planted. For softening rough edges and making highlights in rock surfaces, these succulent leaved rosettes were made as if to order. Where soil pockets are of varying depths, other species of plants are also desirable, but in shallow nooks and crannies with scarcely any soil the houseleek is the easy solution. When planted in strawberry jars or barrels they make attractive ornaments for terraces and porches and require little or no care. The stubby flower stalks studded with rosettes of pink flowers in summer add greatly to their ornamental value.

Houseleeks can be planted at almost any time during the growing season. Drainage is much more vital to their survival than soil. No wet feet for them at any season. Use them first of all in sunny places, but they can endure light shade.

JUNIPER   1–2′   Zones 2–5   *Juniperus* genus

On steep slopes in full sun where grass is difficult to maintain because soil tends to be dry and erosion threatens, few plants are more adaptable and desirable than low-growing junipers. Horizontal in habit, evergreen and soft in texture, these prostrate types are attractive throughout the year. As the branches spread they root, making a wavy carpet. Creeping junipers are often the answer to problems created by the construction of split-level houses, particularly in areas of rolling terrain. Also, when used in masses to link several changes of level on home grounds, they are more effective than grass because of their height, color, texture, and mode of growth.

Most widely planted is the creeping juniper (*J. horizontalis*), which makes a dense mat of gray-green needlelike foliage. For color and variety the blue-gray Waukegan juniper (*J. horizontalis douglasi*) makes a pleasing companion plant. For a stronger blue-green color, you can use the blue creeping juniper (*J. horizontalis glauca*), a slower and more compact grower. Another variety in wide use is the Andorra juniper, valued for its delicate texture and rich purple color during autumn and winter. Where taller kinds are needed, both the Pfitzer and the Hetz types may be used to advantage. These are widely grown and readily available.

153

Junipers and pachysandra make a pleasing textural pattern.

The Sargent juniper (*J. chinensis sargenti*) is of more billowy habit and somewhat taller as it matures. It is grayish green and somewhat bolder in habit than the common creeping types.

The Japanese garden juniper (*J. procumbens*) is darker in color, dense and rather upright in habit, and about 2 feet tall when mature.

The common juniper of rocky soils in upland pastures, listed as *J. communis depressa,* is a widespreading plant that may eventually grow 3 feet tall, but usually is lower. Gray-green and silvery in texture, it is especially desirable where there is space to accommodate it in naturalistic plantings. Bluish fruits add interest in autumn and winter. Of more compact habit, the mountain form (*J. communis saxatilis*) makes broad patches slightly under 2 feet in height.

For sandy banks and slopes, the shore juniper (*J. conferta*), a Japanese native, is a real asset, especially close to the sea, since it is not harmed by salt spray. Bright green shoots grow somewhat upright from low, spreading branches. Plants are 1 foot or less in height and spread 8 to 10 feet across, hugging the ground.

Regardless of how poor the soil is or appears to be, junipers will prosper with proper soil preparation. Assuming that the slope has been raked and graded, dig holes wide and deep enough to accommodate equal parts of garden soil and peat moss thoroughly mixed with a handful of acid-soil fertilizer. Water thoroughly and leave a slight depression around each plant to catch water. Additional water will be needed twice a week until the plants are established. Rooted cuttings from flats, potted plants, or balled and burlapped specimens may be used. In soils of low fertility, an annual feeding produces surprising results.

LAMB'S EARS. See Chapter 11.

LAVENDER, ENGLISH. See Chapter 11.

LAVENDER COTTON. See Chapter 11.

LILY OF THE VALLEY 6″ Zone 2 *Convallaria majalis*

In many gardens where lilies of the valley were first planted in neat clumps, they have spread to become ground covers in sun and shade. Although not evergreen in foliage, they produce a dense mat of underground roots to hold soil. Soft green leaves, fragrant white bell-shaped flowers in May, and golden autumn foliage coloring are assets, but the foliage becomes unsightly as it fades. This point, and the fact that the ground remains bare all winter, are to be considered when choosing a place for lilies of the valley. Yet where there are large bare areas of soil to be covered, this tough, hardy perennial is effective, inexpensive, and desirable. A good ground cover under shrubs, it combines well with ferns. Fortin's Giant is an improved form with larger flower spikes than the type, and there is also a pale pink variety.

Clumps can be divided at any time during the growing season, separating each rooted segment, or pip, as it is called. For a thick planting, set the pips 6 to 8 inches apart. Ordinary soil meets their requirements. Regular feeding with a complete fertilizer improves the size and quality of both foliage and flowers.

In the lower South, particularly in Florida, lilyturf is of prime importance as a ground cover and substitute for grass, especially in sandy soils. The common name lilyturf is used interchangeably for two related evergreen perennials with bulbous roots, liriope and ophiopogon. Both are completely hardy from Zone 5 south and are readily adaptable to a variety of soils, particularly those low in fertility. They endure heat, drought, and salt spray. Carpets of lilyturf are used in all degrees of shade, under trees and shrubs, on slopes and banks, as wide edging plants, and wherever soil cover is required. Plants make solid mats of growth quickly, which adds greatly to their value for erosion and dust control. Both are native to the Orient.

The flower spikes of liriope, which resemble those of grape hyacinth, may be blue or white. These are held well above the foliage, whereas the blooms of ophiopogon are mostly concealed in the leaves. Fruits are blue-black berries that appear in the fall. Of the two, liriope is taller.

There are several distinct types of ophiopogon. *O. japonicus* is a dwarf form usually less than 1 foot tall and grows less rapidly than liriope. In this respect it has merit for use in small areas. *O. jaburan* is taller in habit. Both liriope and ophiopogon have forms with yellow-striped foliage that has definite ornamental value when used for accent.

Ophiopogon has proved itself hardy in Washington, D.C., and can be grown even farther north in protected locations. Liriope is hardier and can be depended on to live through winter in the Boston area. However, in winter its color in no way compares with such cover plants as myrtle, pachysandra, pachistima, and others. Both of these popular Florida ground covers have been widely advertised in the past few years. Their greatest value is in those regions of the country where ice and snow are not a major factor and winters are mild. Many gardeners in the Northeast have enjoyed growing them for limited use because of their attractive appearance, especially those with the yellow-striped foliage.

Neither soil nor exposure nor light conditions are vital factors in growing these plants, but they have special value in shade. Since they make dense, sodlike growth, they need division every few years. They can be reset in fall or spring and require no special care.

Moss Pink. See Phlox.

Moss Sandwort   1″   Zone 2   *Arenaria verna caespitosa*

A mosslike alpine about a half-inch high, widely used as a paving plant throughout the greater part of the United States, sandwort is often referred to as Irish moss. It is most frequently called moss sandwort or lazy-man's lawn. For many years it was listed as *Sagina subulata* and still appears under this name in some lists and reference books. It can be found growing in almost any well-drained soil except heavy clay, seldom requires clipping, and generally is long-lived. It takes the ordinary foot traffic of gardens without damage and is most useful between flags or paving blocks, for walks, terraces, and patios. When grown in broad masses, it occasionally humps up in a mound, but a firm foot puts it back where it belongs. For sunny locations, this and the others listed here also take a fair amount of shade.

A species with a low-creeping, branching habit bearing tiny white cup-shaped flowers in late spring (*A. laricifolia*) does best in sandy acid soil in full sun. Mountain sandwort (*A. montana*), another miniature with glossy foliage, bears large white flowers in late spring on its trailing growth.

Increase of these tiny plants is by division, and most of them have a way of spreading beyond their bounds, providing future supply for places that become worn at times with heavy traffic.

PACHYSANDRA   6″   Zone 4   *Pachysandra terminalis*

Pachysandra, or Japanese spurge as it is sometimes called, rates as one of the four most popular ground covers used in American gardens. Its use in seaside gardens is somewhat limited, for, despite its hardiness, it burns badly during open winters when exposed to sun, wind, and sudden drops in temperature. Soil of better than poor sandy type is essential for vigorous growth. Yet there are many locations where it can be used effectively. The spoon-shaped leaves, arranged in whorls on trailing stems, make a rippling effect when used in broad carpets. Creamy white spikes of bloom top the foliage in May, and old plants produce whitish fruits in autumn, but these are not common. Easy to grow and propagate, it makes a dense mass for shady areas and grows most satisfactorily even where there is considerable sun. However, it is no plant for hot, dry situations. It burns badly during open winters when planted in exposed areas where wind and sun are its enemies.

Because pachysandra makes a superbly rich green carpet, it fits under such trees as maples and other shallow-rooted kinds that tend to rob the soil of nourishment and make cover of any kind a problem. Interplanted among rhododendrons, azaleas, and other broad-leaved evergreens, it gives a pleasing and finished effect. Along steps on banks and slopes, it serves all the purposes of a good ground cover. It also combines with low-spreading junipers, yews, pieris, leucothoe, and many of the broad-leaved evergreens for equally pleasing effects.

Oftentimes there are shady areas along walks, the sides of houses or garages, or other places where it is difficult to maintain grass or other kinds of planting. These are the places for pachysandra. Interest can be added to broad expanses of pachysandra by using low-growing evergreens like dwarf yews, leucothoe, mountain andromeda, Oregon hollygrape, and others for

157

Sedums are planted between the stones; a drift of gray-foliaged catmint with pachysandra for contrast. Lavender, dusty miller, and lavender cotton fill the raised bed. A study in foliage texture.

accent. The large-leaved plantain lilies can be used in a similar manner for contrast in foliage texture.

In recent years a variegated form known as Silveredge has been introduced. Lighter green than the type, the leaves are marked with a silvery white margin, usually ¼ inch or less, outlining each leaf. As with many mottled or variegated foliage plants, Silveredge pachysandra supplies a color contrast that brightens broad expanses of green foliage. It can be used to advantage along margins of broad-leaved evergreen plantings.

A native species known as Allegheny spurge (*P. procumbens*), native from West Virginia to Florida, grows in clumps and is more erect in habit than the familiar Japanese type. Although evergreen in the South, it loses its leaves in northern areas, but the showy spikes of fuzzy white flowers in early spring are very attractive. In regions where it remains evergreen it has some merit, but does not cover so rapidly as *P. terminalis*.

Well-drained soil with plenty of organic material in the form of peat moss, leaf mold, or chopped sod gets pachysandra off to a good start. Incorporate fertilizer with the soil when preparing it. An annual top dressing in early spring is also a good practice until the area is well covered. After setting out young plants and watering thoroughly, a soil mulch at least 1 inch deep keeps weeds in check. Feeding each spring with a complete fertilizer helps to keep growth vigorous.

Few of our ground covers are as easy to propagate or root more rapidly. Cuttings can be taken after the new growth has formed in early June and rooted in a mixture of sand and peat. An easy way to do this is to prepare a little propagating bed in some corner of your garden under a shrub where you will be sure to water it occasionally. Make the cuttings about 4 inches long, using sharp shears. Remove all foliage on that portion of the stem that will be placed in the soil. Usually cuttings root in about 10 days, but they must be kept moist. Sand is also a good medium for rooting pachysandra. Some gardeners simply make cuttings in their own garden soil and shade them until roots appear. Once a good healthy set of roots has developed, the plants can be set out, about 8 to 10 inches apart for intermediate effect. Close planting is worthwhile with rooted cuttings, to eliminate the job of weeding.

PERIWINKLE   6″   Zone 3   *Vinca minor*

Less likely to burn in open winters than pachysandra, periwinkle with its smooth, hard-surfaced leaves is a most useful evergreen ground cover of trailing habit. It is also popularly known as myrtle.

The familiar blue-flowering type is *Vinca minor*. There is also a white-flowering variety which is most pleasing. *V. minor atropurpurea* has purple flowers. A double-flower kind and one with yellow markings on the leaves are sometimes planted. The best of them all is the Bowles variety, with larger and deeper blue flowers and a more restrained habit of growth than the common periwinkle. It spreads from the expansion of its crown rather than by the rooting of trailing stems, typical of the species. A new variety called Miss Jekyll's White is smaller in scale than any of the other kinds described, and notably refined in texture. Not only smaller in leaf, but more restrained in growth, it is exceptionally free-flowering and well suited as a carpet plant in spring-flowering bulbs.

Big-leaf periwinkle (*V. major*), particularly the variegated form, is frequently seen as a trailer in window boxes and other types of plant containers in various sections of the country. In the South and on the West Coast this form serves as a ground cover on slopes, sometimes combined with English ivy because its variegated foliage makes a pleasing contrast.

Ordinary soil, well prepared, gives good results in sun or shade. Easy to propagate from division of the clumps or rooted trailers, it can be transplanted at any time of year. When dividing matted clumps, cut back the runners hard to make the rooted portions easy to handle. Otherwise, a

159

A gentle slope covered with myrtle and juniper, birches, and other native trees shelters the terrace where pot plants flower in profusion.

newly planted area has a messy appearance. Heavy pruning induces new growth from the rooted portions, which makes for denser cover. Annual feeding of newly planted colonies induces more vigorous growth, as does continued fertilizing of established plantings.

PINKS   3–8″   Zone 2   *Dianthus* genus

Hardy pinks are well suited to hot, dry, sunny places and they thrive where there is ample lime in the soil. These loose-tufted perennials are especially appealing when in flower, even if a bit untidy afterward when not sheared. Their conspicuous glaucous foliage is a notable landscape feature. Both single and double-flower kinds, perennial and annual, are prime favorites and deservedly so, for their color and fragrance. There are also several alpine forms that make enduring mats of blue-green foliage, studded with pink, white, or red fragrant blooms. These are neat of habit, require little care, and give a softening effect to rough, rocky ground and spaces between flagstones or along paths. Not all the rock-garden kinds are rugged enough for ground-cover use, but the various dwarf kinds grown together in a rocky area can be treated effectively as rock or ledge cover.

The maiden pink (*D. deltoides*) is decidedly tough and makes a blue-green lawn about 3 inches high as it spreads over the ground with masses of bloom ranging from white to deep red in June. From Finland we have the sand pink (*D. arenarius*), with white, fragrant, fringed flowers. The cheddar pink (*D. caesius*), its hybrids and other tiny species, and named kinds like Little Bob, Little Joe, and Sammy make chummy companions to carpet sunny spots.

Average well-drained soil, especially on the gritty side, in full sun, is best for pinks used as ground covers. Too much plant food is no asset. Soil on the sweet side improved with lime is essential. They can be propagated by seed, cuttings, or division, but the latter is easiest for most gardeners. Set plants or divisions 10 to 12 inches apart. With the exception of the hardy carnations that are sometimes "miffy" in open winters, most of the pinks self-sow readily.

PLANTAIN LILIES   1–3′   Zones 3–5   *Hosta* genus

A century or more ago plantain lilies were cherished as new plant treasures from the Orient. Naturally, they found a place in gardens along the Eastern seaboard where many of them still flourish despite neglect. Late in the Victorian era they were widely used in beds and borders, then, later, they were largely ignored. Because of their vigor, ease of culture, and adaptability to shade, they have been rediscovered by present-day gardeners. They make excellent ground covers under shrubs and trees and in areas where other plants fail to make a presentable appearance. As accent

Ferns, plantain-lilies, and coleus lend a variety of texture and color to shady borders and require comparatively little care.

Taloumis

plants they have few equals among the hardy perennials, since their foliage retains its freshness all season.

Among the plantain lilies there are large- and small-leaved kinds, some with white margins and others with variegated markings. Blue-green and yellow-green types, as well as some with lustrous dark green foliage are to be found among the kinds available. For textured effects, for accent, or for striking contrasts with smaller leaved plants, these plants have value. Flowers are mostly blue, lavender, or purple, but one kind has showy white flowers. Blooms appear from July to September and make an attractive display while they last, but the foliage surpasses them in many ways.

Perhaps the most imposing of all is *H. sieboldiana,* with large broad leaves of notably glaucous coloring, best described as a gray-blue luster. The August or assumption lily, as it is called, *H. plantaginea,* is valued for its polished yellow-green foliage and showy white fragrant flowers in August. Of the variegated sorts, *H. fortunei marginata alba* is outstanding.

Plantain-lilies are well suited to shady situations. Kinds like Hosta fortunei marginato-alba often spread 3 feet wide.

Genereux

Leaves are large, glossy, and irregularly margined in white, making a very showy plant often spreading 2 feet or more in diameter. Another variety, *H. viridis marginata,* is yellow-green when it first unfolds, with a subtle edge of darker green, but the contrast is less obvious as summer approaches.

The most widely planted of the small-leaved variegated forms is *H. undulata,* with wavy leaves of light green splashed with creamy white markings. Of heavier texture and waxy green, *H. undulata univittata* has creamy bands through the centers of the leaves. *H. lancifolia albo-marginata* has a pencil-like, narrow white border on a long, narrow leaf.

Plain green kinds include *H. caerulea, H. erromena,* and *H. lancifolia.* A recent addition to this notable group of plants is a handsome late-blooming kind named Honeybells, with spikes of lavender flowers 3 feet or more in height, and olive-green foliage.

Plantain lilies grow in average garden soil in sun or shade. If planted in rich loam, they grow to enormous size, especially in shade, for which they are well adapted. One feeding a year in ordinary soil produces good results. Plants are easily divided in spring or fall, or at any time during the growing season. They are completely hardy and seldom affected by pests or diseases.

PHLOX, CREEPING AND TRAILING

Moss Pink	6″	Zone 2	*Phlox subulata*
Camla Phlox	8″	Zone 4	*Phlox nivalis*
Mountain Phlox	6″	Zone 4	*Phlox ovata*
Trailing Phlox	6″	Zone 4	*Phlox procumbens*
Creeping Phlox	1′	Zone 4	*Phlox stolonifera*

Creeping and trailing forms of hardy phlox, particularly the varieties of moss pink (*phlox subulata*), are useful soil binders and general covers, valued for their hardiness, rapid growth, and ease of culture. The evergreen needlelike foliage that forms a flat mat has year-round appeal and the sprawling stems develop roots as they spread.

The common type of moss pink with its magenta flowers clashes with other colors in the garden, but when used in broad masses with the white form it can be most pleasing. However, there are so many superior varieties in shades of pink, red, lavender, and purple, that there is no point in using the common magenta form. J. Herbert Alexander of Middleboro, Massachusetts, has introduced many of them. Hybrids resulting from crossing *P. subulata* with *P. nivalis* have greatly enlarged the possibilities of use for creeping phlox. Larger blossoms, clearer color, and repeat flowering in the autumn are among the aims of the plant breeders. Improved habits, including denser growth and better winter foliage color, are of prime concern from the point of use as ground cover. The variety Alexander's Surprise is valued for its bright pink flowers and its repeat flowering in autumn.

For an inexpensive cover in large rocky areas, creeping phlox is prac-

163

tical and easy to handle. It lends itself to use especially on sloping or hilly terrain. A rapid grower, it is easy to plant, quick to multiply, and thrives in full sun in almost any type of soil, among rocks, on slopes or flat areas. During open winters where zero temperatures are prevalent, it suffers from sun- and windburn and has a somewhat ragged appearance; this is not the case where there is ample snow cover or in regions where the winters are normally mild. Occasionally plantings become infested with witchgrass, which thrives and roots deeply under the foliage of this matting perennial.

Similar to *Phlox subulata* in appearance but somewhat taller and more open in growth is the trailing phlox (*P. nivalis*). The best-known variety is the lovely Camla with salmon-pink blooms 1 inch across. It is not a wild or rampant grower and is ideal for small gardens as a ground cover for limited areas. Rock-garden specialists offer several other outstanding forms introduced by Mrs. J. Norman Henry, noted Pennsylvania plant hunter. Among them is Gladyn, a good white with the repeat-flowering habit, but it is tender north of New York City.

Several species of wild forms of phlox and their hybrids, of interest primarily to wild garden enthusiasts, are by nature well adapted to ground-cover use and are not as frequently planted as they might be. Mountain phlox (*P. ovata*) makes an open mat of growth with deep purple blooms on stems 1 foot or more tall. Trailing phlox (*P. procumbens*), with flowers in the same range, grows about 6 inches high with rosy purple color. Several notable hybrids of creeping phlox (*P. stolonifera*), also introduced by Mrs. Henry, have put this phlox in the class of unusual ground covers for places where there is rich, acid soil and shade.

The various kinds of low-growing phlox are of easy culture and free from serious pests. All can be increased by division in early spring or early fall, or at any time during the growing season if they are given the necessary watering after transplanting. Choice kinds can be propagated by cuttings. The native species respond easily to cultivation and make healthier, denser growth if fed annually with a complete fertilizer. These need attention to soil, on the acid side, and are propagated mostly by division.

ROSES, TRAILING AND CLIMBING. See Chapter 6.

SAINT-JOHN'S-WORT. See Chapter 5.

SAND MYRTLE   15"   Zone 4   *Leiophyllum buxifolium*

One of the choicest and rarest native evergreen ground covers is sand myrtle. Its common name suggests its favorite habitat. The glossy boxlike foliage is borne on open, irregular, wiry branches, makes a billowy evergreen mass of miniature growth that is attractive throughout the year. Native from New Jersey to Florida, it thrives under the same conditions as the heaths and heathers and makes a fitting companion for them. Although full sun suits it best, it will do well in part shade. Pink buds in clusters unfold as fuzzy starlike white flowers appear in May and June. During the cold months the enduring foliage takes on a bronzy cast. In addition to the typical form, there is a compact variety known as Allegheny sand myrtle (*L. lyoni*), which hugs the ground, 6 to 8 inches tall. Both types, depending on the height desired, are suited for large pockets of acid soil among rocks and ledges.

Obtain balled and burlapped or container-grown plants, and set them out in well-prepared sandy, acid soil, using leaf mold and peat, spacing them 1 foot apart. Feed with evergreen fertilizer and water frequently until the plants are established. This is not an easy plant to establish, but the record of success with it is most gratifying.

SAVORY   Zones 5–7   *Satureia* genus

Savory is a flowering herb used to give zest to meats and other foods, but there are several related species that make desirable cover plants. These are dwarf shrubs native to Europe that are sometimes grown in rock and herb gardens. Used as ground covers in rocky, sandy soil for hot, dry situations, they fill this need admirably.

Calamint (*S. calamintha*) is a creeper only a few inches high with pungent leaves and purple flowers from late spring through midsummer. The species *S. globella*, listed by rock-garden specialists, is even more dwarf in habit and ideally suited to terraces and paths. A native of Kentucky, its flowers are tiny purple bells on 3-inch stems. Today, West Coast gardeners use yerba buena (*Micromeria chamissoni*, formerly listed as a savory) for a ground cover, whereas the early settlers considered it primarily a valuable culinary herb with a pleasing minty fragrance. Stems often trail 2 feet or more, bearing tiny white flowers. Winter savory (*S. montana*) is a tall-growing kind, to 15 inches, with tiny lavender flowers in summer. The forms *S. montana pygmaea* and *S. montana subspicata* are compact forms, less than 6 inches tall.

Full sun and gritty soil are the easy requirements for savory. Division or cuttings are the methods home gardeners use to increase their stock. Many kinds can be raised from seed.

SNOW-IN-SUMMER   6"   Zone 2   *Cerastium tomentosum*

To many gardeners, snow-in-summer is little more than a weed. Yet when grown where it is needed, it proves to be one of the handsomest of ground covers through most of the year. It came into use as a plant for rock and wall gardens and it is truly at home among the crevices of rocks in hot, dry situations. The gray woolly foliage makes dense mats studded with starry white flowers in May and June, covering sizable areas in a short time. It keeps down weeds satisfactorily and makes a practical, fast-growing soil binder. When it becomes messy in appearance as a result of trampling or animal damage, shear it back to encourage new growth. The same holds

165

for browning, caused by too much wet weather followed by extreme dry spells. Snow-in-summer is practically indestructible and self-sows readily, but it can be kept under control. Gardeners with difficult rocky sites or sandy banks to be covered in a hurry can make the most of this easy perennial. When it outgrows its space or its usefulness, yank it out.

Division of clumps in early spring or fall, or at any season of the year, and the use of seedling plants, are the usual methods of increase. Poor soil and full sun satisfy its needs.

SPEEDWELL   3″   Zone 5   *Veronica* genus

Veronica, or speedwell as it is sometimes called, rates high for its blue flowers of good color, and there are pink forms as well, but these are not spectacular. All are of easy culture, have clean, persistent foliage, and are practically disease-free. Among them are many dwarf kinds admirably suited to ground-cover use, ranging in height from a few inches to 1 foot or more, including the flower spikes. Some nurseries list a few, but most rock-garden specialists grow them in wide variety.

To gardeners who take pride in their lawns and wage a continual battle against carpeting weeds, mention of creeping speedwell (*V. repens*) causes a shudder. They know it as a mean weed. It thrives in shade, makes a tight, flat mat of glossy foliage that roots as it creeps. It is most useful as a paving plant in shade. Pale blue flowers in spring add to its appearance. Another weedy species is *V. filiformis,* with bright blue and white flowers, nearly evergreen in its matting foliage, and most appealing when in flower. A good paving plant, some gardeners use it as an undercover for primroses. Other kinds for paving and crevice use are *V. armena,* with lacy evergreen foliage and vivid blue flowers for shady locations, and *V. pectinata,* with woolly evergreen leaves, for sunny places. A variety of this species has pink flowers.

Taller growing kinds include the woolly speedwell (*V. incana*), valued for its silvery foliage, only 4 inches high, and brilliant blue flower spikes rising some 6 inches taller. There is a pink form also. Germander speedwell (*V. chamaedrys*) is an evergreen type with excellent matting foliage. Flowers are blue or white, according to the variety. See also Chapter 11.

These are among the better kinds that can be used in broad masses in full sun or light shade for colorful flowers in spring and early summer.

As a group, the speedwells are of the easiest culture in ordinary garden soil in full sun or light shade. All are easily divided in spring or fall. They transplant readily and require a minimum of care.

STONECROP   3–12″   Zone 2   *Sedum* genus

Stonecrops or sedums are weedy plants, but in the seaside garden they can be the most useful of soil binders for checking erosion. On stony locations, on slopes or banks, or among ledges where soil is sparse, the sturdy

166

Genereux

Sempervivums and sedums flourish in the sun and are ideal ground covers for exposed slopes near the sea.

stonecrops have a place. Because of their shallow roots, they are easy to eradicate when they attempt to run away with any given area. Low-growing, free-flowering, and requiring little care, they are often of great use, especially in summer places where low maintenance is essential.

Sedum acre, sometimes called mossy stonecrop, actually grows by the acre in a short time. One of the lowest growing of all, 2 to 3 inches, its flowers make a carpet of gold above miniature evergreen foliage. A white-flowering form that grows twice as tall (*S. album*) also makes a good matting

167

plant. *S. lydium* is another white form. Stringy stonecrop (*S. sarmentosum*) produces its yellow flowers in early summer on stems about 6 inches tall. The so-called two-row stonecrop (*S. spurium*) makes mats of dense growth, is partially evergreen in mild climates, and flowers in midsummer with pink flowers fading to white.

Not all the sedums can be considered commonplace and weedy. Because of their ability to flourish in hot, dry situations, hybridizers have developed some notable improved forms. *S. spurium* is the source of a rich red kind known as Dragon's Blood. It flowers from July on and the general effect is one of varying shades of red from the bronzy tones of buds and stems to the carmine flowers that fade to crimson. The species *S. sieboldi,* with its rounded silvery gray leaves edged with red, grows like a great flat rosette, bearing bright pink flowers in September on gracefully curved stems. Capablanca, a form of *S. spathulifolium,* has blue-green foliage topped with flat heads of yellow bloom in late spring. In variety they are legion and in the proper places are well worth growing.

Ordinary dry soil, even on the poor side, suits all the stonecrops. The smallest bit with a root will grow, and they can stand drought and neglect with ease.

Thrift   4–10″   Zone 1   *Armeria maritima*

Well suited to sandy soils, thrift is one of the easiest of ground covers to grow and increase in hot, dry locations or by the sea. Among rocks, in sandy, gritty soils, on slopes or flat ground, wherever there is good drainage,

Sea thrift is at its best when grown in hot, dry, rocky sites.

Taloumis

Thyme makes a pleasant, fragrant carpet to soften this flagstone terrace. Sumac which flourishes in poor, rocky soil takes on brilliant foliage color in autumn.

this tufted plant grows with ease. At iris time and for a month following, the grasslike mounds are studded with pink, bell-shaped flowers on wiry stems held well above the foliage. Common thrift (*Armeria maritima*) has magenta-pink flowers, while the improved form, *A. maritime laucheana,* native to Greenland, has bright carmine flowers in May with occasional bloom throughout the summer. The variety Six Hills is more dwarf, more compact than the type, with light pink flowers. Thrift makes a desirable companion for heaths and heathers as a mixed ground cover.

Easy to handle, clumps can be divided at any time during the growing season, setting the divisions 8 inches apart. Thrift can be used to make a pattern planting over a large area by setting clumps 1 foot or more apart and mulching the areas between with crushed stone or pebbles. As the cushionlike growth expands in size, it sometimes browns in the centers, an indication that it needs dividing.

THYME, MOTHER-OF-THYME   2–4″   Zone 2   *Thymus serpyllum*

This carpet plant has many forms, both species and varieties, but most useful of all for a flat green cover are forms of *T. serpyllum,* known as mother-of-thyme. There are white, lavender, crimson, and reddish purple flowered varieties, one with white margins and another with yellow coloring in its leaves. Lemon thyme has yellow-green foliage and woolly thyme is

169

just what its name implies, grayish in texture. Bees love thyme and honey from its jewel-like flowers is a delight. A true seaside plant, it is found wild in coastal areas in the warmer parts of Europe and it has become naturalized in many places in the United States.

A green rug for slight slopes, a covering among rocks, dry walks, and ledges, a crevice plant for walls and terraces and for uneven ground surfaces, thyme is at its best in the sun. Several kinds, or as many as you can collect, will make a bank that you will enjoy working around. The common thyme (*T. vulgaris*) makes a broad, shrubby mound 6 inches or more in height and the hairy stemmed kind (*T. lanicaulis*) makes a down-covered mound of pinkish lavender, 6 inches high and many times as wide. There are many other kinds, some carpeting and others shrubby, all worth growing.

A hot, dry, rocky soil on the poor side where the sun shines all day is the best place for thyme. Since the smallest portion with a root will grow, there is no need to start it from seed unless the aim is to grow some species not easily available. Thyme likes lime, but grows in acid soil.

VERBENA   8–12″   Zone 2   *Verbena bipinnatifida*

For hot, dry situations there are several perennial verbenas well adapted to rough areas in seaside gardens. *V. bipinnatifida,* from the Dakotas, has crinkly foliage on creeping stems a few inches tall and purple flowers that appear from late spring till frost. A faster growing kind is *V. canadensis,* with reddish purple flowers on 8-inch stems that make roots as they trail. It is free-flowering and vigorous and, like all the verbenas, grows well in sandy soils.

Well-drained locations assure their permanence. Full sun and sandy or gravelly soil are their only requirements. Increase by cuttings or division of the roots, or they can be grown from seed. Once established, these perennials tend to self-sow.

WINTERCREEPER. See Chapter 9.

WOOLLY YARROW   6″   Zone 2   *Achillea tomentosa*

Yarrows are generally thought of as weedy perennials for use in hot, dry places in gardens where space is abundant. The woolly yarrow is valued for its pleasing silvery green, matlike, evergreen habit and the showy heads of bright yellow bloom that appear in early summer on 6-inch stems. Where several kinds of ground covers are needed in rocky areas or sandy places, it is worth growing. It can be used among flagstones for it can be stepped on without harm. A form known as Moonlight is greener in color, slower to spread, and carries flowers of a lighter yellow. There is also a compact form (*A. tomentosa nana*) of tight-growing habit with small white flowers.

Poor soil and a hot, dry location are best for this low perennial. Increase it by division at any time during the growing season.

170

CHAPTER ELEVEN

Hardy Perennials

ARDY PERENNIALS are indispensable in coastal gardens where continuity of color is desired. Many of the sturdier kinds are reliably hardy and long-lived when grown in well-drained locations, but they require considerable care and maintenance. These facts should be borne in mind when making choices and selecting places in the garden where they are to be used. Then, too, a perennial border planned and planted for a succession of bloom from spring until hard frost requires considerable space and should be at least 8 to 9 feet wide if it is to be effective. In fact, the labor required for maintenance often precludes the use of herbaceous plants in this way. However, perennials can be adapted for use in broad masses to create striking effects with low-growing shrubs, in the foreground of shrub borders, with evergreens, in rock gardens, for ground cover, or for naturalizing.

A list of perennials chosen for a protected seaside garden would not differ greatly from a selection made for an inland garden except in one or two respects. Plants with blue-green, gray and silvery foliage are practically a must in coastal gardens, since many of them are native to such sites in their natural habitat. These include several of the artemisias, especially Silver King and Silver Mound, catmint, dusty miller, false indigo, globe thistle, lamb's ears, lavender, lavender cotton, pinks, sea holly, and others. The gray or silvery effect is the result of the fine hairs on the leaves, usually on both surfaces. These hairs reflect so much light as to conceal the true green color of the leaf surface which is more readily apparent on a rainy day when moisture darkens the hairs. The intensity of the gray effect varies according to kind, and young new growth is always more gray or silvery. The tiny hairs protect the leaf surface from summer heat, wind, and salt spray, conserving moisture and lessening transpiration. When doused with salt water, the salt crystals are caught in the hairy surface and cause no damage to the leaf itself.

171

Genereux

Dusty miller is distinctive for its rich texture and gray foliage.

Because of their distinct coloring texture, they have special merit for contrasting and enhancing the appearance and beauty of plants with showy bloom. Gray and silvery textured foliage makes blue flowers appear bluer; pink, brighter and clearer; and yellow, richer and more intense. It adds a lustrous appearance to the various greens and is the great harmonizer and blender of color in any garden, and holds special eye appeal when grown by the sea. It can be used lavishly to good advantage.

Many of our hardy perennials are deep-rooted, vigorous in growth, and reliably hardy, and they are usually long-lived as well. Among them are balloon flower, bleeding heart, day lilies, false spirea, gas plant, hardy asters, iris, Oriental poppies, peonies, phlox, plantain lilies, the various sedums, and other weedy kinds mentioned later in this chapter. On the other hand, the various hybrid strains of delphinium are usually short-lived, and are best grown from seed and treated as biennials. Some types such as chrysanthemum, dianthus, phlox, Shasta daisies, veronica, and violas require frequent division to maintain healthy stock.

A sizable number of perennials, once established, become weedy. While they are most useful in large gardens for naturalizing and for ground cover, especially as soil binders, they soon outgrow the small place. However, in seaside gardens where space permits, they are a notable asset. Choose those you plant thoughtfully, since they are likely to be yours for a long time. Among them are achillea, beebalm, boltonia, evening primrose, false dragonhead, hardy sunflowers, hollyhocks, widow's tears, practically all the sedums, and many others.

Perennials need to be evaluated for their foliage as well as for their bloom. With few exceptions the flowering period of most kinds is brief, but the foliage of the majority of perennials lasts throughout the growing year. A prime consideration is foliage that endures dry weather and wind, is not susceptible to disease, is pleasing in form and texture, and retains a fresh appearance through the summer months. Practically all the plants with gray or silvery foliage fit this category. Peonies, iris, plantain lilies, day lilies, gas plant, balloon flower, and others are also in this group.

When perennials are thoughtfully selected and placed, they are even more ornamental if given a suitable setting or background. This may be a wall, a fence, a hedge, a large rock, or a group of evergreens or deciduous shrubs. Perennials are being used more and more in large planters, urns, pots, and boxes to good advantage. However, desired effects are often lost where one or two each of a dozen kinds are used instead of broad masses of 2 or 3 kinds. Groups of 3, 5, or 7 of a single perennial arranged in broad masses or drifts are preferable for satisfying landscape effects. Consider foliage, time of bloom, intensity of color and combinations of color, to create a harmonious mass in which there is variety in form and texture. By using perennials in this manner, emphasis is placed on their value in the over-all planting scheme.

The problem of succession of bloom with perennials is simplified if some annuals are used. From mid-July through September annuals are at their best, and they can be combined effectively to sustain the continuity of bloom which every gardener longs for.

When perennials are planted in small units, soil preparation includes the addition of organic matter and a complete fertilizer mixed in the usual manner. If plants are set out early in spring while still dormant, or as new growth is emerging, they are frequently sold bare-root. (Later in the season, they are offered in containers.) Holes must be large enough to accommodate roots without crowding. Cut back damaged or broken roots and any exceptionally long stringy segments. Set crowns at the same level at which they grew in the nursery, and firm the soil around roots. When the hole is nearly level with the adjoining soil, fill it with water and allow it to drain away before adding the remainder of the soil. When planting is completed, provision must be made for the settling of the soil so that there are no low areas where moisture can collect after heavy rains or when plants are watered. A few kinds like iris and peonies and poppies are more exacting in their requirements and methods of handling. These are discussed separately.

Drainage is essential for the survival of all perennials. It is a mistake to plant them in places where water stands after heavy rains or during the winter.

Spacing to allow for normal development and to provide air circulation for each plant is essential. The general rule for spacing is half the mature height, which may seem strange when small plants or typical nursery divisions are used. Yet plants need ample space for normal development. Slow-growing kinds and those which do not multiply rapidly may be set closer.

MOVING PLANTS IN BLOOM

Perennials with compact root systems can be moved successfully when in bud or bloom if precautions are taken. Among these are chrysanthemums, coral bells, false spirea, plantain lilies, phlox, primroses, violas, and other shallow-rooted kinds. Avoid this practice with balloon flower, day lilies, gas plant, lupines, peonies, and other deep-rooted kinds unless they are container-grown. Soak the soil thoroughly around the plant to be moved before digging. Use a sharp spade to cut straight down on all four sides; lift with as large a ball of soil as can be obtained, and place it in its new location. Another soaking is then needed. Shade provided by a fruit basket, long-stemmed brush, or lightweight cloth (suspended on stakes) kept on for several days will give the plant an opportunity to become reestablished with a minimum of shock. Then do not allow it to dry out.

Hollyhocks have been favorites in seaside gardens since the 17th century when they were first brought to New England.

GENERAL CARE

Maintenance is essential for top results with perennials and some require more attention than others. To encourage vigor and heavy flowering, remove dead flowers to prevent seed production. Booster feedings with fertilizer in liquid or dry form encourage new growth and improve the size of secondary bloom.

Pinching. With the exception of bleeding heart, day lilies, iris, peonies, plantain lilies, and poppies, most kinds are benefited by pinching out top growth. When growth is 4 to 6 inches tall, remove the top inch or two of growth on each stem to induce side shoots for sturdier stems and maximum

175

Marshmallow with flowers of white, pink, or red borne on 4- to 6-foot stems, brightens the seaside landscape in late summer.

flowering. With chrysanthemums and hardy asters, several pinchings are needed. Sturdy stems mean less staking for tall kinds. Perennials grown in varying degrees of shade need this treatment; otherwise they may become rank in growth.

Thinning. Perennials that produce many stems from the base, such as Michaelmas daisies and phlox, may need to have some growth cut out to allow for good air circulation. This practice helps to check mildew on lower stems and foliage.

Staking. Painted bamboo stakes (available in several lengths) tied with "twistems" make the task of supporting heavy stems easy and keep plants tidy.

Feeding. Booster feedings for perennials (at 2 to 3 week intervals) are usually needed on thin soils, especially those of sandy texture, since plant food is leached out quickly.

Mulching. See Chapter 18.

Watering. Adequate moisture is essential for perennials and the frequency of watering depends on the use of mulches and weather conditions. It is far better to water thoroughly once a week than to give plants a light sprinkling every few days.

PLANTING A BORDER

If a border is contemplated, a rough plan to make placement easy and effective is basic practice. Using a convenient scale, such as 1 inch equals 5 feet, plot the area. Then indicate the placement of each kind, according to height: those for the background, middle area, and foreground. Rules for spacing as outlined above aid in determining the number of plants in each group. Balance can be achieved without making a severely geometric pattern. In fact, masses of each kind can be so arranged as to flow together in irregular drifts. Identify each unit with a key number. The planting key is a list containing plant names, number of plants, distance apart, and time of bloom.

The entire area to be planted needs to be dug and turned over to a depth of 18 to 24 inches. Add organic material and a complete fertilizer as discussed in Chapters 15 and 16.

A SELECTED LIST OF DEPENDABLE PERENNIALS

For the most part, the perennials described in the following pages thrive in average garden soil. A few like iris, peonies, and others require special culture which is given in detail. Practically all the perennials discussed are well suited to full sun and no special mention is made of this fact in describing them. However, a considerable number are suited to varying degrees of shade, under deep-rooted trees, among shrubs, or in the shadows of buildings, fences, and walls. These conditions exist in many seaside gardens and it is important that those best suited to such situations be planted when they give satisfactory results. The relative amount of subdued light the various kinds can endure is indicated by the following code:

LS (Light Shade)   SS (Semi-Shade)   DS (Deep Shade)

Flowering period as indicated by months refers to the appearance of primary bloom and the period during which secondary crops of flowers may be expected normally. It should not be interpreted to mean a continuous display of abundant color for any given kind. Rather, as with day lilies, phlox, and others, if several varieties are planted, continuity of bloom is assured.

Many low-growing perennials well suited to use as ground covers are described in Chapter 10.

ARTEMISIA. See Wormwood; see Ground Covers, Chapter 10.

ASTERS, HARDY. See Michaelmas daisies.

ASTILBE. See False spirea.

Erigeron, a California native, flourishes on the beach at Carmel, California.

BALLOON FLOWER   1½–2′   LS–SS   JULY–SEPTEMBER
Platycodon grandiflorum

There are comparatively few blue-flowering perennials that are more rewarding for the seaside garden than balloon flower. So called because the buds look like tiny balloons, the blue, white, or lavender cup-shaped flowers that may be single or double, according to the type grown, are borne in large terminal clusters. The glaucous foliage carried on sturdy stems remains fresh throughout the growing year and turns golden yellow in autumn. Deep-rooted, permanent, and dependable, balloon flower needs staking in shade unless the dwarf form (*P. mariesi*) is grown. It is more easily grown from seed than divided because of its long taproots. This old standby often self-sows and can be expected to remain in the garden over a long period of years.

BARRENWORT. See Ground Covers, Chapter 10.

BEACH PEA   9′   JULY–SEPTEMBER   *Lathyrus maritimus*

The beach pea (*Lathyrus maritimus*) frequently found growing in pure sand or scrambling over rocks, is native to the Eastern seaboard. Actually a sprawling perennial, given the slightest encouragement it becomes a most attractive vine. Its counterpart on the West Coast is *L. littoralis*. Whatever the location of a seaside garden, there is usually a suitable spot for some native plants and beach pea should be one of them. A related species from Europe, formerly listed in catalogs but now seldom seen, is the perennial pea, *L. latifolius*. Known for its vigor, growing to 9 feet or more, it is rather weedy in habit but highly decorative, free-flowering, and easily adapted to seaside conditions. In fact, it sometimes occurs in naturalized plantings along the New England coast as a garden escape along with globe thistle, day lilies, and other sturdy perennials.

Both the foliage and the blossoms of all these peas have unusual ornamental value and, like many another wilding, were they rare exotics, we would cultivate them with care.

All these hardy peas can be started from seed and transplanted, when large enough to handle, to more permanent locations. The native kinds can be collected with the aid of patience and a long spade. Root divisions can be made in early spring or fall.

BEACH WORMWOOD. See Chapter 11.

BEEBALM   2–3′   LS–SS   JUNE–AUGUST   *Monarda* genus

The showy heads of red, pink, or lavender flowers (depending on the species or named variety) which are borne on sturdy, squarish stems, are loved by bees and hummingbirds. Several improved forms are offered by leading nurserymen. A rapid grower with clean foliage that is minty when crushed, this old-time native perennial is also known as bergamot and Oswego tea. It spreads by underground stems and needs room, but can be kept in place by frequent dividing. Well suited to naturalizing, especially in moist locations, it provides abundant color in early summer. Increase is by division in spring or fall.

BELLFLOWER, PEACHLEAF   1½–3′   LS–SS   JUNE–JULY   *Campanula persicifolia*

The slender spikes of white or lavender-blue flowers rise from tufts of peachlike, durable foliage, providing graceful effects, particularly when grown in sizable drifts. It develops clumps by means of underground stems, and needs division and resetting every 2 to 3 years. Easily raised from seed, it tends to self-sow once established. Effective under trees and tall shrubs with ferns for a background, the peachleaf bellflower is also a desirable border plant in full sun for accent. Divide plants in spring or fall, or after flowering.

BLEEDING HEART   1½–2′   LS–SS   APRIL–JUNE   *Dicentra spectabilis*

The pink heart-shaped flowers of this old-time perennial are borne on graceful, arching stems and make a notable display for 4 weeks or more. Unfortunately, the attractive glaucous foliage dies down in midsummer. Bleeding heart combines most effectively with ferns and an underplanting of blue phlox, Jacob's ladder, spotted lungwort, and other spring flowers. It makes an ideal background plant for spring bulbs. Frequently it self-sows, and numerous small plants may be obtained if the area around an established clump is left undisturbed until late spring. Look for seedlings and move them to desirable locations, since divisions of this perennial are more expensive than most kinds. Large plants are best moved as early in the spring as growth shows or when the foliage is dying down. See also Plumy bleeding heart.

BLOODROOT   6–10″   SS–DS   APRIL–MAY   *Sanguinaria canadensis*

Essentially a woodland plant, the dainty single white flowers appear as the bold, deeply cut foliage is unfolding. An easy wilding to establish in mats with other native plants, it is well suited to naturalistic plantings. The double form bears long-lasting miniature peonylike blooms, which greatly enhance such ground covers as English ivy. It is no plant for thin, sandy soil, preferring woodsy soil rich in leaf mold. Divide roots in late summer when plants are dormant.

BLUE PHLOX   15″   LS–SS   MAY–JUNE   *Phlox divaricata*

Drifts of rich blue or lavender flowers make their appearance on slender stems at tulip time. Once established, it forms dense mats, spreading by underground stems, and makes a refined ground cover by itself or with foam flower and other native wildings of moderate growth. Divide plants after flowering and feed to stimulate growth. Few gardeners ever have too much of it, even when it self-sows freely. Ideal for naturalizing, blue phlox or wild sweet William as it is sometimes called, is notable for its long-lasting blooms that make a show for several weeks.

BUGLEWEED. See Ground Covers, Chapter 10.

CARDINAL FLOWER   3′   LS–SS   JULY–AUGUST   *Lobelia cardinalis*

The showy spikes of rich red flowers are carried on sturdy stems, making stately clumps in beds and borders or among shrubs. Like beebalm, this native is a prime favorite of hummingbirds. The foliage holds up well throughout the season. Although native to moist conditions, usually found along stream banks, it adapts itself well to fertile loamy garden soil. It is easily raised from seed, or established clumps may be divided in early spring or after flowering.

CATMINT   1–2½′   LS   JUNE–AUGUST   *Nepeta mussini*

Catmint is a loose, billowy, moundlike perennial with silvery gray foliage and slender spikes of lavender-blue flowers in early spring. Among the hardiest of perennials, it grows about 15 inches high and spreads as wide, making an attractive border or edging for shrub plantings or big-scale perennial borders. It is also effective in drifts among low-growing shrubs or on rocks for its soft gray effect. Particularly striking with creeping rose and mugho pine, it is a favorite perennial in English gardens and ought to be more widely planted. Catnip (*N. cataria*) to which it is related is a much coarser and taller plant. An improved form of catmint known as Blue Beauty is more upright in habit with larger flower stems, some with 2-foot stems. The species *N. tatarica* offered in recent years grows to 2½ feet with lilac-colored blooms.

Give catmint full sun, ordinary, even poor soil, a well-drained location, and it will flourish. Cut back heavily after first flowering to encourage new growth. Increase it by division of the roots in spring or fall. Cuttings can be rooted easily in early summer.

CHRISTMAS ROSE   1′   LS–SS   NOVEMBER–APRIL   *Helleborus niger*

Whether grown in a seaside garden or inland, this worthy perennial needs a protected location. The single white flowers that change to pink and purple with age are highly cherished when they appear. Many seaside gardeners along the Atlantic seaboard and on the West Coast enjoy the blooms at Christmas. Flowering may be from November to April, depending on protection, size of the plant, location, and the ability to establish it. To enjoy the flowers to the fullest, protect with evergreen boughs or a simple frame covered with glass. A bushel box with the bottom removed and an old window sash will suffice. Well-drained humusy soil, not too acid, and a sheltered location are needed. This may be among rhododendrons, yews, or other types of broad-leaved or needle evergreens. The foliage is evergreen, forming heavy clumps as the plants mature. Plants offered by nurseries are usually small divisions that require several years to develop sufficient size to produce abundant bloom. Feeding with superphosphate induces better flowering. Also consider the Lenten rose, *H. orientalis*, which flowers in early spring. Neither is happy in summer sun.

CHRYSANTHEMUM   1–3′   LS   SEPTEMBER–NOVEMBER

Chrysanthemum genus

The beauty of any autumn garden is greatly enriched by the multitude of chrysanthemum varieties that bloom freely until hard frost. Essentially sun-loving perennials, yet suitable for light shade, they flower well even in semishade if there is adequate direct light. There are so many distinct types worth growing that no garden is complete without a few.

The cushion mums or azaleamums, valued for their moundlike habit, are among the earliest to bloom and are usually exceptionally hardy. Both the single and the double Korean hybrids are equally noteworthy for their winter-hardy qualities. Various double hybrids introduced during the past 20 years include those with buttonlike flowers, the pompon types, and the large decorative varieties. Others have spoonlike ray petals while those called spider chrysanthemums are distinguished by threadlike petals.

The usual practice is to divide clumps annually in spring, setting single-stemmed divisions one foot apart each way. Since this method often perpetuates nematodes, healthier plants result from rooted cuttings. These are taken in early May, selecting sturdy top growth 4 to 6 inches long. Cuttings are inserted in a mixture of sand and peat moss and kept moist until roots form. Young plants need to be pinched hard 2 or 3 times during the growing season from May to August 1st to induce bushy growth and the maximum number of flower buds. Pinching also eliminates staking, except with fall varieties.

Because of their shallow root systems, chrysanthemums often winter-kill due to heaving in mild winter weather or as a result of excess water and ice on the crowns. Growing plants on a slight slope assures good drainage for wintering. After the ground has frozen hard, cover with marsh hay, straw, or evergreen boughs. Roots of favorite kinds can be wintered easily and safely in a cold frame by lifting them after flowering and cutting off tops at soil level before replanting in the frame.

COLUMBINE   1–3′   LS   MAY–JULY   *Aguilegia* genus

The color range of these showy perennials runs the gamut of the rainbow, but the glaucous foliage has little value after midsummer. Well-drained soil is essential for longevity. Many species and strains including the McKana hybrids are easily raised from seed; once established, columbines self-sow readily. Since long taproots make division of clumps difficult, young plants or small seedlings are easiest to handle.

CORALBELLS 1½–2′ **LS** **MAY–SEPTEMBER** *Heuchera sanguinea*

In any list of perennials, coralbells belong among the top ten for their free-flowering habit, disease resistance, and general dependability. The tiny pink, coral, or white bells (depending on the variety) appear in airy racemes on sturdy stems rising from compact clumps of attractive heart-shaped foliage. Colorful, long-lasting, and showy, they are essential even in the smallest garden, both for cuttings and for their landscape value. Use them for trim borders or in generous drifts with other perennials or in the rock garden. Well-drained average soil, even on the gritty side, suits them. In heavily acid soil, add lime annually. Divide every 3 years in spring or early fall.

DAME'S ROCKET 2–3′ **LS–SS** **JUNE–SEPTEMBER** *Hesperis matronalis*

Denizens of Colonial dooryards, the fragrant white, lavender, or purple flowers of dame's rocket or sweet rocket are borne in loose panicles resembling somewhat those of hardy phlox. A good filler plant, it is often short-lived, but self-sows and naturalizes readily, sometimes becoming weedy if not controlled. Effective among ferns and low-growing shrubs, this old-time plant is a desirable cutflower, well suited to gardens where minimum care is essential.

DAY LILY 2–5′ **LS–SS** **MAY–SEPTEMBER** *Hemerocallis* genus

The trumpet-shaped flowers range from pale yellow through deepest red and are held aloft on sturdy stems (scapes), but each lasts only a day. Sturdy in growth, free-flowering, showy, and permanent, day lilies are good

Day lilies are sturdy, long-lived perennials with heavy root systems tolerant of dry soils and full sun or a fair amount of shade.

Taloumis

soil binders because of their heavy roots. Hundreds of varieties are offered by specialists and this makes it possible to enjoy a continuous display of bloom from May through September. These big-scale plants with graceful arching foliage need ample room.

Day lilies multiply rapidly and can be divided every 3 years. Plant in spring or fall; dividing can be done after flowering if desired. Not only adaptable to sun or shade, the common types can be used in hot, dry places, even in poor soil. However, the high-priced hybrids should be given attention until well established. Bear in mind that an individual clump of day lilies requires 3 to 4 square feet of space for adequate development.

DUSTY MILLER. See Ground covers, Chapter 10.

DWARF ANCHUSA   15″   LS–SS   MAY–JUNE   *Brunnera macrophylla*

Frequently listed as *Anchusa myosotidiflora*, the rich blue forget-me-not-like flowers that appear with late daffodils and tulips last several weeks. Although the large, heart-shaped foliage is coarse in texture, it is useful under shrubs as a cover plant. Dwarf anchusa self-sows readily, is hardy, long-lived, and requires little care. A few plants left to themselves usually make a sizable colony over a period of several years.

EVENING PRIMROSE   18–24″   LS   JUNE–AUGUST   *Oenothera tetragona*

An excellent seaside perennial well suited to sandy soil, the evening primrose is often listed as *O. fruticosa youngii*. True, it is a weedy perennial, but is greatly valued for its bronzy green foliage and yellow, cup-shaped flowers borne in great profusion in early summer. Where space permits, it is desirable for its over-all effect. Since it spreads by underground roots, is hardy and long-lived, it can be used to advantage in large plantings, especially for naturalizing and for ground cover.

FALSE DRAGONHEAD   1½–3′   LS–SS   JULY–SEPTEMBER   *Physostegia*

The pink, rose, or white tubular flowers are borne in showy spikes on sturdy stems. This plant makes a sizable mass of growth if not kept in control. Growth is sturdy and the glossy foliage keeps fresh throughout the growing year. Because it spreads rapidly, false dragonhead may become weedy, but is useful for its display of bloom and its easy culture, where there is room. Annual division keeps it within bounds.

FALSE INDIGO   4′   LS   MAY–JUNE   *Baptisia australis*

This stately shrublike perennial bears spikes of indigo-blue, lupinelike flowers, glaucous foliage of enduring quality, and conspicuous, decorative seedpods. Deep-rooted, disease-free, and long-lived, it is highly ornamental until cut down by frost. It makes a desirable backdrop for lower peren-

184

Astilbe is at its best where it gets shade part of the day.

nials and needs ample room for development. Ordinary soil suits it even when sandy in texture. Plants are increased by seed or division of the roots.

FALSE SPIREA   1½–4′   LS–SS   JUNE–JULY   *Astilbe* genera

This plant is one of the highlights of the early summer garden with its showy plumes of white, pink, or red, according to the kind grown. Since a wide range in height exists among the varieties, striking massed effects can be achieved. The fernlike foliage is durable and attractive except in dry weather, but even prolonged dryness does not kill plants. It prefers a moist, humusy soil, and is hardy, long-lived, and desirable. Low kinds make attractive borders or edges. One of the best perennials for shade, stock is easily increased by dividing every 2 or 3 years in spring or fall.

FLEECEFLOWER. See Chapter 10.

FOAM FLOWER. See Chapter 10.

FORGET-ME-NOT   8″   LS–SS   APRIL–JULY   *Myosotis* genus

Favorite border plant of spring gardens, flowers of the forget-me-not may be white, blue, or pink. All have soft green foliage. They thrive in moist soil and self-sow readily, but are well suited to average garden conditions, except in dry situations. Most kinds sold are biennials, but their seeding habit gives them an effect of permanence. Ideal companion plants for spring bulbs, they are also good foreground fillers among taller perennials, or for naturalizing.

FOXGLOVE   4′   LS–SS   JUNE–JULY   *Digitalis* genus

The most familiar kinds (forms of *D. purpurea*) are those with white or pinkish purple flower spikes. Improved forms, the Shirley and Excelsior hybrids, have a much wider color range including apricot. Very showy, foxgloves make dramatic spires of bloom in shady areas. These are all biennials, self-sowing readily, but some plants may live over to bloom a third year. Where space is available they naturalize, creating impressive effects for a month or more in early summer. True perennial kinds include *D. ambigua,* with pale yellow flowers, but not particularly showy.

FUNKIA. See Plantain lily.

GAS PLANT   3′   LS   JUNE–JULY   *Dictamnus albus*

Deep-rooted, long-lived, and dependable once established, gas plant is important in any group of perennials and requires little care. Spikes of white or pink flowers standing well above a shrubby mass of glossy foliage appear at peony time. Each plant requires 3 to 4 square feet when established. When setting out, transplant seedlings or small container-grown plants, since big clumps are difficult to move because of the heavy, deep-rooting habit.

GLOBE THISTLE   4′   JULY–AUGUST   *Echinops ritro*

A rugged perennial with stiff stems and coarse thistlelike leaves that are white on the undersurface, globe thistle bears steel-blue globular heads of bloom, 2 to 3 inches in diameter. It creates a strong accent in borders and belongs in seaside gardens with clumps of pink and white phlox. A popular long-lasting cut flower, it is much sought after for dried bouquets. Suited to sandy soils, it is a plant for full sun. Increase is by root division in early spring.

GLOBEFLOWER   1–2′   LS   MAY–JULY   *Trollius* genus

The large buttercuplike flowers in varying shades of yellow and orange show to good advantage on sturdy stems. Equally attractive, the foliage retains its vigor and freshness in moist, humusy soil, but globeflower is not well suited to naturally dry conditions. Plants make sizable clumps and usually need division every 3 years.

GOLDENROD   2–3′   JULY–SEPTEMBER   *Solidago* genus

One of the most colorful and enduring native perennials found in sandy and rocky places along the East Coast is the seaside goldenrod (*Soli-*

186

Seaside goldenrod blooms among clumps of beachgrass in a sand dune.

dago sempervirens), but few would consider it worthy of a place in gardens unless natural effects are sought. Yet in England and elsewhere in Europe, goldenrod is cultivated and holds a place of honor in beds and borders. Among the improved forms is the variety Golden Mosa that grows 3 feet tall with handsome sprays of lemon yellow plumes in August and September. Peter Pan averages 2½ feet in height and flowers in July with warmer yellow coloring. Primrose Cascade, slightly under 2 feet in height, with primrose yellow bloom of eye-catching beauty, makes a display from mid-August on. Unfortunately, the pollen of goldenrod is troublesome to some people, but, for those who can grow it, the improved forms of this useful perennial belong in seaside gardens.

Full sun and ordinary garden soil suit goldenrod. Clumps may be divided in spring or fall.

HARDY AGERATUM   2′   LS–SS   AUGUST–OCTOBER   *Eupatorium coelestinum*

Easily recognized by its typical ageratumlike blue flowers and foliage in late summer and early fall, hardy ageratum is also called mistflower. This perennial with its matlike root system makes sizable drifts, but it

187

is easily controlled with a sharp trowel or spade. Shallow-rooted, it does best in moist, humusy soil and is good for naturalizing.

GOLD DUST. See Chapter 10.

GOUTWEED. See Chapter 10.

HARDY CANDYTUFT   1′   LS   MAY–JUNE   *Iberis sempervirens*

Actually a dwarf shrub, this low, sprawling plant has semievergreen foliage and fits naturally into seaside gardens. The snow-white flowers are borne in great abundance. Candytuft makes an excellent border or it can be used in large drifts with mugho pines, goldentuft, artemisia, silver mound, and others. There are several improved forms including one called Little Gem. Cut plants back hard after flowering to induce compact new growth. Plants can be divided after flowering or stock may be increased by cuttings.

IRIS   6″–3′   LS   APRIL–JULY   *Iris* genus

There are not only many distinct types of iris suitable for home gardens, but the number of varieties in several categories is ever on the increase.

Bearded or German iris with its extensive color range rivaling that of the rainbow, stands at the top of the list. An individual bloom is composed of 3 upper petals or "standards" and 3 lower petals or "falls." The sword-like foliage remains decorative and attractive from spring to late fall.

Dwarf iris (*I. pumila*) and the intermediate hybrids have flowers and foliage of similar form but are low-growing.

Siberian iris (*I. sibirica*) is distinguished by slender foliage and small purple or white flowers of distinctive form.

Japanese iris (*I. kaempferi*) belongs in the spectacular class, with large flat blooms, rich in color and texture. It flourishes in moist, humusy soil, producing its bloom in June and July.

In addition, there are numerous worthwhile species including the roof iris (*I. tectorum*), the Louisiana iris, the spuria hybrids, the bulbous types, the vesper iris for summer bloom, and others.

Bearded iris is best grown in full sun. Give it a well-drained location and soil of average fertility. Where acidity runs high, an annual side dressing with ground limestone scattered lightly around each clump in early spring is desirable. The most annoying pests are iris borer and rhizome rot. Clumps need dividing every 3 or 4 years and this is best done after flowering, through August, so that the divisions are well established before winter. Late fall transplanting often causes plants to heave unless they are well mulched.

Dig clumps and shake all soil off the roots. Cut the foliage back to 6 inches from the base of the rhizome (as the starchy root is called). Examine carefully for borer damage and decay, cutting out all damaged parts including old shriveled portions of the rhizomes. Select only healthy, firm divisions, resetting them in well-prepared soil. Plant singly or in groups, allowing 8 inches of space each way, and cover the rhizomes lightly with soil (less than an inch). The long stringlike roots can be cut back to a few inches. Water to help settle the soil around the roots.

JACOB'S LADDER   **1′**   **LS–SS**   **MAY–JUNE**   *Polemonium caeruleum*

This spring-flowering carpeting plant with its clusters of soft blue bells and lacy foliage would be a much more satisfactory ground cover were it not for its habit of becoming dormant in midsummer. Effective among ferns, it spreads and seeds readily and is easily divided in spring or fall.

Japanese iris provides abundant color in early summer.

Genereux

Lamb's ears, a neat-growing silvery-textured edging perennial.

LAMB'S EARS   1'   LS   JULY   *Stachys lanata*

The name of this low perennial—lamb's-ears or lamb's-tongue—
vividly describes the appearance of the gray woolly foliage. It is also called
woolly betony. In rock gardens and herb plantings where its texture is
valued, and as an edging plant, it has been commonly grown for centuries.
As a ground cover for limited areas in sunny, well-drained, slightly sloping
areas, it is a plant to remember, giving the effect of coolness in hot weather.
Thinking of heather plantings interspersed with patches of thrift, here is
another companion plant for sandy mounds. Great sheets of lamb's-ears
used in front of pink floribunda roses in a seaside garden created a picture
I shall long remember. In another effective way, this gray-textured perennial has been used as a foreground for coralbells. Spikes of reddish purple
bloom, 1 foot or more tall, appear in early summer, but some gardeners
cut them off, preferring the silvery mats of foliage for their enduring beauty
throughout the entire growing season.

Full sun and ordinary light soil, even of gritty texture, suit it best.
When grown in heavy loam or in a fair amount of shade, it languishes and
rots and looks sick. Division of clumps, which are of creeping habit, can
be done at any time during the growing season.

190

English lavender is one of the best-loved of old-time plants and rates high in the list of fragrant herbs. Actually, because of its woody stems, botanists classify it as a subshrub, but it is usually listed as a perennial in most catalogs. Widely grown in borders and rock gardens, it is sometimes used as a low hedge. No herb garden is complete without it. In bygone days the essential oil was highly prized as a cure for many ailments. The kind commonly grown, *L. spica,* and its various dwarf forms, are not always hardy in the colder regions of the Northeast. In all parts of the Mediterranean regions it grows abundantly in the wild state, while in the south of France and to some extent in England it is cultivated widely for its essential oil. Like rosemary and thyme, it has long-time associations with seaside gardens.

The delightful fragrance of the grayish, evergreen foliage, which persists through the winter, the even more potent scent of the flowers, and the whole aspect of the plant, plus its folk associations, make it a much-cherished plant for gardens. A dozen clumps spaced 18 inches apart each way are the makings of a foliage mass as lovely as any spreading juniper in the silvery effect, and a fragrant, sun-loving ground cover as well. Combined with pink, yellow, and deep blue flowering annuals and perennials, lavender greatly enhances the beauty of these colors.

There are many horticultural forms of lavender, both natural hybrids and man-made, some with broader leaves than others, which may send up flower spikes to 2 feet or more. Dwarf kinds easily obtainable are Munstead, with lavender flowers about 15 inches tall, and Twickle Purple, which grows about 10 inches high with rich purple flowers on a compact, slow-growing plant. Other species for the collector to grow and revel in are numerous, but not easily available. Helen M. Fox tells about them with enthusiasm in her delightful book, *The Years in My Herb Garden.*

Well-drained garden soil, on the light, gritty side, in full sun, suits lavender best. It can be grown from cuttings or from seed, but most gardeners obtain plants bare-root from growers in early spring as field-grown clumps, or in containers. Raising from seed is an easy way to get a good stock of plants. Seed sown in May will produce plants large enough to live through winter in the open except where winters are unusually severe. Pinch seedlings once or twice to develop bushy plants. Go slow on fertilizer.

Shearing established plants in early spring induces dense growth, and division every three or four years is essential to keep plants vigorous. Winter damage sometimes necessitates pruning to the ground. Lavender's lack of complete winter hardiness in cold New England was recorded nearly three centuries ago by John Josselyn, but nonetheless gardeners have been growing it and cherishing it all through the years. Much of the difficulty with winterkill, particularly of the entire plant, can be attributed to heavy soil and poor drainage.

LAVENDER COTTON   15"   *Santolina chamaecyparissus*

This dwarf spreading shrub with silvery gray, pungent, evergreen foliage rates a place in every seaside garden. Native to the Mediterranean region, it became a favorite in herb gardens centuries ago, often as a trim dwarf hedge, since it lends itself well to shearing. However, lavender cotton is at its best when allowed to grow naturally, developing into a loose open mound, 18 inches or more in diameter. Well suited as a ground cover in sunny places, among rocks, or in gritty or sandy soil, it needs the best of drainage to survive winter dampness. Distinctive in appearance and in texture, its effect is heightened greatly when planted with masses of bright green foliage of coarser texture, such as the mugho pine or drifts of brightly colored perennials and annuals. Yellow buttonlike flowers appear in summer, but they are of little value.

Lavender cotton has the same kind of appeal as the various silvery leaved wormwoods, but usually it is not as long-lived in most gardens. Spilling over rocks and ledges, massed on a slope, or planted near a low wall, it blends well with thyme, winter savory, germander, and the various kinds of scented geraniums to create a drift of old-time fragrance. For a trim, formal ground-cover effect in gardens where a distinct pattern is desired, it can be sheared. Sometimes it is planted to make a billowy edging

Lavender cotton, both the gray-leaved and the green form, are valued for their pleasing texture and their drought endurance.

Taloumis

for a perennial or shrub border. A plant of year-round appeal, its pleasing gray texture in the winter landscape is not to be overlooked.

A kind with dark green leaves (*S. virens*), otherwise similar in habit, is most attractive. Also, *S. virens ericoides* is a selected form of emerald green. *S. neapolitana,* from southern Italy, is an unusual and little-known species, formerly listed as *S. rosmarinifolia.* It grows 2 feet tall or more in mild climates. The threadlike, pendulous foliage is silver and shaggy. It is tender and needs protection where winter temperatures go below zero. Cutting it to the ground annually is recommended.

Plants can be set out at any time during the growing season. A well-drained location in full sun and poor soil suit this dwarf shrub. The determining factor in its longevity is the kind of winter weather it must endure. Long periods of thawing and freezing are harmful as is excessive ice and lack of normal snow cover. Rooted cuttings from pots or flats are the most satisfactory way to handle it in quantity. Most nurseries offer 2-year plants, either field-grown or from containers. Old clumps benefit from heavy pruning in early spring, a practice often necessary after an open winter. Increase from cuttings is the usual method of propagation.

Leopard's-bane   1–2′   **LS–SS**   **April–May**   *Doronicum* genus

Showy yellow daisylike flowers rise from a crown of heart-shaped foliage. It flourishes in naturally moist, humusy soil making sizable clumps, but languishes where soil and heat are not to its liking. Divide every 2 to 3 years after flowering. There are several kinds of varying heights that are at their best at tulip time.

Lily of the Valley. See Chapter 10.

Meadow Rue   3′   **LS–SS**   **June–July**   *Thalictrum* genus

The fluffy white, pink, purple, or yellow flowers are of more fleeting beauty than the feathery glaucous foliage. It can be grown in average soil, but makes a superior plant in humusy conditions. A good background plant where lacy texture is desired, it also fits well in naturalistic settings.

Michaelmas Daisies   1–4′   **LS**   **September–October**   *Aster* genera

Like chrysanthemums, hardy asters are valued for their welcome fall bloom and the two are ideal companions in beds and borders. The white, pink, lavender, or purple daisylike flowers, borne in panicles, range in height from 9 inches to 4 feet or more. There are dwarfs for edging or rock gardens; medium-growing forms for combining with chrysanthemums; and tall varieties for background use. Foliage of New England asters is often mildewed and is not outstanding, but plants are generally long-lived, hardy, and showy in flower. Frequent division every other year, periodic feeding as with chrysanthemums, and pinching back several times from May to early August keep the growth of tall types compact and cut down on staking. Thin out heavy growth, allowing several stems for each clump, for better air circulation. Average soil is suitable, but they will take moist conditions if well drained.

MONKSHOOD   3–5′   LS–SS   JULY–OCTOBER   *Aconitum* genus

Loose panicles of purplish flowers are borne in late summer and autumn on long, slender stems with delicately cut foliage. Give it moist, humusy soil in a shady situation and dig in superphosphate to improve flowering. Plants usually need staking. Monkshood is easily divided in early spring, and it usually requires a full year to become established before it blooms, but not all gardeners are successful with this perennial. The root is a source of a deadly poison.

MISTFLOWER. See Hardy ageratum.

ORIENTAL POPPY   2–3′   MAY–JUNE   *Papaver orientale*

Spectacular in color, the Oriental poppy is often spoken of as the noisiest and showiest of perennials. The common forms are notably long-lived and deep-rooted. Scarlet, orange, various shades of red and pink, and pure white are available in named varieties. Allow ample space for each plant to develop (2 to 3 square feet), and provide companion plants to camouflage the short-lived foliage that begins to deteriorate after flowering. Drainage is essential to longevity. Plant in late summer or early fall when roots are dormant. Set the crown 2 to 3 inches below the surface of the soil and dig a hole deep enough for the taproot to be perpendicular. Container-grown plants can be set out anytime. Old clumps may be divided in late summer or plants may be increased by root cuttings at this time. To make cuttings, dig up the entire root; cut into pieces 3 to 4 inches long and plant with wide end up in pots or directly in the ground, setting pieces 3 inches deep.

PEONY   2–3′   MAY–JUNE   *Paeonia* genus

Many old-time gardens by the sea contain this garden heirloom. Once established, the peony is actually one of the easiest, hardiest, and longest lived of all perennials. The flowering period is comparatively short, but the foliage remains effective until fall when it lends further interest as the leaves turn crimson and yellow. Varieties are legion in both single and double flowering kinds.

Full sun and a deep, well-drained, well-prepared location produce the most vigorous growth. Early fall is the ideal planting time. Obtain healthy divisions with 3 to 5 eyes (pointed reddish buds) and dig holes large enough to accommodate the roots without crowding. Place the roots so that the eyes are an inch below soil level. Too deep planting may result in sparse bloom, but other factors may be responsible also.

When old established plants are being divided and reset (every 15 to

Annuals and perennials combined with flowering shrubs and evergreens.

20 years is not unusual), care must be taken to loosen the soil thoroughly by deep digging all around the plant. Lift roots without breaking and divide with a sharp knife. Choose disease-free sections from the outer rim of the clump, with at least 3 to 5 or more large, plump eyes. Make clean cuts on the starchy roots, removing damaged or broken segments. Discard the central part of the crown. Sections of roots with even a single eye will eventually develop into blooming-size plants. Healthy divisions may produce a bloom or two the first year after planting, or it may require two or more years for a creditable display, but they are worth waiting for.

Lack of bloom on established plants is a common complaint and may be attributed to several causes. Deep planting as previously mentioned, poor soil, or root competition from nearby trees and shrubs, lack of sun, small divisions, unexpected spring freezes, or botrytis blight are typical conditions. All are correctable.

PHLOX 2–3′ LS JUNE–OCTOBER *Phlox paniculata*

When viewed against the sea, the bright-colored varieties of hardy phlox always appear much more vivid than those grown inland. Phlox is truly the backbone of the hardy flower border in summer and in its lively array rivals many of our showiest annuals. Named varieties include white, numerous shades of pink, red, lavender, and purple, many with contrasting

195

Hardy phlox is the mainstay for color in summer gardens and the colors always seem brighter at the seaside.

centers. An outstanding early white is Miss Lingard (*P. suffruticosa*) with glossy foliage that remains clean.

There are varieties of moderate height and some that grow 3 to 4 feet tall, as well as early, midsummer, and late flowering kinds. The chief drawback is mildew on the foliage which can be most unsightly. It occurs in humid weather and can be checked by dusting the leaves with sulfur or using a copper fungicide. Allowing clumps ample room for development and air circulation often circumvents heavy attacks of mildew. Given moderate care, including water in dry spells, division every three years, spring or fall, and adequate feeding, hardy phlox is long-lived and most satisfactory. To prevent the production of seedlings that invariably produce unwanted magenta bloom, remove heads after flowering.

PINKS. See Chapter 10.

PLANTAIN LILY. See Ground Covers, Chapter 10.

PLUMY BLEEDING HEART   15″   LS–DS   MAY–SEPTEMBER
Dicentra eximia

The dainty pink or white heart-shaped flowers on sturdy stems appear in profusion above clumps of lacy foliage. Long-flowering, dependable, hardy, and easy to grow, plumy bleeding heart is one of the most adaptable perennials for the shady garden. *D. eximia* is native to the East Coast and a similar species, *D. formosa,* is common on the West Coast. Named varieties are offered by many growers. It is especially useful under shrubs and trees as a cover plant or among ferns. Increasing stock is no problem since it self-sows readily, or clumps may be divided in spring or fall.

PRIMROSE   6–18″   LS–SS   APRIL–MAY   *Primula* genus

All the colors of the rainbow may be had if one is so minded. Species and hybrids vary in height and time of bloom from early April to late June. Primroses are denizens of shade where soil is naturally moist and humusy. Hot sun and dry soil are hard on them, even fatal. Ideal for edgings or carpeting effects, they are well suited to wild gardens, particularly where boggy conditions occur. Divide every 3 years after flowering, or grow plants from seed. Greatest losses occur when plants are neglected in dry summers.

PURPLE LOOSESTRIFE   4′   LS   JULY–SEPTEMBER   *Lythrum salicaria*

A perennial of the salt marshes, widely naturalized, it makes the swamp landscape come alive with color from midsummer to early autumn. Purple loosestrife is at home in average garden soil even when poor, thin, and dry, and flourishes equally in sun or shade. Improved forms include Morden Pink, a good rose pink which many gardeners prefer since it does not set seed, and several other named varieties of varying heights ranging from red to purple. It will grow practically anywhere and is easily divided in spring or fall.

Rose Mallow   4–5′   August–September   *Hibiscus moscheutos*

Saucerlike flowers of enormous size, 6 to 12 inches in diameter, appear in clusters on sturdy stems balanced by big-scale foliage in late summer. Colors, in named varieties, range from white to red with conspicuous contrasting markings. Rose mallow is a spectacular perennial that delights in heavy moist soil, but will flower well even under dry conditions, producing smaller blooms. It holds up well even in windy locations. A deep-rooted perennial, it is best planted bare-root in early spring. Old clumps may be divided at that time and stock may be increased by seed. Growers offer container-grown plants.

Sea Holly   2′   July–September   *Eryngium amethystinum*

Planted among pink, yellow, and white flowers, sea holly with its glossy foliage and oval heads of spiny bloom makes a distinct accent in the summer garden. The flower color is grayish blue changing to amethyst as it develops. Like the globe thistle, it is a cutflower of high ornamental value either fresh or dry. It thrives in hot, dry, sandy soils, endures salt spray, and is increased by division in early spring.

Sea Lavender   2½′   July–September   *Limonium latifolium*

Generous airy sprays of warm lavender flowers rise from rosettes of leathery foliage presenting a delightful effect in summer. Flowers fresh or dry add luster to a bouquet. Several species of varying heights are cultivated and wild forms are found on beaches. Sea lavender belongs in gardens by the sea where it thrives in sandy soil, adding a touch of delicacy to any group of plants throughout the summer. It is a deep-rooted perennial and care is required in moving established plants. Nurseries offer it in containers and it is easily raised from seed.

Shasta Daisy   18″   LS   July–October   *Chrysanthemum maximum*

These glorified daisies, both single and double, usually pay their way with the bloom they produce, but they are not always long-lived in the colder parts of the Northeast. The best of drainage is essential as well as fertile soil. Sturdy, durable foliage and sturdy stems are typical of the majority. For the most part, the single forms live the longest. Many of the doubles and those with frilled petals, while most appealing, are not dependably hardy, a point to remember when ordering. Increase for named kinds is by division, best in early spring or early fall if plants are mulched.

Snakeroot   4–6′   LS–DS   July–August   *Cimicifuga* genera

Stately white spires on sturdy stems rise above clumps of rather coarsely cut but attractive foliage. Dramatic effects can be achieved when

198

Genereux

A spring garden featuring primroses, daffodils and forget-me-nots.

199

snakeroot is used with false spirea in the foreground. Give the plant a moist, humusy soil for best results, but it will grow well even under average conditions and requires little or no special care. Long-lived and hardy, increase is by division of the roots in early spring.

Speedwell   1–2′ LS–SS   June–September   *Veronica* genus

The flower spikes may be blue, purple, pink, or white depending on the kind chosen. Blue is the common color of this perennial and, like the peachleaf bellflower, the balloon flower, and the globe thistle, it is a must for the seaside garden. There is so much variety in height among the species that spectacular effects can be had at various seasons. Clean and attractive with durable foliage, *Veronica* is a vigorous grower, usually neat in habit. Pinching makes stems sturdy and increases bloom. All are of easy culture in average soil. Increase is by division. Many kinds, including creeping sorts for carpet use, are inclined to be weedy except when used for ground cover.

Stonecrop. See Chapter 10.

Viola, Violet   8″   LS–SS   *Viola* genus

Violas are best described as short-lived perennials with blooms similar to pansies but smaller. The color range is wide with several good blues and purples, yellow, white, apricot, red, and bicolors. All are ideal for seaside gardens. Treated as biennials, they often self-sow and naturalize, making good filler plants as well as edgings. Frequent pinching and cutting back by taking long stems for cutflower use keeps plants trim. Violets of many kinds are true denizens of shady places. Not all are weeds, as for example Rosina, pink, Double Russian, double purple, and several other named varieties. Many native kinds are ideal for naturalizing under shrubs and trees as ground cover. If left to themselves, they will run wild. Choose kinds with care to fill a need.

Wake-robin   12″   LS–DS   May   *Trillium* genus

Among the most notable of our native wildings for shady gardens, the great or snow trillium (*T. grandiflorum*) is valued for its white three-pointed flowers that turn pink with age. Other species are also of interest in wild gardens but not as showy. Plant the roots (rhizomes) in fall. Moist humusy soil, slightly acid, preferred.

Windflower   2–4″   LS   September–October   *Anemone* genus

The fall-flowering Japanese anemones of waxy texture in white, pink, and purple tones flaunt their bloom on long slender stems rising from clumps of durable and attractive foliage. Not easy to establish, they require moist, well-drained soil with plenty of humus, a protected exposure, and are sensitive to summer dryness. Best transplanted in spring, they are slow

200

in showing signs of life and their locations need to be marked carefully. It is not practical to plant them unless their needs can be met, but where conditions are right, they are most rewarding, and nowhere are they lovelier than in a seaside garden saying au revoir to summer.

WORMWOOD   6″–4′   LS   *Artemisia* genus

Although the wormwoods in their various forms are among the oldest plants cultivated for culinary and medicinal uses, practically all these plants have considerable landscape value. The interest they lend is often diminished by their weedy nature, and then too, they are largely overlooked because many of them are not listed in catalogs or generally sold in nurseries.

For the most part, wormwoods are filler plants, desirable for their gray and silvery foliage. The textural effect of the various wormwoods offers pleasing and even striking contrasts to large areas of green foliage and they greatly enhance and accentuate the color of annuals and perennials found in summer gardens.

The best known low-growing kinds are Silver Mound artemisia, fringed wormwood, and Roman wormwood (see Chapter 10). A newcomer in nursery catalogs listed as *A. discolor* is described as shrublike in habit and slightly more than a foot high, cottony in texture, and decidedly gray in color. Somewhat taller is another novelty, *A. versicolor,* with silvery gray-green foliage. This plant produces a stately central stem 18 to 20 inches tall with a low, compact mound of foliage nestled at its base. The finely cut spiky leaves create an interesting chain-link effect.

Decidedly woody and pleasantly aromatic, *A. abrotanum,* known by such popular names as southernwood, old man, and lad's love, develops into a picturesque shrub 2 to 4 feet tall with delicately cut, lacy gray-green foliage. Silver King, a form of *A. albula,* sometimes called ghost plant, has silvery white foliage on sturdy stems 3 to 4 feet tall. It suckers freely, becoming weedy if not controlled, but is a most effective perennial. There are several other perennial species including mugwort (*A. vulgaris*) and tarragon (*A. dracunculus*).

All the wormwoods thrive in full sun in sandy or gritty soil, are often low in fertility, and require no special care. Most of them are rapid growers, increasing by underground stems. All are easy to divide and are long-lived.

CHAPTER TWELVE

Annuals

*A*NNUALS produce the predominant bloom in summer gardens and these are the flowers that lure most beginners to start a garden. An annual is a plant that completes its life cycle, from seed to seed, in a single season. Some tend to self-sow and appear as volunteers the following year since the seed, when ripe, drops to the ground, lies dormant through the winter, and germinates when the ground warms up the following spring. In seed catalogs, annuals are classified according to their ability to endure cold temperatures and are referred to as hardy, half-hardy, and tender annuals. The proper time to plant each group is based on this consideration.

Some are started indoors rather than directly in the garden, because they require a longer season to produce bloom than outdoor conditions allow in the colder parts of the country. Others are by nature not true annuals; they may be either biennials or perennials in their native habitat but they can be flowered in a single season if given an early start. Pansies, English daisies, and forget-me-nots are true biennials which, when started early, bloom the same season. Snapdragon is actually a perennial, but in cold climates is treated as an annual.

Hardy annuals are those that endure cold temperatures and may be sown in the open ground as soon as the soil is workable, even before the frost has left the ground entirely. In fact, these may be sown also in late autumn to obtain early bloom the following season. Typical examples include:

Baby's breath	Cornflower	Pinks
Bachelor's button	Gaillardia	Poppies
California poppies	Larkspur	Snow-on-the-mountain
Calliopsis (coreopsis)	Love-in-a-mist	Sweet alyssum
Candytuft	Lupines	Sweet peas

Marigolds and coneflowers provide an abundance of yellow flowers from midsummer
to late fall.

Half-hardy annuals are those that may be planted before the ground has become thoroughly warm since the young seedlings are not usually harmed by light spring frosts. These include:

Annual phlox	Lavatera	Petunia
Calendula	Lobelia	Portulaca
Cleome	Marigold	Salvia
Cosmos	Mignonette	Scabiosa
Everlastings	Nemesia	Snapdragon
Godetia	Nicotiana	Verbena

Tender annuals are those that are so sensitive to frost or severe drops in temperature as to be impeded or stunted in growth when set out too early. Beginners are advised to consult with experienced gardeners before setting out any of the annuals in this group or any tender plants from the window garden or greenhouse. Included in this group are:

Ageratum	Coleus	Saliglossis
Balsam	Cup-and-saucer vine	Scarlet runner bean
Begonia	Datura	Statice
Bells of Ireland	Everlastings	Strawflower
Blue lace flower	Heliotrope	Sunflower
Celosia	Lobelia	Tassel flower
China aster	Morning glory	Tithonia
Chrysanthemum	Nasturtium	Wishbone flower
Clarkia	Petunia	Zinnia

To enjoy early bloom, many are started indoors, or they may be purchased from local growers in small flats or boxes. Despite their susceptibility to frost, a sizable number self-sow. Petunias, flowering tobacco, balsam, and others often appear as volunteers when the soil warms up. The seed remains dormant in the soil until temperatures for germination are ideal. Of all the kinds mentioned, self-sown petunias are the least desirable because of their magenta color.

SOWING HARDY ANNUALS IN THE OPEN

When forsythia blooms, seed of hardy annuals can be sown in the open ground, but the soil must be prepared first. The area to be planted needs to be spaded or turned over with a digging fork, then raked to remove stones and other debris. If the soil crumbles easily when a handful is squeezed, it is in workable condition. However, if it is exceptionally moist, it must be allowed to dry out before seed is sown.

Soil Preparation. Areas that have not been cultivated the previous year require preparation to a depth of 8 to 10 inches and the addition of a complete fertilizer such as 5-10-5 (see Chapter 16) at the rate of 3 to 5 pounds per 100 square feet. This is scattered on the surface and turned under as the soil is prepared. Allow the prepared area to settle for a few days before planting.

Snapdragons are indispensable in gardens by the sea.

Light Requirements. For success with annuals, the site must have direct sunlight for at least half the day. Many, such as zinnias and marigolds, require full sun to produce their best bloom. (See lists at end of chapter.)

Sowing in Open Ground. Since most annuals are easily transplanted, they are sown in rows in a seedbed. However, some that have long taproots do not transplant successfully without special care, and the usual practice is to scatter the seed broadcast where they are to bloom. When large enough to handle, they are thinned to allow ample room for the development of each plant.

Experienced gardeners may take issue with some of the plants in the following list, since with care they can be transplanted, but the effort in-

205

volved is usually not worth the time required. When the delicate roots are damaged or broken, seedlings of the kinds listed below do not survive in most cases. Professional growers offer many of these in plant bands or small flats that can be transplanted safely. Hence, the usual practice for beginners is to sow them where they are to bloom and thin to stand the distances indicated below:

African daisy—12″	Clarkia—8″	Love-in-a-mist—6″
Annual chrysanthemum—12″	Four-o'clock—24″	Lupines—12″
Annual vines—24″	Gilia—12″	Mallow—18″
Baby's breath—6″	Godetia—12″	Mignonette—6″
Bachelor's button—12″	Larkspur—12″	Nasturtium—24″
Chinese forget-me-not—12″	Lavatera—18″	Poppies—12″

Sowing in a Seedbed. Tiny seeds are best mixed with sand before planting. If sown in rows, scatter thinly and press into the soil with a block of wood. Larger seed is distributed as evenly as possible in the row and covered with soil to a depth of twice the diameter of the seed. Cover the seedbed with burlap or cloth and water with a fine spray through this material to prevent washing away the soil.

Broadcasting Seed. When seed is scattered broadcast over a bed, aim for even distribution (mixing fine seed with soil is practical) and rake in lightly. Watering should be done carefully enough not to cause soil wash. Seeded areas must not be allowed to dry out. Keep them moist but not soggy.

Thinning. As seedlings emerge, the tender shoots produce a pair of seed leaves that provide food for the stem. These are followed by a pair of true leaves. When two or more sets of true leaves have developed, annuals sown broadcast can be thinned as indicated above. Moisten the soil before thinning and pull out seedlings not wanted, leaving those showing the greatest vigor.

Transplanting. Those grown in the seedbed are transplanted as soon as they have developed two or more sets of true leaves. Moisten the soil first. Remove seedlings with a putty knife or narrow-bladed trowel, being careful to dig deep enough to get the entire root of each seedling. To avoid wilting, handle them in small groups. In replanting them in their permanent positions, or to a bed for later transplanting, make holes deep and wide enough to accommodate the roots adequately without crowding. Firmly but gently compress the soil around each seedling with the thumb and forefinger of each hand. After transplanting, water and provide temporary shade for several days until the seedlings are established. (Shade may be brush cut from nearby shrubs; or old window screens covered with light-weight cloth supported on stones provide necessary protection from sun and wind.) Keep seedlings moist, but not soggy. After 3 to 4 days, cover may be removed.

206

Using Flats, Plant Bands, Peat Pots. When beds are not ready for seedlings, some gardeners find it practical at first transplanting to place seedlings in flats spacing them 2 to 3 inches apart in rows, or plant bands or peat pots may be used. This step necessitates a second transplanting, but it aids in developing sturdy plants with well-developed root systems. (This is basically the practice of the professional grower who raises annuals for sale.) In removing annuals from flats, soak the soil thoroughly, then lift out with a knife or trowel, removing each seedling with as much soil as possible attached to its roots.

Pinching. After plants have become well established, most kinds need pinching to produce bushy, well-developed specimens for a maximum of bloom. This is done by removing the tip growth with the fingers or shears.

Feeding. If the beds have been prepared and fertilized before transplanting (the usual practice), no plant food will be needed until flower buds begin to form. Scatter a complete fertilizer lightly around the plants and water it in. Two additional feedings may be given at 4-week intervals. Some gardeners use foliar feeding. See Chapter 16.

Cultivating. In most gardens, as summer approaches, soil tends to cake or form a crust, preventing water from penetrating easily. Every 2 to 3 weeks, loosen the soil around plants with a hand cultivator. Long-handled kinds eliminate bending and stooping.

Mulching. The use of a convenient mulch eliminates cultivating, a considerable amount of weeding, and conserves moisture. See Chapter 18.

STARTING ANNUALS INDOORS

Seed of certain annuals needs to be started earlier than is possible in the open because of the time required to produce flowering plants. With others, the purpose of indoor sowing is an early start to obtain early bloom. Most annuals require about 8 weeks from seeding indoors to develop plants large enough to set out. Kinds like petunias, salvia, snapdragon, China asters, verbenas, belong in this category. Local growers usually offer all these kinds in boxes, but often the number of varieties available is limited. Consequently, with many gardeners, the only way to obtain specific varieties is to raise them.

Timing. Schedule seed sowing for 8 weeks prior to time of setting out.

Light Requirements. Unless window space is available that receives sun most of the day, results may be disappointing since seedlings are bound to be leggy. Greenhouse conditions are ideal for those who have them. Electrically heated hotbeds are also useful, provided they are easily accessible. Cold frames are a must if many kinds of annuals are to be raised in this way.

African marigolds, stock, feverfew and sweet alyssum make a lively display.

Some gardeners start seedlings under artificial light. With proper controls this method is successful, but constant care and timing of light are required. For most beginners, it is a specialized and complicated approach but it can be a most rewarding adventure.

Where only a few kinds are desired, a sunny window suffices. Satisfactory results can be expected if seedlings are properly handled from the time of germination until they are large enough to set out.

Equipment. Bulb pans; cigar boxes; flats or plastic trays, 2 to 3 inches deep. 5-inch wooden labels for identifying varieties. Drainage material: broken flowerpots, stone chips, or screened gravel soil mixture (or vermiculite or sphagnum moss); glass or plastic for covering or plastic domes; seed sower.

Bulb pans are wide flowerpots such as used by florists for tulips, daffodils, azaleas, and other plants. They may be clay or plastic. Clay types are porous and the soil dries out more rapidly than in the nonporous plastic. Therefore watering seedlings in plastic pots requires more care, since soil can easily become waterlogged.

Cigar boxes or those of similar size fit conveniently on many window-sills.

Wooden or plastic trays 2 to 3 inches deep are frequently used. Holes must be made for drainage. Cookie tins make good "saucers" for them.

Soil Mixture. $\frac{1}{3}$ sand, $\frac{1}{3}$ peat moss (screened), $\frac{1}{3}$ good garden soil (screened) or leaf mold or soil from compost pile. Some amateurs start seed in sand, others use vermiculite or chopped sphagnum moss.

Vermiculite (A finer grade is known as terralite). This is a mineral substance of light weight valued for its sterile quality. It contains no plant food, is weed- and insect-free, but since it contains no plant food, this must be added in liquid form as soon as seed germinates. Many gardeners find it useful for starting seeds since there is no chance of damping-off.

Sphagnum moss, chopped and treated, offered in packages, is used by some gardeners for starting seed. It is sterile, weed-free, and holds moisture well, but as with vermiculite, terralite, and similar media, seedlings once germinated need feedings of a water-soluble fertilizer every 10 days. However, for starting seeds that are slow to germinate (certain perennials, shrubs, and wild flowers), it has proved most satisfactory. Its value lies in its moisture-holding capacity, and its loose, fibrous texture, allowing for air circulation without becoming waterlogged. Sphagnum moss, vermiculite, and terralite are preferred by many amateurs who garden under artificial light.

Drainage. Before containers are filled with soil, they need drainage in the form of pebbles or pieces of clay pots, broken up small. Use at least a $\frac{1}{2}$-inch layer. Cover drainage with coarse material—screenings from soil, sphagnum moss, rough compost, or coarse soil. Then fill the pot or flat to within $\frac{3}{4}$ inch of the top. Tamp soil with a block of wood to remove excess soil air. Once the surface is flat and even, seeds are ready to be planted.

Damping-off is a fungus in soil that kills seedlings as they emerge. It occurs in the presence of too much moisture or damp weather. To combat it, sterilized soil, a sterile medium, or disinfecting the soil or the seeds are the methods used.

Sterilizing soil can be a chore if certain methods are used. Heating soil in an oven for an hour at 200°F. is one good method. Another is formaldehyde. A teaspoonful is sprinkled into a flat of the soil mixture and stirred thoroughly. Seed is sown, and the flat is placed in water to soak the soil, then covered with wet newspaper until the seedlings push through.

DISINFECTING SEED

The most convenient method for the beginner is to use a chemical solution for treating seed, such as Anti-damp, Semesan, Arasan, or the like, according to the instructions on the package. These materials, which are valuable for the control of damping-off indoors and in the garden, are easy to use.

SEED-SOWING TECHNIQUES

Sowing seed requires patience, but care exercised now makes transplanting easier and more efficient. Seeds vary in size from some as fine as dust to those the size of a pea or bean. The finer the seed, the greater the chance of planting too deep, with the result that germination is faulty.

Metal and plastic seed sowers make the task of sowing fine seed easy, or you can make your own from heavy paper. Before sowing, treat the seed with one of the disinfectants for control of damping-off. Drop a pinch of the powder into the seed packet and shake it thoroughly to coat the seeds. This simple operation is well worth the effort. Scatter the seed as evenly and thinly as possible on the surface.

Handling Fine Seed. Mix tiny seed with finely screened soil, or scatter it on sphagnum moss or vermiculite. These materials provide even moisture, essential to germination. Water from the bottom by placing the pot in a pan of water until bubbles cease to rise from the water. This method of watering is best until germination occurs; then water with a fine spray and cover with a piece of glass, a plastic cover or dome. Place pots in a warm location until the seedlings emerge. Then move them to full sun. Seeds do not require light until the tiny sprouts break through the soil.

Light. Once germination has occurred, pots must be turned daily since seedlings always reach for the strongest source of light. Fresh air is also essential when seedlings have developed a set of true leaves. When large enough to handle, they can be transplanted to flats, peat pots, or plant bands. From now on, full sunlight and fresh air are essential.

Handling Large Seed. Seed of handleable size is sown in rows, using flats, plastic trays, or cigar boxes. Space seed carefully for even distribution. Patience is required, but the effort simplifies transplanting. Cover the seed, firm the soil with a block of wood.

210

Few annuals make a more spectacular display than the pink and white varieties of cleome which self-sows readily.

Watering. It is essential to keep soil from drying out; moist, but not waterlogged.

Transplanting. Use techniques as previously outlined in this chapter.

Peat Pots and Plant Bands. In lieu of flats, some gardeners prefer to use either peat pots or plant bands, placing one seedling in each. When peat pots are used, they are set directly in the ground at planting time since they soon disintegrate. Plant bands are removed before planting seedlings in the ground. In either case, the small plants are saved the shock of a second transplanting since the roots are not disturbed.

BUYING ANNUALS ALREADY STARTED

Many home gardeners find it convenient and practical to buy some or all of their annuals from local growers. Conveniently boxed in wood or plastic, usually 12 to a box, these seedlings are easy to handle. Some growers offer annuals in individual peat pots, plant bands, or in pots of plastic or clay, but these are always more costly. Regardless of the kind used, the soil in the container should be thoroughly watered and allowed to drain before the seedlings are removed for setting out. Well prepared soil and periodic feeding are essential for better than average results. See Chapter 15 for soil preparation and Chapter 16 for fertilizing.

Dusty miller, geraniums, coleus, and the trailing periwinkle combine effectively for use in window boxes and other types of containers.

CHAPTER THIRTEEN

Summer-Flowering Bulbs

$\mathcal{S}$UMMER-FLOWERING BULBS are a source of pleasure for their bloom and the exotic effects they create in the garden. They are ideal for temporary garden effects or for the summer place, since they require little care and can be stored through winter in a frostproof place for replanting the following year. All the kinds described are tender (except where noted) and must not be planted in the open until all danger of frost has passed. Some are true bulbs, others are corms or tubers, but all are commonly referred to as bulbs. In general, prepare soil to a depth of 6 to 8 inches beneath the specified planting depth of the various kinds discussed.

When frost has nipped the foliage, dig the bulbs, shaking excess soil from the roots, and allow them to dry for a week before storing in a frostproof location. Those requiring warmer temperature are indicated. Named varieties should be labeled before storing.

Acidanthera is an awkward name for one of the most delightful and fragrant members of the gladiolus family. Unusually delicate in form, the white petals are marked with red-purple and the buds and blooms are most distinctive as they appear on sturdy 2 to 3 foot stems. Plant in full sun, spacing the corms 4 inches apart in groups of 3 to 5, and cover with 3 inches of soil.

Basket Flower, or ismene, resembles the amaryllis in form, and the greenish white trumpets, rising from straplike foliage, are usually about 18 inches tall. Like all members of the amaryllis family, it needs shallow planting in a sunny location. Barely cover the bulbs, spacing them a foot apart each way. For satisfactory bloom the following season, the bulbs must be stored through winter at a temperature of at least 50°F.

Begonias, Tuberous-rooted. Of all the bulbous plants that flower in summer, none can rival the tuberous-rooted begonias for their free-flowering habit and their adaptability to shade. They are easier to grow than most

213

beginners realize. Tubers already started may be purchased from local growers at planting time, but it is easy and much less expensive to start your own indoors.

Plant them indoors 6 to 8 weeks before they are to be set out. Use flats, small boxes (at least three inches deep), or bulb pans filled with a mixture of 2 parts thoroughly moistened peat moss and 1 part sand. Press the tubers, concave side up, into the mixture, allowing 2 inches between them each way, and water well. Place them in the basement near the heater (60 to 65°F. is ideal). When growth starts, bring them into normal daylight, since growth becomes spindly if they are kept in the dark too long. As soon as plants have developed several leaves, pot them in 6-inch bulb pans.

For potting, use a mixture of equal parts of compost or well-rotted manure, peat moss, and fertile garden soil. To each bushel of this mixture add one 4-inch pot of steamed bonemeal. If soil is on the heavy side, add enough sand to make it crumbly. As you pot the tubers, keep as much of the starting mixture as possible on the roots, and set them no deeper than the first planting. After potting, water the young plants thoroughly to settle the soil. Occasional spraying of the foliage is also desirable, but keep them out of sun until the leaves have dried off, because water spotting disfigures foliage permanently. To avoid waterlogged soil, watering should be done carefully until plants are well established.

Tuberous-rooted begonias are especially tender, and must not be set out until all danger of frost has passed and the ground is thoroughly warm. For best results, the soil mixture in the garden should be similar to that used in potting. Where root competition of shrubs and trees is a problem, pots can be sunk in the ground up to their rims. Never allow plants to dry out, because drought affects growth, foliage, and the size of the blooms. If watered in the morning, there is less chance for mildew to develop. Plants kept in pots or tubs on terraces require constant watering. Feed begonias with liquid fertilizer (low in nitrogen) every 3 or 4 weeks. Too much plant food results in lush growth, causing plants to topple over during heavy rain, and staking may be required.

Few pests trouble tuberous begonias except slugs and snails, which can be controlled with poison bait or handpicking. Stem rot attributed to manure occurs occasionally, but is seldom serious. The most challenging disease affecting the plants is powdery mildew, which disfigures the foliage seriously. Control with Captan or a similar fungicide. Badly infected plants should be destroyed to prevent the spores from spreading. When growth has been cut down by frost, cut it off at the soil level, dig the tubers, and allow them to dry off for several days. Store through winter in dry sand in a frostproof place, 40°F.

Calla Lilies. White, yellow and pink-flowering kinds can be grown in full sun or part shade, provided the soil is on the moist side and rich in organic matter. The white-spotted foliage of the yellow variety is attrac-

214

Snowflakes, like crocuses, grape hyacinths, scillas and other miniature bulbous plants, are effective among ground covers.

215

tive throughout the season. These natives of the tropics need an abundance of water. Cover with 3 inches of soil and space them 12 to 18 inches apart.

Caladiums. Fancy leaved caladiums are ideal for shady parts of the garden and are grown for their richly colored tropical foliage, but they are sometimes grown in full sun. The blooms are insignificant and should be removed. They can be started indoors, but if not given plenty of bottom heat they are slow to root and sprout. Use flats or bulb pans filled with a mixture of equal parts of garden soil, sand, and peat moss. Moisten it thoroughly and barely cover the corms when planting. Place them near a heater or radiator so that they get maximum bottom heat. The dry roots are usually shriveled and lifeless in appearance, but, as long as they are firm to the touch, they will grow. Once roots have developed and buds have broken, give them ample light. Exceptionally tender, they cannot be set out until the soil is thoroughly warm, about the same time as tomato plants. Space 12 to 15 inches apart each way and cover with an inch of soil. Humusy soil suits them best and a mulch of peat moss conserves moisture. Water thoroughly during dry spells and feed occasionally. Dig tubers before hard frost and store through winter in a temperature of 60°F.

Cannas, usually thought of as Victorian bedding plants, are back in favor again. Their tropical foliage and exotic blooms are strong points in their favor, and the new hybrids, that range from soft yellow to deep rose, average 3 feet in height, making them desirable for small gardens. They can also be grown in tubs, provided they are kept well watered. Give them soil with plenty of organic matter and an abundance of water in dry weather. Plant in full sun, spacing the roots 18 inches apart each way and cover with 4 inches of soil. For an early start, set the roots in deep boxes in a warm basement and cover with thoroughly soaked peat moss 4 to 6 weeks before planting out.

Dahlias are planted when all danger of frost has passed. Examine stored tubers and cut them to single divisions, using a sharp knife. Buds appear at the junction of the neck of the tuber and the stem of the previous year's growth. There is no point in planting an entire clump of tubers when one will suffice. If purchased from a garden center or a dahlia specialist, one firm tuber with one or more eyes is the usual method of selling them. Whether setting out named varieties or tubers saved from last year's seedlings, the practice is the same. In feeding dahlias, avoid fertilizers high in nitrogen, since they tend to produce foliage at the expense of flowers. Space dwarf kinds 18 inches apart each way; tall varieties require 2 to 3 feet between plants. Cover tubers with 3 inches of soil, giving them full sun and a well-drained location. Many home gardeners prefer the small-flowered single and double kinds. These are treated as annuals and started from seed indoors 8 weeks prior to planting time, or they may be purchased already started. In late fall, tubers of favorite colors can be dug and stored through winter to flower the following year.

216

Gladiolus. Probably the best known of all summer-flowering bulbs in home gardens, gladiolus is more commonly grown in rows in the cutting garden than for landscape effects. Yet the miniature types are well suited for border use, combined with annuals and perennials or in the foreground of a shrub planting. There are five distinct classes based on the size of the individual florets and the flower stalks range in height from 1 to nearly 6 feet, depending on the type and variety grown.

Few bulbs are easier to grow, provided a start is made with healthy corms that have been treated for thrips. Thrips are tiny pests that disfigure foliage, causing silvery streaks as well as deforming buds and flowers. They are controlled with DDT, dieldrin, or Malathion by spraying or dusting, and, as a protective measure, corms are dusted with 5 percent DDT before storing for winter.

Plant corms in full sun, 5 inches deep and the same distance apart; an inch or two deeper planting is desirable in light sandy soils. Successive plantings made at intervals, beginning as soon as the soil is workable, provide for a succession of bloom. Rotation of crops each year is good insurance against disease. Tall exhibition kinds may need staking, but deeper than normal planting helps to correct this problem.

Summer-flowering bulbs like gladiolus combined with annuals are well suited for temporary effects to provide color on shore properties.

Darling

Midcentury lilies add a dominant note of color from late June on.

Dig in late fall, remove all growth to the top of the corms, allowing them to dry off. Separate old withered corms from those newly formed and inspect for disease before treating with DDT. Store in ventilated bags in a frostproof place. The small cormels can be segregated and planted the following year to increase stock of favorite varieties. Growers grade corms according to size, a point to remember when buying them. Bargain offers are sometimes not bargains since the corms are frequently small in size.

Lilies. Although fall is the ideal time to plant lilies, bulbs are sold for spring planting also, having been stored through winter in cool temperatures with their roots attached. They are offered in Plastolene bags, packed in peat moss to keep the scales firm and the roots from drying out. Plant as soon as the soil is workable, or they can be started in pots indoors and transferred to the garden later. Perfect drainage at all seasons of the year is essential for lilies and humusy soil is preferred. Slightly sloping ground is ideal; areas where water stands after rain or during winter are to be avoided. Bulbs should be covered with 3 to 6 inches of soil, measuring from the top of the bulb; the larger the bulb, the deeper the planting. Mark locations after setting out to avoid damaging the emerging growth which may require two weeks or more to break through the soil. See catalogs of specialists for list of kinds and blooming dates.

Montbretias resemble miniature gladiolus in flower and foliage. Plants average 18 to 24 inches in height and the color range is pale yellow to

218

orange-red. The delicately shaped flowers are diminutive and graceful and well suited for flower arranging. Plant in full sun in groups of five or more, spacing 4 inches apart, covering the corms with 3 inches of soil.

Summer hyacinths (*Galtonia candicans*). These grow to 3 feet in height, producing spikes of white bell-like flowers loosely arranged on sturdy stems surrounded by glaucous straplike foliage. They make pleasing accents in the border, are good cut flowers, and are hardy from Philadelphia south. Set in groups of 3 to 5 in a sunny location, spacing them 8 inches apart, and cover with 4 inches of soil.

Tigridias have gladioluslike foliage and spectacular flat blooms on 2½-foot stems, ranging from pale yellow to bright red with contrasting blotches. Plant them in full sun, 6 inches deep.

Tuberoses, long cherished in old-time gardens for their penetrating fragrance and waxlike texture, are effective in small groups in borders where their sweet scent will fill the air on summer nights. Plants grow 2 to 3 feet tall and require a warm, sunny, well-drained location. Tuberoses may be started indoors 4 to 6 weeks before planting them in the open ground. Give them plenty of bottom heat. Space the tubers 6 inches apart and cover with 3 inches of soil.

CHAPTER FOURTEEN

Planting Techniques for
Trees, Shrubs, Hedges

*T*HE TECHNIQUES for planting trees and shrubs whether for specimen use, in areas adjoining the house, or in borders to form hedges, screens, and windbreaks, are basic to all good gardening. Woody plants are intended to create fairly permanent effects and are usually planted where they are to remain for a period of years. Thorough soil preparation is essential if they are to be given the proper start, especially in coastal areas where soils are usually thin in texture and low in organic matter. Also, adequate amounts of plant food need to be added to the soil. See Chapter 16 regarding fertilizers.

Flowering and shade trees as well as ornamental shrubs are sold bare-root, or as balled and burlapped specimens, or container-grown. Bare-root material is available in early spring before growth breaks or in late fall as it approaches dormancy. At other seasons of the year, balled and burlapped specimens (or those container-grown) make transplanting easy. All evergreens are handled in this manner. Burlap used for balling is usually thin and open-meshed and need not be removed when planting. In fact, while handling and planting a tree or shrub, care must be taken not to break the earth ball around the roots. Such injury causes the soil to become loose, thereby harming the tiny feeder roots.

In handling plant material bare-root, keep the roots moist and well covered during the process of planting. Since tiny feeding roots exposed to sun and wind dry out rapidly, keep them wrapped in wet burlap or plunge the roots into a bucket of muddy water until plants are set in the ground. Prior to planting, remove broken and bruised roots as well as those of unusual length, using sharp pruning shears to make clean cuts. Holes need to be large enough in width and depth to accommodate the root system without crowding. Set the crown of the plant at the same level at which it

Fuchsia Gartenmeister Bonstedt, also called Firecracker, has reddish foliage and brilliant red flowers. This and other varieties flourish under moist coastal conditions.

grew in the nursery. (The soil level is usually apparent on bare-root material.) The remainder of the procedure is the same as for balled and burlapped specimens discussed in the following paragraph.

When planting a balled and burlapped plant, dig a generous hole, allowing for at least twice the width and depth of the root ball. After excavating, fill the hole half full of the best available topsoil or compost, or a mixture of both. Both the needle types and the broad-leaved evergreens as well as all types of azaleas are benefited by lining the hole with moistened peat moss. Mix 2 to 3 handfuls of a complete fertilizer with the soil to provide the plant food needed to get roots off to a good start. Cover with an additional inch or two of topsoil so that the roots do not come in direct contact with the fertilizer. Set the top of the ball of earth level with the

221

Common bush honeysuckle makes an attractive and useful screen for this sheltered seaside garden, located only 50 yards from the shore.

surrounding soil surface. As soil is filled in around it, tamp firmly with the end of a spade handle or use your feet for the purpose. Water thoroughly to eliminate air pockets and to settle the soil around the ball. Leave a depression around each plant for subsequent watering and the full benefit of rain. Mulching newly planted shrubs and trees is sound practice. See Chapter 18.

After planting, top pruning is usually necessary, especially if the specimen is heavily branched or if growth is tall and ungainly. In coastal areas, this practice is advisable for bare-root material and balled and burlapped plants as well. Cutting back the top growth of deciduous shrubs and trees at least one third is sound practice, to induce heavy root growth and to improve the general form. Constant exposure to wind results in excessive transpiration of moisture from both stems and leaves, which places more

222

than normal demands on a newly planted shrub. Since every leaf gives off moisture, reduction of the leaf area at planting time helps to check water loss.

Freshly planted evergreens are benefited by watering the foliage frequently as well as the roots, especially if winds are strong and temperatures are unseasonably high.

Tree trunks may be wrapped with heavy paper or burlap to reduce transpiration. This practice involves labor but is good insurance, particularly on windy sites.

The importance of thorough and frequent watering for newly transplanted shrubs and trees, especially during prolonged dry spells, cannot be overstated.

Staking or guying big shrubs and all trees is also vital to success in establishing them in exposed areas. (All wire used should be encased in pieces of rubber tubing where it comes in contact with branches and main stems.) Careless handling of this procedure may result in serious damage to woody stems as they are blown against stakes, particularly when they rub against the rough surfaces of pipes used as supports.

PLANTING A HEDGE

To plant a hedge, dig a trench wide and deep enough to accommodate the roots of the plants without crowding. Also, the depth must be sufficient for adequate soil preparation beneath the roots. For material like privet, barberry, and the like, a trench 2 feet wide and 1 foot deep should suffice. Prepare soil thoroughly to a depth of 8 to 10 inches in the trench by using the excavated topsoil and a generous shovelful of organic matter, peat moss, or compost for each plant. Add a complete fertilizer, allowing 2 pounds for each 10 feet of trench, and mix it in thoroughly.

For hedge use, shrubs are usually 2 to 3 years, field-grown plants, packed bare-root in bundles of 25. Roots are wrapped in moist sphagnum moss and waterproof paper for shipment. If dry when they arrive, soak them overnight in deep water. Trim the roots, removing all damaged parts, and shorten long stringy growth, since the aim is a compact root system. Before planting, stretch a line to serve as a guide for planting a straight row. Shrubs are set at the same depth at which they grew in the nursery. Soil clinging to lower stems indicates the soil level. To prevent roots from drying out while planting, keep them covered with moist burlap or plunge them into a pail of water. As the earth is shoveled in from both sides, each plant is held firmly as the soil is packed around it, holding the stems perpendicular to the ground. Treading with both feet is an easy way to pack soil. When the trench is half filled, water with the hose (nozzle removed) to aid in further packing soil close to roots and eliminating air pockets. Then the remainder of the soil is replaced in the trench, allowing a depression of an inch for watering until the roots are established.

Using the line as a guide, cut back at least ⅓ of the tops to induce bushy growth at the base. Top pruning is esssential to the development of a strong, many-stemmed hedge.

When balled and burlapped or container-grown specimens are used, as with evergreens like pines, Japanese yew, pittosporum, and others, planting techniques are the same. Usually evergreens are neatly trimmed when purchased, but if not, they need to be pruned to assure that each plant is wider at the base than at the top. If growth has not been trimmed and plants appear to be thin and leggy, cutting back growth ¼ to ⅓, depending on the condition, is advisable. The object is to develop a dense hedge that will be sturdy to break the force of the wind.

TRIMMING HEDGES

To keep hedge plants vigorous and attractive, they need to be trimmed so that the lower branches are slightly wider than those at the top to allow light to reach them. Otherwise they soon die, detracting from the effect sought. The taller the hedge, the more important this principle becomes. This practice should be started from the time the hedge is planted, particularly with evergreens, since they are costly.

Evergreen hedges are much more appealing if not kept too tightly clipped. One trimming with hedge shears annually should be sufficient. This is usually done in early summer when new growth has developed. A second trimming or one done in early spring should consist merely of casual snipping here and there to remove long growth. Treated in this manner, an evergreen hedge has a soft, billowy appearance and the play of light and shadow gives it greater substance and more pleasing texture.

REVIVING OLD HEDGES

Certain kinds of hedges that have outgrown the space allotted to them or have been damaged can be cut back severely. This is particularly true of the various kinds of privet which quickly assume a ragged appearance if not trimmed regularly. Don't be afraid to cut back within a few inches of the ground and then feed and water heavily. The job is best done in early spring. This treatment can also be used on barberries and most kinds of flowering shrubs used for hedges. As new growth develops, it should be pruned into the desired form, keeping it wider at the bottom than at the top. After the second season, the new growth that results will be well on its way toward providing the kind of hedge desired.

Evergreen kinds, particularly the various forms of Japanese yew, can be cut back hard and renewed. Some growth with foliage must be allowed to remain and the task may be performed in two stages. This is a job for spring so that new growth will have ample time to develop. Feeding and watering are advisable after cutting.

CHAPTER FIFTEEN

Improving Soil

OILS in coastal areas vary greatly in their makeup. Seldom are ideal types available for cultivation of all the kinds of plants the home gardener wishes to grow. Yet few soils are so poor that they cannot be improved sufficiently to produce satisfactory vegetation. To a considerable extent, soil types determine what can be grown successfully. Even in regions where soil is known to be acid, areas adjoining the coast usually test alkaline.

Thin sandy soils from which moisture, minerals, and available plant food leach rapidly are commonplace. Thus, the prime need is for loam and topsoil as well as organic matter in some form such as compost, leaf mold, peat moss, or stable manure. Compost must be made and requires several years for production. Leaf mold is not always readily obtainable. Stable manure is usually scarce. Various types of peat moss are in plentiful supply but where considerable amounts are needed, cost may be a factor. In any event, for most seaside gardeners the task of improving soil is a continuing process. The use of mulches that are incorporated with the soil annually is another method of improving such soils. Sowing of "green manure" crops is also sound practice.

Considerable variation may occur in rocky areas in which pockets of loam or clay may exist. All of these factors play a part in the over-all scheme. A careful examination of the kinds of plants that grow naturally in areas along the coast is the key to what may be expected of similar or related cultivated types. Even in the poorest of coastal soils, surprising results can be obtained in a single growing season by constant feeding. Contrary to popular notions, native plants are greatly benefited by the same kind of feeding program given to cultivated kinds. (See Chapter 16.)

Every experienced gardener knows and beginners soon learn that success in gardening, or the lack of it, can usually be traced directly to the soil in which plants are grown. There is more to the makeup of soil than meets

225

Garden ornaments often reflect other interests of the owner.

the eye. Its texture, its moisture-holding capacity, its fertility, and its general makeup are of prime importance. Rich, dark color does not necessarily indicate a high degree of fertility. Nor must soil be heavy in texture to grow crops successfully. This assumption is easily disproved by the great number of flowering plants that thrive in thin sandy soils where water and fertilizer are given frequently. The ability of soils to retain moisture, to make food available to the roots of plants as they seek it, and to be workable after heavy rains, are the factors that determine how well plants grow.

Regardless of its size and the type of soil that exists, a garden is a highly artificial environment and the soundest approach to good gardening begins with the soil. First we must understand the makeup of soil. The breakdown of rock, caused by physical and chemical weathering effected by wind, water, heat, cold, plant growth, and animals produces the miner-

Diana looks out to sea from her pedestal.

als that give soil part of its substance. Soil scientists are continually remind-
ing us that the basic stuff that produces growth is more than a mixture of
tiny particles of sand, silt, and clay held together by organic matter. This
combination of minerals and organic matter teems with microorganisms.
In addition to solids, soil also contains water and air. The water and air
present in soil are distributed in the pore spaces between the solid particles
and consequently they are not continuously in liquid or gaseous form.

The ideal condition for growth is described as that point when soil
moisture is at its highest level. At this point, soil humidity is nearly 100
percent. The various organisms, bacteria, fungi, and others become active,
chemical reaction is hastened, and the magic machinery of growth is in
full operation. Since soil processes are biological in nature, the adding of
organic matter and the breakdown or decay of this material that follows

227

are essential to the continuing fertility of soil. All in all, the makeup of soil is far more complex than is generally realized. The interaction of the various components and the part that plant foods play in stimulating growth are only apparent in what shows above the soil. For the gardener, this is one of the wonders of nature.

Types of soil are commonly described on the basis of their physical makeup. These are referred to as sand, silt, clay, and loam.

Sandy Soil. The individual particles, or grains of sandy soil, are easily seen with the naked eye. Water and air pass through it quickly, and it absorbs heat readily. Sandy soil is coarse in texture, heavy in weight, and light in substance because it is deficient in organic matter. Because it dries out quickly, it needs organic matter to absorb and hold water and to retain the plant food the gardener applies to produce healthy plants.

Silty Soil. As grains of sand wear slowly away, they form a powdery dust referred to as silt. We see it on the surface of newly turned fields, along the roadside, in pools of water, and in the air, carried by the wind. When it settles, it is found in the bottom of riverbeds, lakes, brooks, ponds, and even in puddles. Few gardens have great quantities of pure silt, but it is a valued component of loam.

Clayey Soil. This is made up of the tiniest particles of silt of exceptionally fine texture. It forms lumps as it dries, because the surface of each particle is colloided or sticky, so that little aeration is possible. As a result of its makeup, clay soil holds water too well, since the grains cling to one another when moist. Although referred to as being heavy because of its moisture-holding capacity, it is actually light in weight when thoroughly dry.

Clay soil needs improvement in texture to allow for good circulation, drainage, and the ability to absorb heat more readily. This last factor is of prime importance since soil of fine texture is slow to warm up in spring and cannot be worked as early as other kinds. The addition of coarse materials like sand and fine gravel as well as organic matter, changes the soil structure. Improvement is essential for vigorous growth since typical clay soils remain cold and wet for extended periods after heavy rain. In summer, the heat of the sun causes it to crack in streaks. Under these conditions, soil organisms do not function normally and the roots of plants are unable to obtain essential nutrients.

Loamy Soil. This is the ideal type, for which most gardeners long. It is a balanced mixture of sand, silt, and clay, soil particles of different sizes, which combine to produce a gritty texture. This is known as crumb structure. Because the individual particles vary greatly in size, the pressure of water and organic matter holds them together, making this type of soil retentive of both moisture and plant food. Yet it crumbles easily, indicating that air can move through it readily. By bulk, nearly half of the makeup of loam is soil water and soil air.

Basically, the structural makeup of soil is more vital than its richness or fertility, since plant foods are easily added. With few exceptions, loam is usually a relatively thin layer of soil on the earth's surface, commonly referred to as topsoil. With gardeners, the aim is to increase its depth for the benefit of plant roots. The task of building and improving soil on the home grounds to obtain good garden loam is a continuing process, accomplished by spading, adding organic matter and plant food.

DRAINAGE

Drainage is vital to the successful growth of plants, even those that thrive in naturally moist soils. Waterlogged soils exclude air which normally circulates around the individual soil particles and the roots of plants. When subjected to this condition for any period of time, roots are killed, growth is checked, and plants eventually die. Even plants growing in boggy and swampy areas are usually found on hummocks of soil, enabling them to have air circulation around their roots at various times during the year. Most cultivated trees and shrubs, perennials, and bulbs are not adapted to soils that are constantly wet. Flat surfaces where water tends to stand after a heavy rain during winter sometimes can be drained by excavating the area and putting in a layer of gravel. If the area is lower than its surroundings, raising the grade is the answer. The problem of drainage often presents itself in heavy clay soils. Where it cannot be corrected by improving the texture of the soil, agricultural tile can be utilized to carry off the surplus soil water. Hardpan subsoil beneath the surface may be a cause of poor drainage. When this condition exists, the subsoil can be loosened by excavating the topsoil and using a pick mattock to break the hard surface. Electric drills are sometimes used when large areas are involved.

IMPROVING SANDY SOIL

Those who garden by the sea are often faced with the task of building up sandy soil; this is usually a task of gradual improvement. Because of its loose makeup, fertilizers must be applied frequently since rain and the constant use of sprinklers cause plant food to be leached out of the soil. Thus, the answer to the problem of feeding is "little and often." There are several ways to approach the problem. Sandy soils can be improved by growing a crop of green manure or sheet composting, as it is sometimes called. Topsoil may be added. Organic materials like peat moss, compost, sawdust, wood chips, or other materials can be dug in before the area is planted. A fourth method is thorough preparation of the individual holes as each tree and shrub is set out. Still another approach is the annual turning under each spring of the mulch used the previous year. However, unless the mulching material is peat moss or leaf mold and the layer turned under is at least an inch deep, the effect sought may not be realized. Thin sandy soil needs sizable amounts of either topsoil (8 to 12 inches) or compost (6 to 8 inches) to hold moisture, particularly during long dry spells. Otherwise, constant watering is essential.

The planting of such crops as Italian rye grass, buckwheat, and winter rye is a most effective means of improving sandy soils. This procedure, commonly referred to as green manure, requires effort in the way of digging, seeding, and turning over, but the results in terms of long-range gardening are well worth the work required. It is an excellent and inexpensive way to improve large areas for lawns, but green manure requires a full growing season before the grass seed can be sown.

The soil is prepared in late summer or early fall. A complete fertilizer is scattered at the rate of 50 pounds per 1,000 square feet. Seed of the crop chosen is planted at the rate of one ounce per square yard. This can be applied with a lawn seeder and raked in. The following spring the area is sprinkled with a complete fertilizer and the crop is turned over before it has matured. When sulfate of ammonia is scattered on the surface before the crop is turned over, decay of the vegetable matter is hastened. When broken down, the result is humus.

THE IMPORTANCE OF HUMUS

Humus may be defined simply as decomposed vegetable or organic matter. The leaf mold or woods soil on the forest floor is the prime form found in nature. Gardeners make their own in compost piles, by growing cover crops as previously discussed, and by adding to the soil various types of organic matter that break down with the aid of the microorganisms present. When the breakdown is complete, humus provides the energy beneath the soil that compares to photosynthesis in green plants. This process refers to the activity carried on by plants in light. Leaves aided by the sun and the green coloring matter which they contain produce sugar and starch, essential for plant growth. Thus the importance of humus for the building of healthy soil is apparent.

HOW TO MAKE A COMPOST PILE

A compost pile can be a sound and practical means of obtaining organic matter for the home garden provided it is properly made and maintained. Some gardeners build a concrete bin or make one of brick and cement or wood. Easier still, simply mark out an area 3 by 5 feet or larger in the service area or in some part of the garden where the pile can be screened from view. Dig out 10 to 12 inches of soil to make a shallow pit. Use disease-free garden refuse such as leaves, grass clippings, discarded plants, bits of sod and the like, building it in layers 8 to 10 inches thick. Coffee grounds, tea leaves, trimmings from vegetables, bones, and other forms of greaseless garbage can be added. Separate each layer with 1 to 2 inches of soil and stable manure if available. As the pile is built, layer by layer, add a thin covering of a complete fertilizer. Ground limestone, super-phosphate, and wood ashes scattered thinly may be added from time to time.

Piles are usually 3 to 4 feet tall and are always kept covered with soil. Soak thoroughly and turn the pile every few months. Bacterial agents (such as Adco) to hasten the breakdown of plant materials are worth using and should be applied as directed on the package. These are especially valuable when animal manure is not available. To provide for ventilation, make two or more holes in each pile, using a stick or a tube made of hard-ware to allow for air circulation. Strips of burlap can be used for cover. By keeping the compost pile well covered with soil and in a moist condi-tion, the breakdown of the various ingredients is hastened.

Heather, lavender cotton, rock saxifrage, juniper, thyme, sedum, cotoneasters, sea pinks, mugho pine, bearberry, and other rock plants lend a variety of form and texture to this slope planting.

Taloumis

When fresh or raw sawdust, wood chips, ground bark, straw, ground corncobs, or other waste materials of this sort are added to soil to improve its organic content, it should be remembered that these materials rob the soil of some of its existing nitrogen as they break down. Therefore, it is essential to add nitrogen. For each cubic yard of raw sawdust, wood chips, or similar material used, add 1½ pounds of ammonium nitrate or ammonium sulfate or 3 pounds of nitrate of soda. The same procedure should be followed when using these materials for mulching. However, if they have been thoroughly composted before they are dug in, the addition of nitrogen will not be necessary. Many of these materials now are packaged commercially with the nitrogen added. To be effective, organic matter of this type needs to be spread and turned under in layers at least 2 inches deep.

ADDING PEAT MOSS AND COMPOST

When peat moss or compost is used to improve soil, a two inch layer is essential in order to obtain any degree of improvement. Half the amount turned under in spring and half in the fall may prove more convenient for most beginners. Soil improvement of any type of soil is a process of gradual and continuing development.

IMPROVING CLAY SOILS

For centuries lime has been used to improve the structure of clay soils, since the reaction that occurs when lime is added aids in the formation of crumb structure. The tiny particles are united to make larger units, thus allowing air to penetrate and improve drainage. The amount of ground limestone required may vary from 20 to 40 pounds per 1,000 square feet, depending on the stiffness of the clay. Often, the amount needed can best be determined by consultation with the local county agent. Since spring weather is often uncertain and garden operations must be started early, fall is the ideal time to begin an improvement program on clay soils. Furthermore, if the soil is turned over and left in a rough state through winter, the action of weathering will be of value.

The addition of sand is another means of improving clay soil, but a sufficient amount must be added to achieve the hoped-for results. Stiff clay requires a considerable quantity of sand for effective conditioning. A layer 2 inches deep, turned over, may not be sufficient to produce the desired texture. It may take an additional inch or two to produce friable soil—the type that crumbles easily when a handful is squeezed into a ball.

For large areas needing improvement, such materials as sifted coal ashes, medium to fine gravel, or cinders from power plants are useful. When cinders are used, they need to be weathered through a winter and, if unusually coarse, they may need screening. On the other hand, small flower beds can be improved with the addition of vermiculite or Perlite. These materials

232

An old millstone makes a shallow fountain with an appropriate aquatic motif.

are light, easy to handle, and slow to disintegrate so that they perform the function of conditioning efficiently. The extent to which they are used is determined largely by the cost involved.

At best, all of these methods are concerned with the improvement of the physical structure of clay soils. Therefore, humus in some form is also essential. The methods for adding it in various forms are the same as those recommended for sandy soils previously discussed.

Chemical soil conditioners produced by reliable firms have merit but are costly and, in the long run, accomplish no better and no more permanent results than the traditional practices used by home gardeners for generations. However, in combating heavy clay soils, it is sound practice to improve thoroughly only areas large enough to be handled efficiently in any given season.

ACID, ALKALINE, AND NEUTRAL SOILS

Gardeners usually discuss soils with reference to their degree of acidity or alkalinity, because certain plants have distinct needs and preferences with regard to the kind of soil in which they grow. Soils may vary somewhat, even within the small area of an average garden. For example, in a

233

A wall made of concrete slabs protects this windswept garden.

garden where the soil is known to be acid, the degree of acidity may be greater on a flat surface than on a slope where it tends to leach. Most home gardeners think of only two kinds of soil—acid or sour, and alkaline or sweet. Yet soils that are neither decidedly acid nor alkaline are spoken of as neutral.

The degree of acidity or alkalinity in soil is determined by a system known as pH. Soil reactions as revealed by simple chemical tests are expressed by numbers. For example, neutral soil has a reading of pH 7. Soil tests showing indications higher than 7 are on the alkaline or sweet side; those lower than 7 are on the acid or sour side. Tests may indicate an extreme situation on either side of the neutral scale, resulting in a toxic condition, but this is not common.

Home gardeners are rapidly learning the value of soil testing, and there are test kits available for home gardeners that are simple and easy to use.

234

However, where a serious soil problem exists, the usual practice is to have tests made by competent analysts at the various county or state experiment stations. This service is available free or for a small fee.

Many of our native plants, as well as azaleas, rhododendrons, and other broad-leaved evergreens and deciduous plants such as blueberries, require an acid soil. While most garden soils where these plants are commonly grown need little preparation to make them suitable, it is sometimes necessary to increase soil acidity for successful culture. Acidity in the soil can be increased by the use of acid leaf mold (easily made from oak leaves), hardwood sawdust, sulfur, and fertilizers such as ammonium phosphate, ammonium sulfate, and urea. Commercially prepared acid-soil fertilizers, sometimes referred to as rhododendron and azalea plant food, often solve the problem.

With most plants that require acid soil, a lack of acidity is indicated by pale green to yellow coloring in the leaves, contrasting with the darker green of the veins, giving the effect of an unhealthy appearance. To verify the symptoms, make a soil test with one of the handy kits available, or send a soil sample, together with a statement of the condition to be remedied, to your county or state testing station. Lowering of acidity may be due to an alkaline condition in the local water supply, drainage from walls in which plaster has been used, or rubble left in the soil by builders. Certain types of fertilizer are known to produce salts that are toxic to acid-loving plants. Then, too, when plants are grown on sloping ground, the acidity tends to leach out of the soil.

To counteract these conditions, the use of aluminum sulfate is widely recommended, but prolonged use may cause a toxic condition in some soils. An easy and safe method to increase soil acidity in the home garden is by the use of ordinary dusting sulfur. Apply it in late spring or early summer by scattering ¼ pound around an average size rhododendron, azalea, or any other broad-leaved evergreen needing it, and water it in. Too much sulfur can be injurious to plants, but scattered in the proportion recommended, no harm is likely to result.

Lime has been used for improving soils for centuries. It has many valuable properties which, when clearly understood, make its use of prime importance in various types of soil. Many curious notions are held as to its merits and not all of them are sound. The term "lime" is used loosely to cover the following specific kinds. Hydrated lime, which is air-slaked (containing at least 70 percent calcium oxide), is light in weight, easy to use, and rapid in its reaction. (Some types of agricultural lime, commonly sold at low prices, are not up to standard.) Ground limestone is composed

Taloumis

A pair of old ships' figureheads looking out to sea and a carved eagle add a nautical touch to this garden terrace.

of larger particles, is slower acting, and requires ⅓ more by weight to obtain the results of hydrated lime. Finely ground oyster shells are equal in value to ground limestone.

Improving Clay Soil. Lime acts as a conditioner reducing the sticky quality of clay and improving soil structure by building the crumb structure. Thus, air can penetrate and drainage is improved enabling the soil to warm up more rapidly.

Improving Sandy Soil. Lime makes sandy soils more compact, enabling them to retain more moisture.

Counteracting Acidity. Sour or acid soils in which rhododendrons, azaleas, and other plants of the heath family (Ericaceae) thrive, together with most woodland and bog plants, are not suited to many types of annual flowers, some perennials, and vegetables. Lime is added to alkalize or sweeten such soils for the purpose of growing specific crops.

Lime for Lawns. When new lawns are made or established sod is renewed in areas of known acidity, lime is applied to sweeten the soil, to improve its texture, to aid in the liberation of plant food, and to check certain types of pests in the soil.

Lime Liberates Plant Foods. When lime acts on existing humus or organic matter in soil, it liberates soil chemicals that supply plants with essential food. In soils of heavy texture, it makes potash available.

Effects on Insects and Diseases. Lime aids in counteracting certain soil diseases and is injurious to slugs, wireworms, and other pests. However, it is not a panacea for the control of insects and diseases generally.

Lime as Aid to Plant Growth. Many plants require a certain amount of lime to flourish, particularly vegetables, but lime is not a fertilizer. Such plants as clematis, dianthus, chrysanthemums, columbines, and delphiniums are greatly improved by the addition of lime when grown in soils known to be heavily acid. Testing soil to determine these needs is important.

Plants That Dislike Lime. As previously mentioned, certain plants have a strong dislike for lime and are adversely affected by it. Thus, its use must be avoided in soils for rhododendrons, azaleas, blueberries, and other members of the heath family which includes many of our native plants. Occasionally lime is applied to these plants by accident and the results are immediately apparent.

How to Use Lime. Generally, hydrated lime is applied at the rate of 3 to 5 pounds per 100 square feet. If ground limestone is used, increase the quantity by one third. Scatter it evenly over the surface of the soil and turn it under lightly. A lawn seeder makes the task of spreading easy. If soil is dug in the fall and left rough, lime can be scattered and left to the action of weather. When larger amounts are required to correct specific conditions, they are best determined by a soil test.

It is of vital importance to remember that hydrated lime is not added to the soil simultaneously with animal manures or commercial fertilizer because the nitrogen in these plant foods is likely to be lost. At least two weeks should elapse before lime is applied under these conditions.

CHAPTER SIXTEEN

What and Why We Feed Plants

*T*HE basic practices for feeding plants are the same whether one gardens by the sea or inland. However, with light sandy soils it is sound practice to apply smaller amounts than generally recommended, but more frequent applications are needed since plant food leaches rapidly from soil of thin texture. The addition of organic matter as recommended in Chapter 15 will aid materially in reducing the amount of plant food that is normally lost in heavy rains.

For the most part, it is useless to recommend the use of stable manure for home gardens since it is seldom obtained easily. We must depend on compost, organic, and commercial fertilizers in the proper balance to provide the essential elements our plants need. In most home gardens, commercial fertilizers are the chief source of plant food. A "complete" fertilizer includes nitrogen, phosphorus, potash, and minor trace elements. It may be either chemical or organic in its makeup, or a combination of both. By law formulas must be printed on bags and packages that indicate the proportions of the various elements used. For example, the formula 5-10-5 means that it contains 5 parts nitrogen, 10 parts phosphorus, and 5 parts potash. Minor elements include magnesium, iron, boron, aluminum, and other so-called trace elements for the general well-being of plant growth.

NITROGEN, PHOSPHORUS, POTASH

Nitrogen is essential to the production of foliage for flowering plants, vegetables, fruits, and grass. Highly soluble in water, it disappears rapidly during heavy rain. Phosphorus stimulates root growth, hastens the maturity of plants, and the production of flowers and fruits. Potash is the element that provides plants with the vigor they need to tolerate changing weather conditions and build up resistance against diseases. Since it helps in the manufacture of starch and sugar, it aids the plant in developing firm stem growth. All three basic elements may be obtained separately in various concentrated forms, but they should not be used carelessly lest they damage the plants.

238

On the whole, complete fertilizers are packaged for general garden use and these should be applied at the rates specified on the container. (The amount is usually 3 to 5 pounds per 100 square feet.) Manufacturers package a wide variety of formulations in containers of varying weight. It is sound economy to buy 50-pound bags of the kinds commonly used, since packages of smaller amounts usually cost more per pound. Highly concentrated fertilizers are usually more expensive than the standard kinds offered, but the amount required for use in a given area is considerably less.

ADDING SUPERPHOSPHATE

In some soils, phosphorus may be lacking or unavailable to plant roots. Flowering or fruiting can be hastened by adding it to the soil in the form of superphosphate, a quick-acting fertilizer. It needs to be dug or watered into the soil so that it is as close as possible to the root area of the plant being fed. Use it at the rate of 3 to 5 pounds per 100 square feet.

MANURE AND OTHER ORGANIC MATERIALS

The nature of manure and other organic fertilizers, as contrasted with the commercial or inorganic types, is sometimes puzzling to beginners. Organic plant foods are raw materials that become accessible to the roots of plants only with bacterial action. These include rotted manure, mushroom compost, dried manure, bone meal, cottonseed meal, dried blood, treated sewerage sludge (Milorganite), and others. The bacteria which break down these organic substances are low forms of plant life that become active in the soil as it warms up in the late spring. In light sandy soils they begin their work much sooner than in heavy clay soils. Therefore, early applications of plant food to stimulate growth require the use of commercial or inorganic plant foods. Where organic materials are used exclusively, they often need to be supplemented periodically with balanced commercial fertilizers that contain all the essential nutrients required by plants.

CHEMICAL FERTILIZERS

Chemical fertilizers are salts mixed with inert ingredients that are readily absorbed by plant roots once they are in solution. In fact, they can only benefit plant growth when they are soluble, thus the need for thorough watering after applying them. When they are added to compost piles, they are absorbed by the bacteria in the pile and are returned to the decomposing matter when the bacteria themselves die. Thus, commercial fertilizer scattered in a compost pile aids in the breakdown of vegetable matter and is returned to the garden when the compost is added.

WHY FERTILIZERS BURN PLANTS

The statement is made that commercial fertilizers may burn plants if they come in contact with foliage and roots in dry form. The term "burn" refers to injury in the form of dehydration which occurs when the chemical

239

salts absorb water from the green tissues of stems and leaves, or from the roots. Therefore, the recommendation is made to water the soil thoroughly after applying commercial fertilizer so that the salts contained in it are in the solution. Then the fertilizer becomes effective as plant food and plant roots absorb it. Furthermore, instructions which refer to thorough mixing of fertilizers with soil before planting are based on this premise. Organic fertilizers, derived from sewerage, can also cause burning. Common occurrences of this condition are seen when lawns are fertilized and seedlings are given side dressings of fertilizer without watering; hence the importance of watering immediately after application.

WHEN AND HOW MUCH TO FEED

In feeding plants, bear in mind that most perennials need at least two applications of commercial plant food annually. The first should be applied early in the spring and the second about eight weeks later. A formula like 5-10-5 or 4-12-4 is well suited to most perennials. Kinds like chrysanthemums, hardy asters, and others that bloom in autumn, need at least three feedings to produce top quality bloom.

In the interest of economy, fertilizer applied to annuals and vegetables can be scattered around the plants and watered in. Feed 3 to 5 times during the growing season, depending on the quality of the soil. This is sound practice for plants grown in containers.

Flowering shrubs, including roses and most kinds of trees, can be fed in the same manner as perennials. Roses fed in late summer (after August 1) are encouraged to produce new growth which may not harden before winter. This practice often results in winterkill, since new growth produced late in the season does not have sufficient time to harden before cold weather sets in. Booster feedings of liquid manure and foliar sprays applied prior to midsummer are also desirable.

ACID-SOIL FERTILIZERS

Ordinary types of commercial fertilizer are not suited for use around acid-loving ericaceous plants such as rhododendrons, azaleas, pieris, blueberries, and others, since the salts are inclined to produce toxic residues in the soil. Use the specially prepared acid-soil fertilizers that are generally available. These contain organic nitrogen, preferred by acid-soil plants. Cottonseed meal is also good; it is high in nitrogen with a small percentage of phosphorus and potash. When feeding broad-leaved evergreens, plant foods are best applied early in the growing season so that new growth stimulated by feeding will have ample time to harden before cold weather sets in.

PEAT MOSS—NOT A FERTILIZER

Because peat moss is widely used in home gardens everywhere, some beginners believe that it is a form of fertilizer. To be sure, some types may

White speciosum lilies, nicotiana, petunias, and Madagascar periwinkle make an appropriate and pleasing setting for a lead figure of Pan.

241

Peppermint geranium and heliotrope predominate in this window box.

contain plant food in small amounts, but it should be considered primarily a soil conditioner. After all, the function of peat moss is to absorb water and keep soluble plant food available to hungry roots as well as to improve the soil structure for better aeration.

FOLIAR FEEDING

Concentrated plant foods that are readily soluble in water have made foliar feeding a popular method of feeding certain types of plants in recent years. The liquid plant food is absorbed by the leaves and stems through tiny openings (stomata) not visible to the naked eye. These concentrates, applied with a watering can or sprayer, have merit for stimulating growth and there is actually little waste, since the liquid which falls on the ground is absorbed by the roots. Where an immediate effect is desired, foliar feeding, although somewhat costly, produces good results. Applications are made at 10-day intervals. Although roses and chrysanthemums have been the object of wide experimentation with foliar feeding, it is used on all types of ornamental plants, fruits, vegetables, and lawns by home gardeners and commercial growers. The various types offered should be applied specifically according to the instructions on the container. Otherwise, using high concentrations of plant food, improperly diluted, can ruin a crop.

CHAPTER SEVENTEEN

Winter Protection

INTER protection in seaside gardens varies according to site and exposure, and the type of plant material used. Where native materials predominate, little protection is usually required once plantings are established. But with new plantings or when abnormally dry summer and fall seasons occur, watering and mulching are necessary. The care that is given a newly made garden during the fall and winter following planting often determines the success with which plants become established.

Many strange notions exist regarding winter protection of plants and the reasons for the various methods used. Basically, neither woody plants nor herbaceous kinds have need for warmth, as with animals. Fundamentally, an understanding of the meaning of the term "hardiness" makes the purpose of winter protection clear.

Hardiness in a plant refers to the ability of a specific kind to endure low temperatures and to survive provided it is in prime condition as the dormant period approaches. Dormancy in the growth cycle is the rest period, a normal condition that begins when leaves fall in autumn and lasts until soil warms up in spring. Severe fluctuations in temperature, notably periods of alternate thawing and freezing, may affect the normal period of dormancy adversely. Sporadic soft growth appearing in late fall or early winter and too early a start in spring are factors that can upset the normal dormant period. Then, too, plants that may have proved hardy over a period of years may not survive an unusually cold winter without adequate snow cover or one in which excess rain falls. A prolonged January thaw can be harmful if followed by a sudden drop in temperature. On the other hand, mild forms of damage may occur when flower buds are blasted but these are not considered serious in the long run, since the plant itself survives.

Thus the object of a protective mulch is to keep the soil frozen and to maintain an even temperature, not to keep the roots warm. Since fluctu-

243

ations in temperature are usually more frequent near the ocean than inland, mulching is sound practice. The function of protective cover and shading around and above stems and foliage is to provide insulation against wind and sun, and the damaging effects of windblown sand. Actually, exposure is concerned as much with windy sites as it is with those parts of the home grounds where winter sun is reflected from a building or shines directly on evergreens. Wind causes excessive transpiration, resulting in the drying out of stems and leaves. The play of sunlight has a similar effect on foliage and the plant, unable to draw water from the frozen soil, tends to dry and burn. Winter damage is usually most severe when temperatures remain abnormally low for extended periods and snow cover is sparse or nonexistent.

When drought has been serious during any given summer, heavy watering of established plantings of flowering and shade trees, shrubs, and all types of evergreens applied in *early* fall is essential. However, woody plants that drop their leaves and particularly those that flower late in the season can be harmed if watered too late in the fall, since excess moisture may stimulate soft growth which is bound to succumb to winterkill. If tender new growth appears, it is best removed by pruning. Such conditions may occur in years when Indian summer is late or prolonged.

Soaking at intervals during early fall is even more important to the survival of newly planted trees and shrubs of all kinds. Otherwise, losses from winterkill may be considerable. Winter damage occurs during prolonged freezing spells followed by periods of alternate thawing and freezing, especially when snow cover is light. Winter winds also cause evergreens to dry out when the ground is frozen.

Mulching of newly planted trees, shrubs, and evergreens is best done in coastal gardens at planting time, but mulches of a permanent nature may be applied in autumn for winter protection and allowed to remain permanently. The soil around well-mulched plants freezes more slowly and less deeply than bare ground. This fact is of prime importance in the culture of all types of evergreens, for unlike those woody plants that drop their leaves, evergreens are never completely dormant. Thus, they require available moisture to combat the drying effects of winter wind and sun. Wood chips or any coarse material not easily disturbed by wind may be used. For mulching materials, see Chapter 18. It is a mistake to apply lightweight mulches since they are easily blown away. When oak leaves, pine needles, and the like are used, they need to be anchored with chicken wire, boards or preferably with evergreen boughs.

PROTECTING TENDER PLANTS

Many gardeners, both beginners and experienced amateurs, delight in growing plants known to be of questionable hardiness and they are often successful in keeping them over a period of years by providing adequate

A wrought iron gate designed to enhance the beauty of a walled garden. The old pear tree provides flowers, fruit, and shade, and English ivy softens the brick wall.

protection. This practice is commonplace with gardeners who live by the sea, since winter temperatures are usually several degrees milder than those inland and plants of borderline hardiness often survive. Young hollies, the mop-head hydrangeas, boxwood, crepe myrtle, camellias, tender magnolias, and other treasures usually require special winter care when grown in areas beyond their limit of hardiness. Heavy watering, followed after the ground freezes by mulching with straw and leaves, and wrapping with

Taloumis

Autumn Elaeagnus makes a dense, shrublike tree, ideal for windbreaks.

burlap, are necessary. Some gardeners use building paper or chicken wire to form a protective barrier. Wooden frames, plastic and polyethylene covering are also used. However, no cover should be applied until the ground has frozen.

USING PLASTIC SPRAYS

A transparent plastic spray (as used by nurserymen for wiltproofing when transplanting) is being more widely used by home gardeners for all types of evergreens, especially the broad-leaved kinds, for winter protection. These include andromeda, azaleas, holly, laurel, rhododendrons, and others. Although most conifers have greater endurance than the broad-leaved kinds because their leaves are smaller, various forms of Japanese yew that tolerate seaside conditions surprisingly well are greatly benefited by this treatment, particularly in windswept locations. Transparent plastic sprays are most effective in reducing transpiration when applied in late November or early December on days when the temperature is approximately 50°F. Recent experience has proved that a second application in midwinter, prior to March, is worthwhile on windy, exposed sites. Directions for application are specifically stated on the container and should be followed carefully, including a thorough cleaning of the sprayer after use.

Using Mulches to Advantage

ULCHING is of prime importance in the seaside garden since wind is usually a major problem, affecting both soil and plants adversely. In a matter of a few hours, constant wind dehydrates plants and dries sandy soil more rapidly than an equal amount of exposure to the sun. Then, too, it should be remembered that sandy soils are light in texture and warm up quickly. Under abnormally dry conditions when prolonged droughts occur, sandy soils actually may become too warm for many of our cultivated plants. Most kinds thrive when soil temperatures range from 60° to 70°. The easiest and most efficient way to combat these and other maintenance problems is by mulching.

To mulch means to supply a protective cover for the soil around and between plants. It is a practice gardeners have adapted from nature's way of forming quick growth on bare ground. Among the materials commonly used are peat moss, buckwheat hulls, sawdust, rotted manure, wood chips, oak leaves, pine needles, and others discussed herein. Wood chips have special value where soil is constantly windswept since they are less likely to be blown away than other kinds of mulch. However, where fences, windbreakers, and hedges are used to check the wind, almost any of the mulching materials can be used to advantage. These materials are derived from some form of plant life itself—leaves, stems, flowers, fruits, pods, bark, or roots. They keep the soil temperature even, conserve soil moisture, allow moisture to enter the soil easily, reduce the growth of weeds, and make it easier to pull those that appear. Mulches aid greatly in maintenance by eliminating the necessity for cultivation, by preventing the formation of soil crust, and by adding to the appearance of a planting. Also, mulching newly set plants and those already established is an easy and effective way to provide the organic matter that practically all soils need.

What to use for a mulch depends primarily on the type of area to be covered, what is available, the cost involved, and the desired result. When large areas need to be mulched, the item of cost must be kept in mind, as well as the amount of attention the mulch will need. For example, if sawdust, wood chips, or chopped bark are used, nitrogen must be added, since these materials remove existing nitrogen from the soil as they break down. However, once deterioration is complete, the nitrogen cycle is reversed and this essential plant food becomes available to the roots of plants.

To compensate for the loss of nitrogen in soils where such mulches as sawdust, wood chips, chopped bark, grass clippings, straw, hay, and corncobs are used, give the soil an application of a complete fertilizer such as 10-6-4 before the mulch is put on, using 2 to 3 pounds per 100 square feet. Some gardeners mix nitrate of soda or ammonium sulfate with these materials before they are spread. To each cubic yard of mulch applied, add 1½ pounds of ammonium nitrate or ammonium sulfate or 3 pounds of nitrate of soda. If organic materials are preferred, use 5 pounds of dried blood or hoof and horn meal.

Feeding plants before any type of mulch is applied, especially in large areas, is another point to consider. If fertilizer is applied before the mulch is put on, time and labor are saved. Actually, the best time to mulch new plantings is immediately after they are planted. However, if plants are partially or well established and mulches are needed to control weeds and conserve moisture, these are best put on in early spring when the plants are beginning their growth and before weed seeds have germinated. How much mulch to use is another important point to consider. If the mulch is not put on thick enough, it will not accomplish the purposes for which it was intended.

Tests have proved that mulches applied 2 to 3 inches deep actually insulate the soil, a point of vital importance to gardeners where summers are exceptionally hot and dry, and particularly in seaside gardens where wind is a constant factor. In addition, it should be remembered that many plants have comparatively shallow root systems. With some plants, roots do not penetrate more than 6 to 10 inches below the soil, and others extend only an inch or two deep.

Peat moss is easy to handle and obtain. Cover should be at least 1 inch deep. The coarse brown peat sold in bales (usually imported) is derived from sphagnum moss and makes a satisfactory cover. However, it tends to cake when the top surface dries. This condition can be overcome by mixing soil with it. Peat from local bogs is often more desirable since it is finer in texture and often can be obtained at moderate cost if purchased in quantity. The finer grades of peat are easier to spread than the sphagnum type, which is fibrous in texture, and they are also easier to soak. Peat absorbs ten times its weight in water, and this point should be borne in mind when applying it. Never apply bone-dry peat to the soil as a mulch, or incorporate it with fairly dry soil, since the dry peat tends to pull the moisture from the soil as it comes in contact with it. Therefore,

248

Taloumis

A two-inch mulch of beach stones makes an attractive and effective soil cover to conserve moisture on this seaside terrace.

it is essential to soak peat thoroughly before applying it as a mulch or adding it to soil to improve its texture.

Sawdust makes a practical mulch and is being more widely used by home gardeners throughout the country. Usually it is obtainable by hauling from any local sawmill. The coarse grade is preferable, because it does not pack together and crust as quickly. The use of nitrogen, as previously discussed, is essential. Fresh sawdust is apt to be unsightly when first applied because of its light coloring. However, it can be piled and allowed to weather before using or it can be mixed with soil. Sawdust does not blow around easily and does not absorb moisture from the soil like dry peat. It allows the rain to penetrate and it is gradually added to the soil as it deteriorates. If applied at least $1\frac{1}{2}$ inches deep, it controls weeds satisfactorily and functions as a useful mulch.

Wood chips make an excellent mulch for permanent use. It should be remembered that they are slow to deteriorate, depending on the size used. Because the particles vary in size, water can penetrate the soil easily. This material weathers in appearance as it ages and its rough texture is by no means objectionable. Apply it at least $1\frac{1}{2}$ inches deep. When new, it can be darkened by scattering a thin cover of native peat over it. As previously mentioned, provide for adding nitrogen.

249

Taloumis

Coarse wood chips make an ideal mulch for seaside gardens since they retain soil moisture, check weeds and are not easily blown away.

Well-rotted stable manure and spent mushroom compost are ideal for level ground or easy slopes. These materials have the advantage of supplying plant food as well, but they are not always easily obtainable everywhere. Apply at least an inch deep.

Leaf mold in various stages of decomposition is a good and useful mulch. In its coarser forms it can be used on slopes, especially if mixed with the surface layer of soil. Spread it at least 1 inch deep; otherwise, use peat or some other material on top of it to achieve the effect desired.

Pine needles, when obtainable, are the best of mulches for acid-soil plants, particularly the various types of broad-leaved and needle evergreens. This kind of cover is always good to look at and allows moisture to penetrate easily. If the mulch can be applied thickly enough, it can be used on fairly steep slopes. One to two inches of cover are desirable.

Composted bark and redwood bark are readily available. This material is not blown away by wind, allows water to penetrate easily, breaks down slowly, and is dark in color. Nitrogen is sometimes included in packaging; otherwise it must be added as previously mentioned. Coconut and yucca fiber are also considered useful mulches on the West Coast.

250

Oak leaves are a natural mulch for acid-soil plants. They break down slowly and have strong eye appeal as well for naturalistic settings. Use 2 to 3 inches around rhododendrons and azaleas and other ericaceous plants.

Sugar cane, shredded, often used for poultry litter, has its group of advocates. Although somewhat light in color, it weathers with age, and allows moisture to penetrate easily.

Straw, provided it is free of seed, and *salt marsh hay* are adaptable and practical for large surfaces and sloping areas where erosion is a factor. However, these materials are fire hazards. As with sawdust, add fertilizer to the soil before the hay or straw is used.

Ground corncobs serve in areas where they are plentiful. Extra nitrogen must be added to the soil before the mulch is applied, and the general use of these has perhaps more disadvantages than good points.

Spent hops make a good soil cover but have an objectionable odor, although this will not be offensive if the material is not placed too close to windows or sitting-out areas.

Buckwheat hulls have long been at the top of the list as an ideal type of mulch, particularly for roses. The one objection to these is cost, but the dark brown color and the light weight make them a joy to handle. As a mulch they absorb little or no moisture from the ground, allow the rain water and water from sprinklers and hoses to penetrate easily. They are ideal because they are rich in organic content and decompose slowly. Buckwheat hulls do not have any apparent effect on nitrogen depreciation in the soil. Gardeners who have used them for years simply add more each year, keeping the thickness of this mulch to 1½ inches, with amazingly good results. Normally they do not blow away except in exposed areas, but they are not practical on sloping ground, being too light in weight.

Grass clippings are desirable because they are easy to obtain and it is a good way to add the leaves of this most important of all ground covers to the soil. However, they are not particularly pleasing in appearance and they break down so rapidly that considerable quantities are needed to make a heavy application. During moist, humid weather they give off a rather unpleasant odor as they decay, and they pull needed nitrogen out of the soil, a point to be remembered. Yet they add vitally important organic material to the soil. Two inches of grass clippings are essential if the mulch is to have any real effect.

Black plastic film, aluminum foil, and tar paper are used commercially for mulches, and these, while quite effective, are hard to handle and not easy to look at. They are satisfactory and may be necessary on severe slopes where erosion is a serious problem. In limited areas, strips of burlap

251

may be used. All these materials are fairly costly if sizable amounts are needed.

Coffee grounds are rich in organic matter and contribute to the acidity of sour soils. People who use great quantities of coffee find it more convenient to put their grounds in a can in the garden until they have a sufficient amount, or place them where they can do the most good immediately.

Tanbark makes a most attractive and useful mulch as well as a good surface to walk on. However, it is not easily obtainable, but it is included in this list to remind those who can obtain it not to overlook its value.

Cocoa shells have been widely used in the gardens at Hershey, Pennsylvania, and elsewhere in areas close to chocolate factories. They make a coarse-looking but effective mulch.

Walnut shells, particularly those of ground black walnut, are sometimes used where available. They break down slowly and make an attractive appearance.

Crushed stone, pebbles, and washed gravel give a certain finish and pattern, as well as contrast to the plantings. These materials are well suited for tailored gardens where flat areas need mulch. If certain color effects are desired, colored gravel can be obtained. If light shades or white gravel or pebbles are used, the harsh effects can be softened by the planting of ivy or some other trailing plant that breaks the surface and makes a pleasing kind of tracery. This is a way of achieving unusual patterned effects.

Stone mulches are particularly appropriate and practical in rock gardens, especially where they are exposed to wind. Peat moss is actually harmful to most alpines, a fact that some gardeners learn too late. Actually, many of the choicest alpine plants grown in American rock gardens are afforded the best kind of prolonged life in summer and winter with the use of stone chips.

Ground cover plants, discussed in Chapter 10, are nature's own mulch. In many ways they are superior to the majority of the materials listed in this chapter, but they require care and maintenance that in some instances are not warranted. However, in large shrub plantings, on slopes and banks, and in places where grass cannot be handled easily, ground covers serve as the best of mulches.

CHAPTER NINETEEN

Pruning

P

RUNING is truly an art and reflects more than any other single phase of gardening the amateur's skill or lack of it in understanding plants and how they grow naturally. The purpose of pruning is to improve the appearance of woody plants and to control their growth with relation to the area in which they are grown. This practice also increases the flowering and fruiting habits of ornamentals and fruit-bearing kinds. Yet pruning shears can be a dangerous weapon in the hands of those who use them thoughtlessly. Actually, the basic principles involved are simple and, once understood, are easy to practice. Such descriptive phrases as "whiffle-cuts" and "shear horror" describe only too well much of the present-day pruning done by many local landscape service and maintenance crews.

For decades, hedges, flowering shrubs, and evergreens have been butchered and barbered into grotesque shapes, patterned somewhat after the topiary of old-world gardens, but often lacking completely the imagination, skill, and placement which made the art of topiary a kind of living sculpture. Settings around certain types of houses call for formal planting, and in such locations clipped shrubbery, particularly evergreens, has a distinct place. Formally trimmed hedges also are highly ornamental and add greatly to the beauty of a tailored landscape planting.

However, shrubs sheared formally, either as specimens or hedges, should be handled with the idea of encouraging new growth all the way to the ground. All too often, the tendency is to trim them wider at the top than at the base, causing the lower branches to die out. The effect is a leggy, unsightly mass of foliage, often topheavy.

Frequently, in an attempt to control the growth of big-scale evergreens, they are sheared and barbered until only the outer tier of growth is green while all the branches within the framework are brown and bare. Severe drought, a heavy infestation of insects, or the damage created by low temperatures during an unusually severe winter are causes of dead growth frequently appearing in large patches on mature evergreens that have been tightly sheared. The result is an unsightly effect, and often they are fit only for the rubbish pile.

RETAINING NATURAL FORM

On the other hand, pruning shears in the hands of the thoughtful gardener can be used skillfully to thin growth, to emphasize the significant lines and shape of a tree or shrub and, generally speaking, to retain its natural aspect, whether pyramidal, global or columnar. The distinct forms of Japanese holly (*Ilex crenata*), when allowed to grow naturally, develop typical mound shapes. Certain arborvitaes have a definite globular habit of growth, while others are columnar in form. Many of the evergreen azaleas are compact in habit, moundlike, and low-spreading by nature. Such shrubs as these require only light pruning annually. It is done by shortening new growth to retain the typical form, but allowing the entire surface to remain fluffy and irregular. To trim shrubs of this sort by close shearing is to detract greatly from their natural beauty.

PRUNING TOOLS

Use sharp shears or a saw to make clean cuts, and be sure that the blade of the shears you use is adequate for the size of the branch you attempt to cut. Long-handled pruners are used for big-scale shrubs that produce heavy wood. Several handy-to-use types of pruning saws are sold in hardware stores and garden centers. These are comparatively inexpensive and most practical for cutting big branches since they have interchangeable blades in several sizes. For removing tree limbs out of normal reach, there are pole pruners and pole saws. Keep tools clean, well oiled, and sharp, and have a convenient place for storing them.

USING TREE PAINT

When sizable branches (more than ¾ of an inch in diameter) are removed from trees or shrubs, wounds should be treated with tree paint which can be applied by using one of the new aerosol-type sprays. These are most efficient and easy to use since none of the paint is wasted and spraying covers the surface evenly. If moisture is present on exposed surfaces after cuts have been made, allow it to drain away before applying tree paint.

FORSYTHIA—RIGHT AND WRONG

Forsythia is often a victim of unfortunate treatment. It has a natural fountainlike, vase-shaped form. Although some types are stiffer and more upright than others, a few are notably pendulous. In either case, there is distinct grace and beauty in the appearance of a well-grown specimen of forsythia that has been pruned to preserve its natural habit. Most kinds reach a height of 8 or 9 feet when mature, often spreading even wider

French pussy willow becomes roundheaded with constant wind pruning.

than their height. Frequently the space required may be greater than is desired. However, by shortening the individual stems and branches to the desired size, the entire shrub can be kept within bounds. Branches are cut back at varying lengths, while preserving the typical character of the growth. In the process, some of the old growth is removed entirely from the base. The time to prune forsythia is after flowering.

What happens when a forsythia is trimmed in geometric fashion? In summer it looks like a green ball, pyramid, or block, whereas in winter it has the appearance of a bunch of ugly sticks. The same is true of spirea,

255

Wintercreeper, cotoneasters, junipers and other low-growing shrubs soften the outline.

mock orange, and any number of other flowering shrubs, trimmed (not pruned) in this manner.

BASIC RULES FOR SHRUBS

A basic rule in pruning most flowering shrubs is to remove the oldest stems at ground level to encourage new growth from the base. The ideal time to prune is immediately after flowering. However, there are times when pruning must be done during the dormant season and some flower buds are bound to be cut away. Sometimes new growth or lateral branches are awkward in habit, or they detract from the symmetry of the plants. These need to be removed, together with all dead, diseased, and weak growth, branches that rub against one another, and gnarled wood. Then the growth of the remaining branches is shortened individually, all the while bearing in mind the natural habit and form of the shrub being pruned.

Actually, few plants grow in perfect symmetry without some manipulation by the gardener, but within the structure of any well-grown shrub or tree there exists a basic symmetry of form that can be followed after a little study.

Since most beginners are a bit wary about pruning shrubs as drastically as is often essential, the following procedure may prove helpful. First remove less of each branch than is desired; pull out or "tuck under" the branch to be removed before actually cutting. Then stand back and ob-

256

serve the effect before you cut. In most cases, it is best to make two cuts rather than one drastic one, which might eliminate an important branch that can never be replaced.

PRUNING SHADE AND FLOWERING TREES

Flowering and shade trees often need pruning to improve form, as well as the removal of lower branches and those damaged by insects and weather. If stems are unusually large, several cuts may be required for removal, taking sections one at a time. Remember that the final cut should be made flush with the main trunk, taking care not to skin the bark as the limb is severed. Any damage that occurs to the bark surface should be trimmed clean and painted. Where large trees are involved, the job may be more wisely handled by a skilled arborist. It usually involves climbing and, with trained help available, the tree can be attended to at the same time.

HANDLING LILACS

Lilacs are often disappointing in the bloom they produce, even after they have reached a fair size. Many times this condition is the result of allowing too many suckers to develop at the base. When these suckers develop in quantity, the large flowering stems do not produce the bloom that should be normally expected of them. Therefore, keep lilacs clean at the base if free-blooming plants are desired. With neglect, old growth may become borer-ridden and this should be removed entirely. Then, too, lilacs are often allowed to grow taller than is desirable. Reducing height involves drastic cutting which is best done immediately after flowering.

REJUVENATING OLD SHRUBS

Through neglect, shrubs often become decrepit and overgrown. The question often arises, Shall they be removed or replaced? In many instances they can be revived by judicious pruning. First remove the least desirable growth. Considerable thinning may be required and the immediate result may be to make the plant look a mere skeleton, but this is often the treatment needed for renewal. When the operation is done in early spring, new growth quickly transforms the appearance of such a shrub. Feeding and watering after pruning will stimulate growth. Practically all flowering shrubs that lose their leaves in winter respond to this treatment. Examples include:

Beauty bush	Kerria	Shrub roses
Flowering quince	Lilacs	Viburnums
Forsythia	Mock orange	Weigela
Honeysuckle	Rose of Sharon	Winged euonymus

PRUNING AND TOPPING EVERGREENS

Evergreens, particularly yews, are often victims of bad pruning. It is an easy matter to study their natural habit of growth and to snip here and there to check rampant growth and at the same time preserve the natural appearance.

In controlling the height of evergreens, small flowering trees, and big-scale shrubs, topping is often necessary to retain good scale in a planting. One or more leader branches may need to be cut. Then several side-growing branches will develop. These in turn need to be headed back, as the expression goes. This type of pruning controls growth effectively.

REPLACING LEADERS IN TREES

Sometimes leaders (the tips of main stems) are damaged by borers, storms, or heavy snow. The damaged part should be cut back to healthy growth, and the wound treated with tree paint if it is more than $\frac{3}{4}$ of an inch in diameter. This precaution prevents insect attack on the cut surface. Usually a vigorous side branch can be induced to form a new leader by staking it to grow upright. If leaders are split so that the bark is not seriously injured all the way around the stem, they can often be taped and with the aid of a splint, made secure. In many cases they will continue to grow after the wound heals.

CREATING HIGH SHADE

Shade is a handicap to bloom in many gardens where trees are allowed to develop dense growth, preventing light from entering sizable areas. Crab-apples, elms, lindens, locusts, maples, oaks, tree of heaven, and others are offenders in this respect. Branches can be cut back to the trunk without disturbing the appearance of the trees concerned. The process may have to be repeated every few years. Thinning heavy growth and lifting or removing low limbs produces what is known as high shade, an ideal condition for growing azaleas, rhododendrons, and a host of perennials, as well as annuals. This job requires two people, one to do the cutting and one to direct it. By increasing light, undergrowth will produce more bloom that lasts longer than in full sun.

PRUNING GRAPES

Pruning grapes should be done as soon as possible in spring. No matter how old a vine may be, it can be revived to a productive stage by skillful and severe pruning. This is often a hard lesson for beginners to learn but hard pruning is essential to encourage new growth for a crop of grapes. In some gardens, grapes are grown solely to provide shade or for ornamental effects rather than for fruit. In these instances, heavy pruning may not be desirable, nor is it necessary.

Newly planted grapes are easy to handle since there is only a single stem or trunk to contend with, and it should be cut back to three buds. Pruning an old grapevine may appear to be complicated at first. The easiest way to train grapes is to provide strong support in the way of posts and wire for a two-branched candelabrum effect. Remove all but one strong shoot to serve as a trunk and allow two sets of arms that emanate from the main trunk. Cut each of these back to four or five buds for each arm and tie the arms securely to the support.

Fruit is produced on young growth from the previous year's buds but not every shoot can be expected to yield. As the young shoots develop and flower clusters appear, it is interesting to note that they are arranged alternately along the shoot at the axils or the leaves. Usually three to five flower clusters appear on each new shoot, which may extend 10 to 15 feet or more in length during a single growing season.

In reviving an old grapevine remember that the wood of the previous year's growth, needed to make the arms, is smooth, whereas the bark of older wood is loose, with a shredded or stringy appearance. Regardless of the age of your grapevine, do not be afraid to cut a heavy, gnarled trunk out completely if you have a young shoot emanating from the base, since this can be trained to become a new trunk. It will bear repeating to state that unless grapes are pruned hard, fruit cannot be expected.

RASPBERRIES

Raspberries produce fruit on stems that developed the previous year; after fruiting, these canes die. As early in spring as possible, remove all canes that have produced fruit and all weak growth. Allow at least six inches between stems and be sure to remove any that are bruised or broken. Raspberries need to be topped at this time and some varieties can be cut lower than others. The average height for topping in spring is four feet. If strong supports of posts and wire are provided, canes can be tied to the wire and grown as a compact hedgerow. This treatment makes raspberries easy to handle and care for. Under normal conditions, the canes can be expected to grow six feet tall or even higher during a single growing season. Every effort should be made to keep the growth tidy for easy spraying and harvesting. Otherwise, the canes become a tangled mess.

BLUEBERRIES

In pruning blueberries, remove only dead and damaged twigs and such growth as will make for more shapely plants. This is a spring operation.

FRUIT TREES

Fruit trees need attention in early spring. The aim in pruning is to develop a balanced, open-headed tree that will permit ample sunlight to reach all the branches and allow for free circulation of air. First remove all diseased or broken branches and top vigorous young shoots produced the previous year by cutting them back. Then clean out all water sprouts or suckers that appear along the sides of the branches. These are easily recognized by their rank growth and whiplike appearance. Growth that crosses or rubs should be removed. Spray large cut surfaces with tree paint; cuts made in removing smaller growth heal quickly and need not be treated.

Old fruit trees that have had little care in previous years may look somewhat stiff and ungainly after severe pruning, but once they have leafed out the marks of pruning are soon camouflaged by foliage. A carefully pruned fruit tree of balanced form is less likely to break under the weight of fruit or to suffer severe damage in a heavy snow or ice storm than a tree that is one-sided.

CHECKING RODENT DAMAGE ON FRUIT TREES

The bark of fruit trees is sometimes damaged by rabbits, mice, and other rodents during winter months, but the ravages are seldom discovered until pruning time. Trouble usually occurs near the surface of the soil or within a foot of the ground. A protective collar of hardware wire inserted two inches below the surface of the soil and allowed to extend at least a foot aboveground is the simplest and most effective means of protection. However, if this practice has not been followed and bark has been girdled, clean away the rough edges of the bark with a knife and spray with tree paint at once. Unless the tree has been completely girdled, it can be expected to survive. To help revive it, dig in a generous shovelful of fertilizer and water thoroughly. Severe pruning of all top branches will reduce the leaf area and aid a damaged tree in revival. Then, too, foliar feeding applied as the buds break will provide the buds and foliage with the readily available plant food they need without overtaxing the weakened stem.

The art of pruning is easier to master than is generally believed. By first studying woody plants that require attention and analyzing their needs, one soon develops a critical eye. Surprising results can be achieved in reviving neglected shrubs and trees as well as maintaining the youth and vigor of those recently planted.

A dooryard garden featuring clematis, English lavender, heather, campanulas, pinks
and other perennials.

261

CHAPTER TWENTY

Controlling Pests and Diseases

Bugs and blights are the biggest headaches that most gardeners
have, and sometimes they can be challenging enough to be discouraging. Yet these pests have always been with us, and the chances
are that they are here to stay. But there are ways to control them. Undoubt-
edly, Adam and Eve knew the tribulations of bugs and bothers. One noted
entomologist delights in recalling a passage from Joel 1:4: "That which
the palmer worm hath left the locust eaten; and that which the locust hath
left the cancer worm eaten; and that which the cancer worm hath left, the
caterpillar eaten."

Quotations from the Bible offer little consolation when Japanese beetles descend in great numbers on roses, grapes, marigolds, zinnias, and a
host of other plants, or cutworms lay waste a whole row of newly set seedlings. Yet systematic efforts to control plant pests are comparatively recent.
It was only a little more than a hundred years ago that New York State em-
ployed its first professsional entomologist, and two years later the federal
government did likewise. During the past two decades, with the aid of
scientific research, materials and equipment have been improved to such
an extent that the physical effort involved in checking pests is not as great
as it once was, and efficient control is more easily assured. However, not all
the latest chemicals are without shortcomings, nor has any panacea yet
appeared on the market. In any event, garden health is easier to maintain
if pests and diseases are checked before they have made headway, as with
Japanese beetle control. Keeping plants healthy by adequate feeding, watering, and mulching is basic to all good garden practice and helps to make
them more resistant to common plant diseases.

Control of garden pests has been made comparatively simple in recent
years with the appearance of all-purpose sprays and dusts. These are available in many forms including aerosol types that are easy to apply. Then,
too, for overall spraying, attachments made for the garden hose assure the
gardener of adequate coverage with little effort. Instructions are carefully

262

printed on insecticide containers and materials should be used as directed. Since some spray materials are highly toxic, they must be kept out of reach of children. Federal and state regulations require that all ingredients used in a formula must be printed on the container, together with any special instructions essential for their handling.

The pests discussed here are the common kinds most likely to be encountered in the average garden. However, no attempt has been made in this brief chapter to describe all of the common plant pests and diseases. Rather the presentation is aimed at description and control of typical kinds.

FRIENDLY INSECTS

Not all the insects we see in the garden are harmful, but would that there were more friendly ones to help in checking those that ravage our plants.

Ladybugs. Rejoice when you see ladybugs, for they live on the various kinds of aphids or plant lice, mealy bugs, and tiny scale insects that appear on the stems and leaves of practically all kinds of plants. Several California firms advertise ladybugs for sale and they have been used most effectively in ridding large shade trees of heavy infestations of aphids and other kinds of pests as well.

Praying Mantis. It resembles a giant grasshopper, is light green in color, and often blends with the surrounding foliage. It poses motionless among plants and waits patiently for its victims. While waiting for its prey, it secures itself firmly and holds armlike tentacles upward as if in prayer, hence the common name. Actually, the praying mantis should be known as the *preying* mantis for it preys on a wide variety of injurious insects ranging from aphids to various kinds of beetles and flies. The female produces a gummy fluid in which to lay her eggs and this dries on the stems of plants and looks like a bit of brown or tan dried foam. Because of its curious shape and color, it is easily noticed. Sometimes in cleaning the garden in autumn, these egg masses are accidentally cut off. Do not destroy them; simply tie them to a nearby shrub and they will hatch out the following spring. Egg clusters are advertised in the garden pages of metropolitan papers and in garden magazines.

Fireflies. On summer nights fireflies, also known as glowworms, appear in gardens. Like the ladybug and the praying mantis, this insect is one of the gardener's best friends. It eats tiny pests of various kinds, as well as snails, slugs, and cutworms, in addition to making its presence welcome by a streak of light in the dusk.

Birds. Berry-bearing shrubs, bird feeders, and bird baths help to attract birds to a garden and every effort should be made to encourage their presence since they eat quantities of insects in various stages of development.

Lady Washington geraniums at Carmel-by-the-Sea, California.

ELIMINATE BREEDING PLACES OF PESTS

Maintaining order and neatness on the home grounds by clearing away debris frequently helps to eliminate breeding places of various kinds of pests. Areas where trash containers are kept, those adjacent to compost piles, or where peat moss, soil, sand, pots, stones, bricks, or lumber may be stored are likely breeding places for earwigs, slugs, and other pests. Destroy by burning all disease- and insect-ridden vegetation and woody stems removed in pruning as well as discarded plants.

SOME COMMON PESTS AND DISEASES

Ants on Peonies and Roses. Although their appearance is often disturbing, ants do little damage since they are seeking the sweet secretions given off by the buds or by aphids often found on the buds. Actually ants

264

do no harm, but if infestations are heavy, they may damage other plants and should be traced back to their nests, which can be destroyed with chlordane or one of the aerosol bomb-type sprays.

Aphids. These tiny sucking insects attack the new growth of practically all types of plants from the tallest tree to the smallest annual. In some seasons they are more annoying than in others. When they appear in great numbers, they weaken new growth considerably by sucking the sap and they often disfigure foliage, fruit, and flowers. Furthermore, aphids spread diseases. Control with contact sprays, such as nicotine sulfate or one of the aerosol types. See also Roses, Chapter 6.

Bagworms. Early spring is the time to look for bagworms on evergreens. Bagworms appear on junipers, cedars, arborvitae, larch, hemlock, spruce, and pines. They are brownish in color and look like tiny elongated bags. Since they harbor eggs of ravaging caterpillars, they should be cut off and burned before they hatch in late spring.

Blackspot. See Chapter 6.

Borers in Trees and Shrubs. Evidence of borers in dogwood, lilacs, birch, as well as many kinds of evergreens, shade trees, and flowering shrubs is usually detected by tiny piles of sawdust at the base of the plant, or particles may adhere to the bark. Use a flexible wire and work it into the hole as far as you can push it, then plug holes with soap or borer paste so that additional eggs cannot be laid by flying insects.

Brown Canker. See Chapter 6.

Caterpillar Nests. These appear as cobwebby masses in the crotches of apples, cherries, and crab apples and should be destroyed before they hatch. In suburban areas, examine wild cherries which are favorite nesting trees for the webbed caterpillar, a most annoying and destructive pest if not checked. Nests in high branches can be removed with a torch on a long pole.

Cutworms are an annual plague in many home gardens, and spraying does not always do away with them. The soil can be treated with chlordane before young plants are set out, or poison bait may be used where the infestation is serious. Since poison bait can be harmful to children and animals, its use is not always advisable. While it takes time, the simplest and most effective practice is to put a paper collar around each seedling. Bury it at least an inch below the ground. This serves as a barrier to cutworms, who usually do their damage just below the surface of the soil.

Cyclamen Mite. Delphiniums are particularly subject to infection from the cyclamen mite, which causes the leaves to curl and become distorted and the lower stems to turn black. Spray with a miticide such as

Aramite, making sure to hit the undersides of the leaves and the crowns of the plants where these tiny black pests congregate. If a number of choice delphiniums are being grown and only a few are infected, it is best to dig up and destroy infected plants by burning, and spray those remaining to avoid infection.

Earwigs. The European earwig, which looks like a water bug on springs with long, pincerlike appendages at its tail, moves rapidly indoors or out. In addition to being repulsive in appearance, it is an omnivorous eater of plants. Furthermore, this pest is easily brought indoors on flowers, clothing, or on any article left on the ground, even for a few minutes. Once inside, earwigs may be found around the kitchen sink, in the bathroom, or even in beds and overstuffed furniture.

One of its most annoying characteristics is its tendency to hide during the sunny hours of the day, becoming active in the early morning and evening hours. It feeds on most flowering plants, many kinds of vegetables, and also attacks fruits.

Earwigs can be controlled with poison bait scattered in beds and borders, using an ounce of Paris green to each pound of moistened bread crumbs. Several insecticides can be used for control. Among these are DDT and chlordane, both available either in powder or liquid form. Use according to instructions on the container. Any control measure is best applied before the earwigs are fully developed, usually from early to mid-June. Spray around the foundations of buildings, under shrubs, near compost piles, or wherever there is decayed vegetable matter, in which these insects find food. Fortunately, the European earwig is affected whenever it comes in contact with the insecticides mentioned, but when infestation is heavy, several sprayings may be necessary.

Elm Bark Beetles. To check the ravages of these pests, which spread the deadly Dutch elm disease, spray thoroughly with DDT in early spring before the buds begin to swell. Early spraying checks the beetles before they penetrate the bark. With trees more than 10 to 12 feet tall, this is a job for a tree surgeon and is well worth the cost. Urging your neighbors who have elms to do likewise is good community effort in order to check the ravages of this serious disease.

Fireblight. A disease that attacks cotoneasters, hawthorns, pears, crab apples, and other members of the rose family, it is easily recognized by darkened stems with a burned look, dieback, and defoliation of the infected parts. Cut and burn diseased parts immediately and sterilize the pruning shears after use to avoid spreading.

Iris borers become active in early summer. If iris foliage looks sickly or flower stems topple, examine the stems or roots (rhizomes) at once for these pests. Use a sharp knife to remove the offender and cut out all soft growth. Dust wounds with sulfur.

266

Beach plum on Cape Cod.

Japanese Beetle. See Chapter 6.

Lace bugs attack rhododendrons, evergreen azaleas, and other broad-leaved evergreens during late spring. These are tiny insects approximately ⅛ inch long and are so called because of their lacelike wings. Evidence of their damage is indicated by a mottled grayish appearance on the upper sides of the leaves and usually they are most troublesome to plants in full sun. Spray with Black Leaf 40, hitting both sides of the leaves. For heavy infestations several sprayings may be necessary.

Leafhopper. See Chapter 6.

Mildew. See Chapter 6.

Red Spider. A tiny mite known as red spider attacks all kinds of evergreens, particularly spruce and junipers, causing the needles to turn brown, and such broad-leaved types as azaleas, rhododendrons and others, giving the undersurface of the foliage a rusty appearance. Red spider is found also on the undersides of the leaves of annuals, perennials, and

267

flowering shrubs, and causes rose foliage to turn yellow and drop off. Few gardeners have ever seen a red spider, because it takes fifty of them stretched end to end to cover one inch of a ruler. When infection is suspected, test by placing a piece of white paper under the foliage and rub your hands on the undersurface. The tiny mites look like specks of red dust.

Where infestations on evergreens are light, the cobwebby nests made by these pests can be washed away easily by a strong spray of water from the hose, every few days. However, to control these pests where infestation is serious, use a miticide like Aramite. Follow instructions carefully in applying and be sure to hit the undersides of the foliage where these pests tend to nest.

Rose Chafer. See Chapter 6.

Rose Midge. See Chapter 6.

Rust. See Chapter 6.

Scale. The commonest and most annoying scale insect is the euonymus scale which commonly attacks wintercreeper (euonymus), pachysandra, and other broad-leaved evergreens. This encrusted insect collects along the stems and on the undersides of the leaves. Apply a dormant oil spray in early spring, coating the infected areas thoroughly. Where infection is heavy, spray with Malathion later, when the tiny pests begin to crawl. If only small areas are infected, branches or stems can be cut out and burned. Without control, this pest causes serious damage. Various kinds of scale that attack other shrubs such as lilacs are controlled similarly.

Slugs nest under boards and debris around compost piles and other parts of the garden where it is damp. Remove litter where they nest and spread lime around plants where slugs are numerous. They cannot crawl over it without injury.

Tent Caterpillar. See Caterpillar Nests.

Thrips. See gladiolus, Chapter 13, and Roses, Chapter 6.

A protective picket fence closely set shields the garden.

CHAPTER TWENTY-ONE

Special Plant Lists

HARDY SHRUBS AND VINES FOR BELT I, NORTH (on the shore)

Kinds useful for hedges are designated with an asterisk (*).

*Barberry	Groundsel bush	Salt tree
*Bayberry	Hall's honeysuckle	Sea buckthorn
*Beach plum	*Honeysuckle	Seaside rose
Bittersweet	Juniper	Shadbush
Broom	Matrimony vine	Sumac
*Buckthorn	*Mugho pine	*Tamarisk
Buffalo berry	Pea tree	Virginia creeper
Coralberry	*Rugosa rose	Willow
Cotoneaster	*Russian olive	*Yeddo hawthorn

SHRUBS FOR BELT I, SOUTH (on the shore)

Kinds useful for hedges are designated with an asterisk (*).

Acacia	*Glossy privet	*Milk bush
*Australian pine	Gold dust tree	Mirror plant
Bay cedar	Gray butterfly bush	*Natal plum
Beach heliotrope	Groundsel bush	Saltwort
Box-leaf Eugenia	Hymenanthera	*Sea box
Butcher's broom	Japanese laurel	*Sea grape
Chile barberry	*Japanese oleaster	Seaside croton
Cotoneaster	*Japanese pittosporum	*Tamarisk
Daisy bush	*Japanese privet	Wax myrtle
*Dildoe	Jaquinia	*Wax privet
Fuchsia	Lophomyrtus	*Yeddo hawthorn
	Marlberry	

SHRUBS FOR BELT I, WEST (on the shore)

Acacia	Bottle brush	Broom
Barberry	Brewer salt bush	Carmel ceanothus

Chaste tree	Japanese oleaster	Rugosa rose
Cherry laurel	Japanese pittosporum	Russian olive
Coastal wattle	Japanese privet	Salal
Cotoneaster	Juniper	Salt bush
Daisy bush	Lantana	Sea box
Desert willow	Lemonade berry	Smooth sumac
Euonymus	Melaleuca	Strawberry tree
Gold dust tree	Mexican blue palm	Sugar sumac
Greenleaf aucuba	Mirror plant	Tamarisk
Heath banksia	Mugo pine	Toyon
Honeysuckle	Natal plum	Windmill palm
Hooker manzanita	Pacific wax myrtle	Zabel laurel
	Pindo palm	

Note: Shrubs suited for Belts II and III, North, South and West, may be selected from those discussed in Chapter 5.

PAVING PLANTS

Miniature plants for use in the crevices of walks, flagstone paths, terraces, and patios must be of compact habit and matlike in their growth, and have the ability to endure traffic. It is an easy matter to pull up bits of sedum and tuck them here and there in the crevices, but these are seldom satisfactory. They are soft and succulent, and become slippery when trodden. Spaces between paving stones are sometimes a problem. Grass and weeds work their way into these tiny crevices, develop a well-established root system under the moist stones, and become difficult to eradicate. If witchgrass or any other deep-rooting kind gets a foothold, it is often necessary to lift the entire walk to remove these pests.

To attempt to grow ordinary lawn grass between these crevices is not satisfactory, because the grass can be kept low only where there is constant traffic. Where grass is used, corners and edges of walks need constant shearing by hand. Creeping plants that stay an inch or so in height are the answer. If there is considerable space between stones, use soil mixed with sand as a filler before planting. Those marked with an asterisk (*) can be walked on easily. The others in this list are suggested for decorative effects in corners and along the edges of paved surfaces.

Aubretia	Kenilworth ivy	*Speedwell
Auricula (primula)	*Mazus	Stonecress
*Baby tears	Moneywort	Stonecrop
*Bluets	*Moss sandwort	Strawberry geranium
Bugleweed	*Mountain sandwort	Thrift
*Camomile	*New Zealand bur	*Thyme
Creeping baby's	Phlox	*Turfing daisy
breath	Pinks	Wall rock cress
*Creeping mint	*Pussytoes	*Whitlow grass
Harebells	*Snow-in-summer	Wire plant
Houseleeks		*Woolly yarrow

Seaside Ground Covers

Bayberry	Fleeceflower	Roman wormwood
Beach wormwood	Fragrant sumac	Rugosa rose
Bearberry	Fringed wormwood	St. John's-wort
Bergenia	Hall's honeysuckle	Sandwort
Bird's-foot trefoil	Harebell	Savory
Bittersweet	Heath	Silver mound
Blue fescue	Heather	artemisia
Broom	Houseleek	Snow-in-summer
Cinquefoil	Juniper	Stonecrop
Cotoneaster	Lantana	Sunrose
Creeping baby's	Lavender cotton	Sweet fern
breath	Lilyturf	Sweet Woodruff
Day lily	Matgrass	Thrift
Dwarf rosemary	Memorial rose	Thyme
Dwarf willow	Moss sandwort	Verbena
English lavender	Mugho pine	Wire plant
Evergreen candytuft	Oregon holly grape	Woolly speedwell
Fig marigold	Potentilla	Woolly yarrow

Ground Covers Requiring Acid Soil

Many plants that thrive in acid soil are widely adaptable and often found where acidity is low or where tests indicate a neutral condition. The plants listed below include many members of the heath family that require acid soil in order to flourish.

American barrenwort	Cowberry	Mountain andromeda
Barrenwort	Creeping snowberry	Pachistima
Bearberry	Drooping leucothoe	Partridgeberry
Bloodroot	Ferns	Sand myrtle
Bluets	Galax	Trailing arbutus
Bog rosemary	Heath	Trillium
Box huckleberry	Heather	Twinflower
Bunchberry	Japanese holly	Wild ginger
Cinquefoil		Wintergreen

Ground Covers with Evergreen Foliage

Plants with foliage that remains green throughout the year are of prime value at all seasons and particularly during the winter months. Not all the plants listed below are completely evergreen where winters are severe, but their foliage is of sufficient substance to be considered partially evergreen. Most of the perennials in this list fall into this group.

Akebia	Broom	Cinquefoil
Bearberry	Bunchberry	Common polypody fern
Bog rosemary	Carmel creeper	Cotoneaster
Box huckleberry	Carolina jasmine	Cowberry
Braun's holly fern	Christmas fern	Drooping leucothoe

Dwarf rosemary	Japanese holly	Partridgeberry
Dwarf yew	Lavender cotton	Periwinkle
Ebony spleenwort	Marginal shield fern	Sand myrtle
Evergreen candytuft	Mountain andromeda	Sarcococca
Evergreen shield fern	Mountain holly fern	Star jasmine
Germander	Mugho pine	Trumpet honeysuckle
Hall's honeysuckle	Oregon holly grape	Western sword fern
Heath	Pachistima	Wintercreeper
Heather	Pachysandra	Wintergreen

PERENNIALS WITH EVERGREEN FOLIAGE

Barren strawberry	Galax	Speedwell
Barrenwort	Houseleek	Stonecrop
Coralbell	Lilyturf	Woolly yarrow
	Snow-in-summer	

GROUND COVERS WITH DISTINCTIVE FOLIAGE

Gray or silvery foliage, leaves with variegated markings, and those with bronzy tones are of special value for contrast when tastefully used. Others with large leaves, the finely cut kinds like the ferns, and the extensive list with small leaf pattern are typical of foliage types among ground-cover plants. Fragrant-leaved kinds provide additional interest.

GRAY OR SILVERY FOLIAGE

Aubretia	Fringed wormwood	Silver mound artemisia
Beach wormwood	Gold dust	Snow-in-summer
Bloodroot	Ground morning glory	Sunrose
Blue fescue	Lamb's ears	Wall rock cress
Dwarf willow	Lavender cotton	Woolly speedwell
English lavender	New Zealand bur	Woolly thyme
Fig marigold	Pussytoes	Woolly yarrow
	Roman wormwood	

VARIEGATED FOLIAGE

Big-leaf periwinkle	Goutweed	Silveredge pachysandra
Bugleweed	Heather	Strawberry geranium
Dead nettle	Lilyturf	Thyme
English ivy	Lungwort	Wintercreeper
	Plantain lily	

AROMATIC FOLIAGE

Bayberry	Fragrant sumac	Savory
Camomile	Fringed wormwood	Sweet fern
Creeping mint	Gill-over-the-ground	Sweet Woodruff
Dwarf rosemary	Lavender cotton	Thyme
English lavender	Roman wormwood	Woolly yarrow

273

Index

275

276

DANIEL J. FOLEY

has spent a lifetime working with plants, flowers and shrubs. A graduate of the University of Massachusetts, this landscape architect and horticulturist is the author of *Garden Flowers in Color, Vegetable Gardening in Color, Annuals for Your Garden, Ground Covers for Easier Gardening* and is the co-author of *Garden Bulbs in Color*.

For seven years he was closely associated with Dr. J. Horace McFarland and supervised the planting and development of the famous Breeze Hill Test Gardens at Harrisburg, Pennsylvania. He served as editor of *Horticulture* magazine from 1951 through 1957.

Widely known as a lecturer, he has appeared before hundreds of audiences, is a frequent contributor to leading gardening magazines and newspapers, with more than 600 articles to his credit, and he has conducted his own radio program. During the past ten years, he has traveled more than fifty thousand miles visiting gardens and nurseries in various parts of the United States and Great Britain, often in the capacity of garden consultant and landscape designer.

Mr. Foley holds membership in more than twenty professional societies and maintains an extensive correspondence with horticulturists in this country and Europe.

Among his other books are *Little Saints of Christmas, The Christmas Tree, Christmas in the Good Old Days, Christmas the World Over* and *Toys Through the Ages*. With Priscilla Sawyer Lord he is co-author of *Easter Garland*.